RESEARCH METHODS
FOR
MANAGERS

Dr John Gill is Reader in Management in Sheffield Business School. He has wide experience of the successful supervision of management research projects at all levels from diploma to doctorate. He has been a member of the (then) Social Science Research Council's Management and Industrial Relations Committee and chair of the Research Degrees Sub-Committee of the Business and Management Board of the CNAA. Currently he is a member of the Research Committee of the CNAA and chair of Sheffield City Polytechnic's Research Degrees Committee. He has published two books and more than forty articles on management topics.

Dr Phil Johnson is a Senior Lecturer in Organization Behaviour in Sheffield Business School. He has undertaken and published research mainly in the areas of the behavioural aspects of accounting and the impact of technological innovation upon organizations. He has experience of supervising management research projects from first degree to doctorate.

RESEARCH METHODS
FOR
MANAGERS

JOHN GILL AND PHIL JOHNSON

P·C·P

Paul Chapman
Publishing Ltd

Paul Chapman Publishing Ltd
144 Liverpool Road
London N1 1LA

British Library Cataloguing in Publication Data
Gill, John
  Research methods for managers.
  1. Research and development. Management
  I. Title II. Johnson, Phil
  658.57

ISBN 1–85396–119–1

Typset by Inforum Typesetting, Portsmouth
Printed by St. Edmundsbury Press, and bound by W.H. Ware

A B C D E F G 7 6 5 4 3 2 1

Contents

Preface

This book had its inception in our concern that the teaching of research methods to management and business students, faced with project work and dissertations, is hampered by the absence of a suitable text.

What we believe is required is an introductory text as guidance to methodological issues of use to students at whatever level their project work is undertaken, from diploma to doctorate.

We have a number of objectives. First, we wish to address key philosophical matters that are basic to any real understanding of the methodological approaches to management research. Second, we attempt to make the text very practical in that examples and exercises are drawn from management and business. Finally, we wish to ensure that the text will enable students to take their first steps in project work confident that they are on firm ground in their choice of methodological approaches.

These objectives were reinforced by the content of a consultative paper, *Research Training for the 1990s*, by the Economic and Social Reseach Council's Training Board (October, 1989). It deals with the content of research training as part of Ph.D. programmes and recommends first a general training in methodological issues; second, training in specific methods; third, training in strategies and techniques; and; finally, in an appendix, it offers suggested contents of the general training package which includes the need for philosophical underpinning.

We also wish to challenge the widespread advocacy of particular approaches to management research as being 'the best'. Advocacy of one approach or another, often irrespective of context, is commonplace in business and management research. These debates are frequently acrimonious probably reflecting fundamental cultural and ideological differences and the defensiveness arising from the need to advance careers. For example, we recently came across the following statement from senior academics in a well known business school who were responding to the Economic and Social Research Council's consultative paper mentioned above: 'In our view, much of the weakness of business and management research has been its over-emphasis on ethnographic methods yielding knowledge of use to the observer, rather than the development of clinical/engineering methods yielding knowledge appropriate for both practitioner and observer.'

Such a view probably arises from a misinterpretation of Schein's (1987) comparison between what he calls the 'clinical' approach and ethnography, work we discuss in some detail in Chapter 5 under action research. In addition, however, it is surely erroneous to maintain that ethnographic approaches are predominant in management research when even a cursory review of the leading management journals would reveal that quantitative, deductive methods are most in evidence. More to the point, an advocacy of 'clinical' methods, or what we include in this book under action research, as being most helpful to practitioners is very debatable and depends of course very much on context and time scale – as we show in later chapters. At this stage it is perhaps sufficient also to mention ethnographic studies that have been influential in bringing about major change (e.g. Lupton, 1963; Goffman, 1968; Beynon, 1973). Such work does not of course solely yield 'knowledge of use to the observer' but has been influential precisely because its methodology, by its very nature, ensures that practitioners can readily relate to it and compare it with their practice as a first step towards making changes.

Our position is to make clear that the main approaches to management research – namely experimental research design, action research, survey research and ethnography – are all imperfect. Each has advantages and disadvantages in the kinds of data it affords and in its vulnerability to particular kinds of error. One way of overcoming each method's weaknesses and limitations is deliberately to combine different methods within the same investigations, a strategy we call 'multimethod research' and which we elaborate in the final chapter. We have another subsidiary and related aim: to see a more balanced approach to research methodology in management by correcting the current bias towards deductive approaches and introducing intending researchers to a wider range of options.

The material presented in this book has been discussed with many people over the years – sometimes only inferentially, often controversially. Those who have so stimulated us are colleagues; academics elsewhere and especially managers and students (the last two often combining both roles). We particularly acknowledge the following: Chris Argyris, Peter Ashworth, Tony Berry, Steve Fineman, David Golding, Dan Gowler, Chris Hendry, Rita Johnston, Karen Legge, Clive Ley, Tom Lupton, John McAuley, Ian McGivering, Iain Mangham, Stuart Manson, John Morris, Nigel Slack, Stuart Smith, Ian Tanner, Pat Terry, Doug Thacker, Dave Tranfield, Don White and Sue Whittle.

We also gratefully acknowledge the help of Janet Green, Martin Cooper, Patsy Wilson-Smith and Peggy Hall, who rescued us from tangles with the word processor; the first also being responsible for producing the figures and tables from very rough drafts. Thanks, too, to all the librarians at Totley for their help on many occasions. Last, but by no means least thanks for Brenda's and Carole's tolerance of our obsession over many months.

John Gill
Phil Johnson
Sheffield, 1990

1
Introduction

Aims and purposes

This book is designed to help those about to undertake research in business and management either in connection with their jobs as managers or as a research project requirement as part of a taught course at undergraduate or postgraduate levels. It will also be particularly appropriate to those working for master's and doctoral degrees by research.

Few books are written with this specific audience in mind, and fewer focus on research methods in business and management. In our experience students undertaking a research project have most difficulty deciding which approach or strategy to use to address the research problem they have set themselves; and then how to employ methods of data collection in undertaking fieldwork, frequently in organizations.

We aim therefore to provide an introductory text to enable students to make an informed start on project work. With such help they are not only likely to be made more aware of the appropriateness of the range of available approaches to research but are also more likely to be in a position better to justify their choices and evaluate their subsequent findings.

The book presents students with a wide range of approaches to management research and their philosophical bases sufficient to be readily applicable to managerial problem-solving.

Managerial problem-solving

Management and business students have been subjected to much controversy over the years about the most appropriate approaches to the study of management as an academic discipline and these dilemmas include issues concerning management research. To some extent this has been due not only to the emergence of different schools of management thought but also to the development of different approaches to research methodology, especially so in the social sciences. One of the major themes of this book is that there is no one best approach but rather that the approach most effective for the resolution of a given problem depends on a large number of variables, not least the nature of the problem itself. Research methodology is always a compromise between options and choices are frequently determined by the availability of resources. In this book we will advance criteria for choice of methodology by reviewing the major approaches to management research and, through examples, their appropriateness to finding answers to particular research questions.

First we need to place management research in context. In a discussion of the historical development of management studies, Whitley (1984a) describes it as being in a fragmented state; as a field characterized by a high degree of task uncertainty and a low degree of co-ordination of research procedures and strategies between researchers. This seems particularly attributable to the wide variations in the quality of management publication media, the multiplicity of validation standards and the variety of recipients of research findings in management. It is also, of course, attributable to the multi-disciplinary nature of management as a field of study and the variations in approach in disciplines as different, for example, as operations research and sociology. As Tinker and Lowe (1982, p. 332) comment, 'management science must hold the record among the sciences for the rate at which it has fragmented into factions and specialisms'.

Research in the United Kingdom comparing attitudes towards research of managers and management developers revealed that managers believed research was initiated by academic researchers often insufficiently familiar with the managerial culture and so lacking credibility. For the most part managers seemed to believe that management research was not only not cost effective but also, more critically, largely irrelevant to the problems they faced. Many managers confessed, however, that they did not know how to use research findings and that clearly utilizable research would be more helpful to them (Bennett and Gill, 1978).

By contrast, Whitley (1984b p. 387), taking an academic view, goes on to suggest that management research seems to have adopted 'a naïve and unreflecting empiricism'. Remedially he suggests that what is required is the means to free researchers from lay concepts and problem formulations and to provide them with a more sophisticated understanding of the epistemological and sociological sciences. This book is an attempt to achieve this and, simultaneously, to bridge the gap between academic and managerial views of what constitutes appropriate research.

The management research process

Harvey-Jones (1989, p. 240), in his bestselling book *Making it Happen*, advises managers when setting about tasks to distinguish content from process. What he means by this is that it is helpful conceptually to separate the content of the task from the way the task is accomplished; that is, to separate the content (what) from the process (how). Research methods on this analysis are

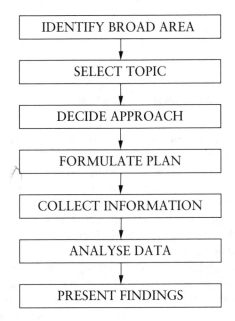

Figure 1.1 The research sequence

then primarily concerned with how (process) to tackle tasks (content).

Despite the variety of approaches to management research they all in essence share a problem-solving sequence that may serve as a systematic check for anyone undertaking research at whatever level. At this point we introduce a cautionary note in qualification. An idealized representation of the research sequence will help the naïve researcher at this stage to review the research process as a whole and make a start; however it rarely accords with actuality. It should be borne in mind that 'the research process is not a clear-cut sequence of procedures following a neat pattern but a messy interaction between the conceptual and empirical world, deduction and induction occurring at the same time' (Bechhofer, 1974, p. 73). We will return to this critical matter in the concluding chapter.

Nevertheless, the seven-step sequence proposed by Howard and Sharp (1983) which builds on earlier work by Rummel and Ballaine (1963), may be found particularly useful (see Figure 1.1), and is referred to again in the next chapter.

These seven steps should be useful to all students at whatever level they are undertaking project work, from diploma to doctorate. It is recommended that each step in the sequence be given equal attention if time is to be saved in the longer term. For example, it is commonplace to give insufficient attention to defining clearly the research topic. This may especially be so when using deductive research strategies; the differences in topic specification when working inductively or deductively are elaborated in Chapter 2.

Lack of clarity may become apparent at later stages of the process, either when planning the project or deciding on methods of collecting data. As a consequence time may be lost recycling to earlier stages of the sequence or the work may fail to meet its objectives. These issues will also be explored in more detail in the following chapter, concerned with starting research projects.

Management development and management research

It should of course be clear that in essence many managerial activities and the research process outlined above are similar. Managers need to be competent in investigative approaches to decision-making and problem-solving and this has been recognized in practically all management development programmes and business education by the inclusion of project work involving problem-solving as part of taught courses. The research process, while being the means of advancing knowledge, also serves as a disciplined and systematic procedure of help in solving managerial problems.

Both management and research activities require a decision as to what to do; followed by a planning stage concerned with making judgements about ways of collecting valid information to tackle the issue. Finally the information gathered will need to be analysed and assessed, and action taken.

Both managerial and research processes are uncertain and risky, and necessarily entail considerable self-initiated endeavour involving co-operation with others and skills in managing all the factors inherent in finding and implementing solutions to complex problems. Not only are the findings of the research important, then, but it is suggested that the processes of systematic discovery have clear benefits to the manager's self-development as a manager or problem-solver.

These parallels between the research and managerial processes as action sciences are recognized both in project work and dissertations as a significant part of most taught programmes, and also in the merits of research training as a component of higher degree programmes in management.

At the diploma and undergraduate levels in business and management the project usually forms a significant part of the final assessment demanding independent inquiry and judgement. Taught master's programmes in management vary widely in their dissertation requirements. Some relatively uncommon programmes are guided by an action learning philosophy pioneered by Revans (1971) and are taught solely around project work based in the student's own organization. More usually a wide variety of MBA programmes exist where the requirement is generally for the dissertation to be completed in about six months part time as part of a largely taught course. Nevertheless, in most cases the MBA dissertation forms a significant part of the assessment and is almost invariably preceded by a taught research methods component.

Typically the MBA dissertation aims to allow the student to develop and demonstrate powers of rigorous analysis, critical inquiry, clear expression and independent judgement in relation to an area of business activity. Most MBA dissertations are normally based on an in-depth investigation into a managerial problem within the student's own organization. The most usual requirement is for more than just problem-solving typical of management consultancy since it requires the student to stand back from the problem, conceptualize it, and explore its wider implications for other managers outside the particular case.

Some taught master's programmes designed for specialists, such as operations researchers and organization development practitioners, may make even greater demands on students in terms of the dissertation requirement. The time devoted to the dissertation may be as much as one third of that spent on the taught programme as a whole and the dissertation may have the same assessed weight as the taught component. Commonly such dissertations are concerned with the student's management of a consultancy project where the student is required not only to find a solution to a particular problem but also to reflect on and generalize the consulting approach and the problems of implementation. For instance, the philosophy supporting the research methods component of such a master's programme in organization development is outlined by a colleague who advocates respect for data, the appropriateness of the research strategy to the problem confronted and the use of a hermeneutic approach in understanding the theories and philosophies of management held by both managers themselves and by self-aware researchers (McAuley, 1985).

The requirements for master's degrees imposed by research and doctoral projects are similar except that the doctorate is a much more demanding piece of work requiring an independent and original contribution to knowledge. In both degrees, however, there is a need to demonstrate an understanding of research methods appropriate to the chosen field and require students to defend their theses by oral examination.

At this final stage attention is given to the quality of the methodology; the thoroughness of the bibliographic search; the depth of the analysis and conclusions; and the standard of presentation of the thesis. Finally, the extent of the contribution to knowledge is assessed: clearly, the contribution made by the master's thesis will be of some importance and will probably at least serve as a reference work. Work at master's level is, however, to be distinguished from the doctorate by the requirement placed on the latter to provide a distinct and original contribution to knowledge.

We now turn to the broad approaches or strategies to management research covered in this book. It is clear that methodological choices are determined not only by the nature of the topic being investigated and the resources available but also by the particular training and socialization processes to which the researcher has been exposed. It will therefore be helpful at this point to diagnose your own predispositions towards particular research approaches, by doing Exercise 1.1.

Exercise 1.1 Self-diagnose your research approach

Say whether you agree or disagree with the following statements by placing a tick (agree) or a cross (disagree) in the box against each statement.

1. Quantitative data is more objective and scientific than qualitative data.

2. It is always necessary to define precisely the research topic before data collection.

3. Of all methods the questionnaire is probably the best by which to collect objective data on management topics.

4. Field experiments such as the Hawthorne Studies, effectively determine cause and effect relationships.

5. A good knowledge of statistics is not essential for competence in all approaches to management research.

6. A case study is an inappropriate way to undertake management research as it cannot be generalized.

7. Anthropological methods are obviously fine as a means of studying exotic tribes but have little utility in management research.

8. Laboratory experiments, such as studies of decision-making in groups, should be used more widely in management research as they can be closely controlled by the researcher.

9. Research into management issues is best achieved through the accumulation of qualitative data.

10. As a management research method observation is too prone to researcher bias to be valid.

Method of scoring: For the method of scoring see the instructions at the end of this chapter.

Approaches to management research

It has been suggested that a common stereotype firmly held by managers is to regard researchers as remote, ivory-tower individuals working on issues of little practical relevance. This stereotype, by analogy with the 'boffin' scientist, may of course be partly defensive and serve to preserve managers from the study of difficult philosophical concepts necessary for a comprehensive understanding of research methodology (Gill, 1986; Gill, Golding and Angluin, 1989).

Managers are not alone in this, for most people associate the word 'research' with activities which are substantially removed from daily life and which usually take place in a laboratory. Further, research – and its connection in many minds with 'science' – is often understood to refer to the study of problems by scientific methods or principles. Management is no exception and there is an influential body of writers who all apparently believe that science is basically a way of producing and validating knowledge which can be applied to managerial problems without too much difficulty.

For example, House (1970), discussing 'scientific' investigation in management, suggests that there is a requirement of public demonstration to prevent the construction of theories and the formulation of general laws on the basis of inadequately tested hypotheses.

The requirement of demonstraton is satisfied, he believes, when the research design includes:

1. a priori hypotheses;
2. a priori criteria that can be used to measure the acceptability of those hypotheses;
3. isolation and control of the variables under investigation; and
4. methods of measuring and verifying the variables in the investigation.

This positivist approach suggests that management research is essentially similar to that used in the natural and physical sciences, whereas the assumptions on which this view is based have been challenged on at least three main grounds:

1. that there is no single method which generates scientific knowledge in all cases;
2. that what may be an appropriate method for researching the natural or physical world may be inappropriate in the social world given the inherent meaningfulness of management action and its contextual nature;
3. that knowledge generated is affected by the goals of managers and their validation criteria.

The distinction between science ('normal science') and non-science ('pseudo-science') is essentially blurred. In the West this line of demarcation is relatively clear; for something to be scientific it must use the agreed set of conventions, that is to say, it must use the scientific method. In other cultures, by contrast, alternative forms of inquiry are acceptable, for example meditation, and it seems inappropriate to reject them simply because those cultures are different from ours.

The conventions we agree to are simply those which have proved useful in the past. If these conventions, and so our scientific process, cease to be successful, however, it would be time to re-evaluate them. This is the point some commentators believe to have been reached in research in information systems (Hirschheim, 1985), and it may also be true more broadly of research in management studies. An exponent of this view, from 'management science' or operations research, believes that the extreme complexity of managerial problems, and attempts to apply scientific methodology to real-world, essentially social problems, have been responsible for the limited success of management science (Checkland, 1981).

Similarly, Bygrave (1989) endeavours to account for what he regards as the unhelpful tendency for researchers to use the methods of the physical sciences in the context of research into entrepreneurship. He points out that many of the key contributors to business strategy have educational backgrounds in engineering, natural science and mathematics and are steeped in Newtonian mechanics at a very impressionable age. Amusingly he makes a plea for less 'physics envy' in approaches to research into the emerging field of entrepreneurship.

The main contemporary criticisms of positivism are well summarized by Burrell and Morgan as follows:

> Science is based on 'taken for granted' assumptions, and thus, like any other social practice, must be understood within a specific context. Traced to their source all activities which pose as science can be traced to fundamental assumptions relating to everyday life and can in no way be regarded as generating knowledge with an 'objective', value-free status, as is sometimes claimed. What passes for scientific knowledge can be shown to be founded upon a set of unstated conventions, beliefs and assumptions, just as every-day, common-sense knowledge is. The difference between them lies largely in the nature of rules and the community which recognises and subscribes to them. The knowledge in both cases is not so much 'objective' as shared.
>
> (Burrell and Morgan, 1979, p. 255)

Accordingly, we may need to change our conception of science to one of problem- or puzzle-solving, where science is simply regarded as a problem solving process which uses certain conventions in that process (Kuhn, 1970). In this respect Pettigrew's (1985a) view of problem-solving as a craft may be inadvertently misleading because if researchers are regarded as 'tool users rather than as tool builders then we may run the risk of distorted knowledge acquisition techniques' (Hirschheim, 1985, p. 15). An old proverb says 'for he who has but one tool, the hammer, the whole world looks like a nail'. For the most part, the way we currently practise research in management leads directly to that view, but times are changing and we hope to facilitate these changes.

In view of these concerns it is unsurprising that there are a number of approaches to management research and several ways of classifying them as a means to clarify the available approaches to research.

Research may be classified according to its purpose. It may primarily be concerned with solving theoretical issues; something capable of wide generaliz-ation but difficult to achieve. On the other hand, it may be concerned with solving a very specific practical problem in one company; this may be achieved more readily but have little application outside the particular case.

Similarly, research may be classified according to the broad approach taken to the problem. Such classifications are often placed on a continuum of increas-ing rigour; from laboratory experiments to what may be termed field research using ethnographic methods based on single cases. In the former approach there is a relative emphasis on deduction firmly based in what is known as positivism which relies on the highly structured methods employed in the natural sciences. These, as has been mentioned above, have as their basis a hypothesis testing process using standardized instruments and controls and most usually generating quantitative data.

Ethnographic methods, on the other hand, are within an inductive tradition which accuses those working deductively of imposing an external logic upon phenomena that have their own internal logics. There is then in this approach an emphasis on the analysis of subjective accounts which are generated by 'getting inside' situations and involving the investigator in the everyday flow of life (see Burrell and Morgan, 1979, pp. 5–6). Emphasis is on theory grounded in empirical observations which take account of subjects' meaning and interpretational systems in order to explain by understanding. This approach generates and uses mainly qualitative data and minimum structure.

Lying somewhere between these extremes are survey research and field experiments, for example involving the test of a new product, but where the variables cannot be so carefully controlled as in the laboratory. Similarly, use may be made of naturally occurring events in the field, which exist without the researcher's direct intervention and which are known as quasi-experiments.

There is a further category in this intermediate group of approaches, known as action research, which, as with quasi-experiments, borrows the logic of experimentation but applies it to natural settings outside the laboratory. In this case, however, the solution of the problem, frequently some aspect of organizational change, is both an outcome of the research and a part of the research process. Action research may or may not involve control groups. For example, if it were decided to research the relationship between zero-based budgeting and organizational effectiveness the action researcher would introduce zero-based budgeting into an organization and would then monitor its effects, ideally using control groups. Action research would claim both to solve idiosyncratic problems for clients and simultaneously to add to the stock of general knowledge about change processes.

It will be clear from the foregoing that one of our main aims in this analysis is to challenge the physical science model as the only approach to knowledge acquisition, particularly for management studies. Our approach is rather what some have described as 'methodological pluralism'; the assertion that there is no one best method but many methods contingent on the issue being studied regardless of epistemological biases (Kuhn, 1970; Giddens, 1978; Johnson, 1989). To quote Eilon, (1974):

> one finds that many researchers are committed to a particular school of thought or methodology, either because it has affinity with the academic discipline from which they have originally come, or because of a combination of habit and conviction. It is very often the lack of understanding of the precise nature of each archetype that generates a great deal of criticism and cynicism, some of which is undoubtedly justified, but some embedded in prejudice. Each archetype has a contribution to make, but each suffers from certain limitations and weaknesses that sometimes assume magnified proportions in ad hoc circumstances, with implications for the ability to generalise and advance our knowledge in the field of management science. One hopes that an informal debate on the strengths and shortcomings of alternative approaches to research, and their underlying attitudes and philosophies, will prove profitable.
>
> (Eilon, 1974, p. 9)

In this book we hope to achieve this goal.

The book's structure

The book is not primarily concerned with such issues as selecting and justifying the research topic or with literature searching except in so far as these activities may interact with decisions on the approach to the investigation. To that extent, these are outlined in the next chapter.

In the same way, means of presenting research findings will not be considered in any detail. Rather, we propose to address the methodological issues entailed in the various approaches to managerial research and managerial problem-solving. While to some extent we will at times be prescriptive, we hope to avoid a 'cookbook' approach with an emphasis on how research should be done by discussing many examples of how management research is actually done (Burgess and Bulmer, 1981).

In Figure 1.1 we outlined the research process and within this process we will be particularly concerned with stage 3, deciding the approach or strategy; stage 4, formulating the plan; stage 5, collecting data; and stage 6, interpreting and analysing the data.

The approaches to management research outlined above structure the chapters that follow. In Chapter 2 we begin by offering some help to the new researcher who wishes to make a start. Then, in Chapter 3, we address the important role of theory in underpinning practical research activities. We believe this is fundamental to understanding, especially so for vocationally orientated, management students, who may be inclined to regard some philosophical matters basic to any real appreciation of methodological issues, as unnecessarily theoretical and academic.

In the subsequent chapters we consider approaches to management research using the structure already suggested above. Accordingly, we follow a logical sequence from Chapter 4, concerned with experimental research design; Chapter 5, with quasi-experiments and action research; Chapter 6, with survey methodologies; and Chapters 7 and 8, with ethnographic approaches. In Chapter 9 we discuss some fundamental philosophical issues concerning the choice and justification of research approaches and, in a concluding chapter, some recurring themes which have been addressed throughout this book, including particularly the practical decisions involved in making and justifying choice of research strategy.

Method of scoring Exercise 1.1

Count each tick as a plus and each cross as a minus. Subtract ticks from crosses. The greater your minus score the more you are disposed towards inductive research approaches and, conversely, the greater your plus score may provide some rough indication of how easy you will find it to be flexible about your choice of method(s). There are of course no right or wrong answers, and in any case the exercise should not be taken too seriously.

2

Starting Management Research

As we explained in Chapter 1, this book is primarily concerned with offering guidance on the appropriate approach to take to a particular research topic. From experience we have discovered that this matter is generally the most problematic for the researcher. However, we also suggested earlier that research invariably proceeds in roughly the sequence outlined in Figure 1.1, and such a systematic procedure is clearly a useful way of clarifying matters at the outset. However, as also mentioned, it should be recognized that these stages are usually not so clear cut in practice and frequently may be recycled; for example, both the topic and the approach taken to address it may be modified iteratively as the work is planned and action taken.

Primarily, then, in this book we will be concerned with selecting the research approach, and collecting and analysing data; that is stages 3 to 6 in the sequence in Figure 1.1, and these matters will be the main concern of later chapters.

However, this chapter considers some preliminary matters essential to making a start. These are the selection and justification of the topic, planning the project and reviewing the literature. The rest of the book is then devoted to methodological issues. Nevertheless, it is of course recommended that the whole book should be read at least once before starting a research project.

Topic selection

Until a topic for the research is identified the work cannot of course start. This obvious point is made to emphasize that so much research, particularly for research degrees, founders because students do not take a systematic approach to topic selection.

At the risk of complicating this matter at so early a stage, there are fundamentally two ways of formulating research topics. One is by analysing the literature, formally stating the problem and the major questions, and only then collecting relevant data; the other suggests that this way of formulating problems tends to stifle questions that a more open-ended approach to the topic might stimulate. Both ways have merit and choice depends upon the research approach(es) selected. Broadly speaking, action research and ethnographic approaches exert open-ended constraints on formulating problems while programmed constraints are placed on those using surveys and experiments. Brewer and Hunter (1989) suggest that multi-method strategies may help overcome these constraints upon problem formulation, and we will consider this matter in more detail in Chapter 10.

Students may of course be allocated a research topic. This is less likely in projects that are part of taught programmes in business and management, where students are generally encouraged to find their own topics with supervisory help. However, much depends on the disciplinary traditions and the immediate research setting. For example, if the student is working as a member of a research team this may entail fitting into an existing programme of research. Further, in such areas as the natural sciences and engineering the student apparently has less influence in topic selection than is commonly the case in the social sciences (Young, Fogarty and McRae, 1987, p. 21).

On the other hand, topic selection may be a somewhat risky process if left entirely to the student, and it would seem that an arrangement whereby student and supervisor work together to define the topic is ideal. There is otherwise a danger that, through lack of experience, topics chosen solely by students may prove impracticable, or alternatively, that the student who is allocated a project will feel no sense of ownership and commitment.

Sources of research topics

Topics may arise in a number of ways. For example, many part-time students in business and management derive topics from their work experience often in consultation with superiors. In effect they offer to work as internal consultants on some problem in their own organization and then, when studying at, say, master's level, stand back from the work so that it becomes generalizable to other cases.

Topics may also arise from articles in academic and professional journals, and ideas for research may be stimulated by reports in the media, where an unsupported assertion may provide a fruitful line of inquiry. Such assertions are not confined to the media; authorities in the field may also make assertions which are not well founded. For example, an established researcher may assert that capital budgeting techniques are used not for decision-making but only as a control mechanism – an assertion that may be readily tested by accumulating research evidence from practitioners.

Experts or authorities will frequently write articles or make speeches commenting on the absence of research in a particularly fruitful area and in the same way committee reports may also refer specifically for the need for research in an area under investigation.

Groups of managers at local meetings of professional bodies, such as the British Institute of Management or the Institute of Marketing, may also be useful sources of research ideas and access to research them. Such suggestions do need to be regarded with a degree of caution, for practitioners are often unaware of research that has already been done, but nevertheless they may often be a useful starting point for a research inquiry.

Research projects in management have also often originated from consultancy, where research questions have arisen in the course of the work. An example was consultancy in a large, nationally known chemical complex to help management commission a technically very sophisticated plant, where the research issues were concerned with the staff's resistance to implementing the new technology. Consultancy helped clarify the topic area as well as lend credibility to the research group in their search for funding in a competitive field in which they previously had little experience.

Finally, many theses and dissertations contain suggestions for further research. Journal articles sometimes refer to the need for further work – and since these appear only a year or so after the study they are generally more up to date than books.

Some characteristics of a good research topic

In looking for a research topic certain important characteristics need to be kept in mind. It is unlikely that all these can be satisfied and each student will place them in a different order of priority, but all the following factors should be checked against each topic proposed.

Access

The possibility of access is generally a fairly easy matter to assess. Nevertheless, students often start with ideas for projects where accessibility will clearly prove difficult if not completely impractical. For example, a Ph.D. project to investigate the role of personnel departments in acquisitions and to make comparisons between the UK and North America clearly posed insurmountable problems of accessibility, not least because of the unwillingness of organizations to provide access to such sensitive and traumatic events. Further, and probably for the same reasons, secondary data seemed sparse – but this took a little longer to assess before the topic was drastically revised. In addition, of course, such a topic was also probably too broad – a common fault and one we will address below.

Similarly, topics concerned with, for example, redundancy, competitive markets or managerial stress, while potentially interesting and useful research areas, may be difficult to access. One internationally known research worker once told one of the authors that one of the fundamental problems in carrying out investigations into managerial stress was to gain access to individuals to interview. After many rejections the conclusion was reached that many managers were too stressed to talk to him about it! It has sometimes been cynically remarked that the potentially most rewarding research topics are often those which are also most inaccessible and often considerable ingenuity and persistence may be required to research further in such areas. Some ways to achieve this are addressed in more detail in Chapters 5, 7 and 8.

However, it should also be borne in mind at this stage that, as Drummond (1989) has pointed out, the use of lateral thinking to concentrate on objectives rather than on obstacles to gaining access to data is a useful technique. In this regard she provides an example from her own Ph.D. research, which seemed to demand access to coercive organizations such as prisons. Much time and wasted effort were taken up trying to gain access to such organizations through official channels, when a focus on what was actually needed to meet the research aims led to fresh thoughts on how to obtain the necessary data. It was found instead to be comparatively easy to obtain access to released inmates through the National Council for the Care and Resettlement of Offenders, to enable the completion of questionnaires. Similarly, we will see in Chapter 7 that Spencer (1980) gained access to non-executive directors by interviewing some who performed the role part time in the course of their work as business school academics and were as a consequence probably more sympathetic to a researcher working for a Ph.D.

Achievable in the time available

With limited time available there is a temptation to select a topic before doing the preliminary groundwork suggested here; this temptation should be resisted and time will be saved in the long run.

In general the time taken to accomplish a piece of research is frequently underestimated. The time actually spent on the project is lengthened by delays due to such matters as illness, domestic pressures and part-time work; and, for part-time students, by job changes and pressures. There is a further potential difficulty for students undertaking research part time in their own organization. While it may be advantageous for the research to be undertaken as part of their normal duties, there may be difficulties if the research depends on the researcher's superior and the organization remaining unchanged throughout the period of the work. Such a case occurred in research being conducted in a region of the National Health Service, where an original plan, based on strategies largely determined by a powerful superior, had to be changed radically following organizational changes. Fortunately, the research design was flexible and the researcher sufficiently resilient to regard such changes as an opportunity rather than a hindrance. This of course has frequently to be the approach in research concerned with complex problems in the relatively uncontrolled conditions found in organizations.

These potential delays are made more manageable by drawing up a research plan, which will indicate the phases of the research and the dates for its completion; an example is given later in this chapter.

Symmetry of potential outcomes

A way of reducing the risk entailed in any project is to try to ensure that, whatever the findings from the work, the results will be equally valuable; this is known as symmetry of potential outcomes.

For example, a research project to explore the effects on managers' careers of holding a postgraduate qualification in a management subject would have symmetrical potential outcomes. If no correlation were found this would be at least as interesting and important as if there were found to be a high correlation. On the other hand, an example of a non-symmetrical outcome might be research which aimed to investigate a possible link between psychoanalytical factors, such as the mid-life crisis, and the personality of the entrepreneurial individual. Establishing such a relationship would clearly be an interesting and potentially useful contribution, but if no relationship were found the result would not be nearly as interesting. The matter of symmetry is particularly important in doctoral studies, where the contribution to knowledge is a principal criterion for the award and the risk entailed in a relative lack of symmetry needs to be minimized.

Student capabilities and interest

This seems an obvious point: clearly, a student with strong capabilities in the behavioural sciences and low numeracy should hesitate before choosing a topic, needing, for example, complex statistical analysis even though it might otherwise be a good one. Similarly, a student with poor descriptive writing skills might be unwise to embark on an ethnographic study.

Finally, it is obviously important for the student to be able to sustain interest in work which may continue for long periods; in the case of higher degrees for a number of years. In these circumstances it is essential that the topic be of particular interest to the student. Thus the student should carefully assess his or her interests and abilities to ensure they match the proposed research project.

Financial support

In most student projects it is usual for the matter of financial support to have been resolved before the project begins but, even then, there are frequently problems for full-time students in ensuring continuity of support; for example, the curious rules of the research councils sometimes cause problems of continuity for the researcher. (*Independent*, 21 September 89).

It is therefore particularly important for the matter of cost to be examined before a topic is finally selected; the lack of funds for travelling, expensive equipment or subsistance may prejudice a successful outcome.

Value and scope of the research

In projects which form part of taught courses the value of the work may usually be judged primarily by its suitability in demonstrating sufficient research competence or problem-solving ability to fulfil the criteria judged necessary to pass the course. For a higher degree by research both problem-solving ability and research competence are needed, and, additionally, the findings should add to the general body of knowledge – without necessarily being of value to the community at large.

There are, however, several reasons why the value of the research should be considered when topics are selected. Both students and supervisors are likely to be more highly motivated if the work has obvious value and examiners, too, are likely to be more interested – and award higher marks if the work is clearly making a contribution to the solution of a significant problem. Furthermore, there is growing concern by government and public funding bodies that publicly funded research should be devoted to problems judged to be important and of practical application.

Closely related to the issue of value is the extent to which the topic has the scope to challenge current beliefs, to be surprising and to affect public policy. For example, personal research for a higher degree into risk-taking by decision makers had considerable scope, particularly when it was fortuitously discovered that decisions taken by groups were apparently more risky than the same decisions taken by individuals. The implications of such findings, if confirmed, were clearly enormous and led to considerable research activity (Brown, 1965, chapter 13.)

Findings with this degree of scope will rarely present themselves to the student researcher but topics low in both surprise and value should if possible be avoided and the search continued for topics which better meet these criteria.

Techniques for generating research topics

When defining a research area most researchers move from a wide field to a manageable topic using some of the criteria mentioned above. We suggested earlier that such criteria are best applied systematically, and the same is true when narrowing down what may be a rather vague list of early ideas into something capable of being researched. On the other hand, some researchers may have already defined their topics and, while this may at first sight seem ideal, the work may be impractical or have already been done; either way, the inexperienced researcher may not be aware of the position.

Techniques which may be used to clarify topics owe much to work on creativity by, for example, De Bono (1971), Parnes, Noller and Bondi (1977) and Miller, (1983).

Simplistically, one might start by using brainstorming methods to provide a list of first thoughts in a particular topic area and then reviewing items on the list by deciding what is meant by each idea. For example, if it were proposed to investigate managerial stress in a particular organization, questions which might arise in a non-evaluated, brainstormed list might be:

1. What is managerial stress?
2. How is it to be identified?

3. Do 'managers' include 'supervisors'?
4. Might some managers be more stressed than others?
5. Will this be a function of the individual?
6. Or of the job?
7. Or of the supervisory style?
8. Might the investigation be focused on particular departments?
9. If so, which?
10. Does stress increase at particular times?
11. Is it possible to predict stressful events?
12. What remedial measures may be appropriate?
13. Is managerial stress openly discussed in organizations?

The next step with such a list is to analyse it carefully and ensure that it is clear what is meant by the terms used and what is to be discovered and why. In this way the aims and objectives of the study will become clearer, as will the tasks which require to be performed; irrelevant topics will also stand a better chance of being eliminated at this stage.

As well as checklists some authors (e.g. Howard and Sharp, 1983) suggest a more systematic approach to topic generation, by the use of particular techniques employed in the management of research and development Jantsch (1967). Such techniques have as their foundation the use of analogy, which may usefully indicate a line of inquiry by its resemblance to the one under consideration, or it may suggest a methodology that, having been employed in one field, may be applied to another. An example of the former was useful in suggesting approaches to consultants who were studying the implementation of computer-aided design into small businesses. Such a specialized topic had apparently had little research attention but when looking into related fields, such as the implementation of high technology in large manufacturing companies, it became clear that advances made there could, by analogy, provide useful insights in the field under study. Similarly, the methodology used to study marketing managers (Grafton-Small, 1985) was helped by analogy with the methods used by Watson (1977) in his study of personnel managers (see Chapter 7).

Other analogy-based techniques that may be employed to generate topics are forced relationships, attribute-listing, relevance trees and morphological analysis. Most of these techniques are best performed in a group, where the synergy introduced by an effective group process usually stimulates creativity. While research is often thought of as an individual effort, particularly in relation to student research projects, the usefulness of working in groups at particular stages of the work should not be underestimated.

Forced relationships involve attempting to relate anything in one's awareness to the problem at hand. It may be a particularly useful technique when an individual is temporarily bogged down and needs to be helped to bring back a flow of ideas. Attribute-listing, another technique to aid the flow of ideas, involves identifying particular aspects, or attributes, of the research area and then focusing on one of them.

Relevance trees are used to suggest ways of developing related ideas from a broad starting concept. As groups of related ideas are produced it becomes possible to identify manageable research areas. Relevance trees are therefore particularly useful for producing alternative areas for research or for helping to bring into focus otherwise vague ideas for a research topic.

Morphological analysis applies the notions of attribute-listing and forced relationships in a matrix, with the purpose of generating a large number of alternative ideas. For example, a morphological analysis of types of management research projects might produce three lists of attributes under factor headings as shown in Table 2.1.

Table 2.1 Morphological analysis

Objective	Method	Target
Exploratory	Experiments	Individuals
Explanatory	Quasi-experiments	Professional group
Clarification	Action research	Department
Theory	Surveys	Interdepartment organization
Problem-solving	Case Studies	
Conceptual	Longitudinal	Interorganization
Predictive	Ethnographic	National

Different research projects can then be generated by taking one attribute from each of the three columns. For example, an exploratory survey might be made of a professional group to define some research issues.

Such an analysis can be useful in offering insights and may be of particular help in focusing topics, although it is advisable to keep the number of factors low as morphological analysis is capable of producing a large number of alternatives.

All these techniques create many alternatives, which are of course useful only when carefully evaluated. (The ideal creative individual may be the manic-depressive who generates ideas in his manic phase and evaluates them later!)

Planning the project

In their book, *How to Get a PhD*, Phillips and Pugh (1987) refer to the need for planning as a means of overcoming some of the main difficulties inherent in such a large individual undertaking. What they have to say is also true of research in general, for a lack of systematic planning is likely to be at the heart of many difficulties.

These difficulties stem from initial enthusiasm, perhaps leading to over-ambitious projects, followed by periods of alienation as the earlier excitement diminishes, deadlines become increasingly irksome and the boredom of concentrating on a particular project for a long period becomes predominant. There are periods of feeling stuck, often towards the middle of the research, and other times when the work proceeds speedily and purposefully, especially when the end of the work is in sight. While all this may seem part of the very nature of such endeavour, the remedy for many of these problems is to manage time carefully by systematic timetabling and planning.

Virtually all research projects are best set out in the form of a proposal, which will generally be a summary of the researcher's more detailed plan. Some experienced researchers advocate the use of network analysis, a technique often applied to the planning of construction projects and which seems easily applicable to research work, particularly if students are already familiar with this approach (Howard and Sharp, 1983, p. 48).

The essentials of a research plan are contained in the questions asked, for example, in the CNAA's application form to register a higher degree and for most well organized master's courses having a dissertation component. Candidates are asked to define their field of interest, then their aims, and finally a plan, clarifying the proposed phases of the work, with dates; outlining the state of current knowledge and how the proposal intends to add to that knowledge; and, finally, the methods that will be used to research the topic. For example, a Ph.D. proposal (Noble, 1989) was structured as follows:

Title: Organisational Design and the Implementation of Office Information Systems

Aim: To identify the effects of different organisation design strategies on the implementation and successful exploitation of office systems.

What is known: The exploitation of office information systems is much less than anticipated in the early 1980s, in part because senior management are unsure of the strategic benefits of office automation, where to start, or how to manage the change process (Price Waterhouse 1988/89). Research on the organisational effects of office automation has focused on the introduction of word processing and the work and attitudes of typists and secretaries (Wainwright and Francis, 1984). Less is known about the effects of computerised office systems on interdepartmental relations and organisational structure and performance, and when they are used by managers and professionals (Olson and Lucas, 1982). The research will focus on the managerial issues involved in the successful introduction of new technology, which seem to depend on the interaction of technical and organisational factors and the quality of the implementation process (Marcus and Robey, 1983).

Plan of work

Phase One

1–4 Months
Literature searching on the nature and types of office systems; the strategic use of information technology; implementation approaches and methodologies; and qualitative research methods. Literature searching to continue throughout the project but particularly intense throughout this period.

1–6 Months
Comparison of implementation methodologies used by consultants, vendors and user organisations, with particular attention to organisational design implications.

Locating and entering six organisations which have recently implemented office systems.

6–12 Months
Three of the six organisations accessed in depth.

Phase Two

9 Months
Literature survey to be extended to analogous topics such as the management of innovation and methodological approaches widened to include, for example, Pava (1983); Mumford (1985); Checkland (1981) and Eason (1982).
Survey results analysed.
Fieldwork in the three organisations to continue and to be extended to three additional sites to represent differing implementation approaches and organisation types.
An original contribution to knowledge is expected to lie in the relationship between technology and organisation structure; the role of different management strategies in determining the outcome of technical change; and the identification of those environments and organisational constraints which inhibit the use of 'best practice'.

Phase Three

7 Months
Completion of Ph.D. thesis. Word processing and editing.

Methods

Research methods will be employed to build up case material from which generalizations will be made.
Semi-structured interviews will be conducted with senior management, IT staff, users, and heads of user departments.
Documents such as, for example, training manuals will be analysed.
A postal survey of 250 managing directors of leading UK companies will be conducted to discover the state of the art, i.e. the relevance of office systems to business strategy and the problems encountered in introducing it.

References
Checkland, P. (1981) *Systems Thinking, Systems Practice*, Wiley.
Eason, K. (1989) *Information Technology and Organisational Change*, Taylor and Francis.
Marcus, M. L. and Robey, D. (1983) The Organisational Validity of MIS. *Human Relations* 3, 6, 203–206.
Mumford, E. et al. (eds.) (1985) *Research Methods in Information Systems*, Elsevier Science Publishers, BV.
Olson, M. H. and Lucas, H. C. (1982) The impact of office automation on the organisation: some implications for research and practice. *Communications of the ACM*, 25, 11, Nov.
Pava, C. (1983) *Managing New Office Technology; an Organisational Strategy*, The Free Press.
Price Waterhouse (1988/9) Information Technology Review.
Wainwright, J and Francis, A. (1984) *Office Automation, Organisation and the Nature of Work*. Gower.

Clearly, then, planning is an important factor in determining the effectiveness and efficiency with which research is carried out. It is especially useful and motivating for students when stages in the work can be identified and dates agreed with supervisors. As with all plans, it will need to be revised from time to time but with an adequate plan progress can be assessed at any time, problems are more likely to be foreseen and contingencies can be taken care of.

Reviewing the literature

Whatever its scale, any research project will necessitate reading what has been written on the subject and gathering it together in a critical review which demonstrates some awareness of the current state of knowledge on the subject, its limitations, and how the proposed research aims to add to what is known. Indeed, one of the criteria for any research degree is to demonstrate a critical awareness of background studies and matters relating to the thesis.

While literature searches and reviews take place early in the research sequence, keeping up to date with the literature on the topic of course continues throughout the period of the research. The *Contents Pages in Management* published fortnightly by the Library and Information Service of Manchester Business School is a most useful means of ensuring current awareness as it contains copies of the contents pages of all journals received by the library. At this stage it is appropriate to make three important cautionary points. First, it is not uncommon for researchers to become bogged down in reading the literature so that it not only becomes a means of avoiding the tough process of writing, but also often seems to become unhelpful in advancing original ideas, as the student becomes submerged in those of other people. Accordingly, the state of the literature search needs to be kept under close review, in consultation with supervisors and colleagues, to avoid becoming over-concerned with other people's work at the expense of creativity.

Second, writing literature reviews can be a demanding exercise, for a critical review should provide the reader with a statement of the state of the art and major questions and issues in the field under consideration. Often they seem to be uncritical catalogues of all that has been found which vaguely relates to the topic regardless of the merits of the work. What is required is an insightful evaluation of what is known which leads naturally to a clarification of the gaps in the field and the way in which the proposed research is intended to fill them.

Third, it is most important when embarking on a literature search to ensure that everything that is read is noted systematically at the time. After quite a short period the likelihood of remembering is remote and much time may be wasted at later stages of the research, for example in locating a precise reference that has not been recorded when read. Such records are best kept on a card index or, even better, on a computerized file so that they can be searched, added to and sorted in multiple ways as required. Once a system is decided upon it is advisable to stick to it.

G. M. Smith (1975) offers a still useful guide to the information network open to researchers in business and management studies in Britain. The article, is structured in thirteen sections: general sources; economics; statistical data; company information; marketing; accountancy; behavioural sciences; industrial relations; personnel management; computers; quantitative methods and operations research; production management; mechanics of research and publication.

Each of these sections then contains subsections on bibliographies, such as *British Books in Print*; indexes, such as the *Social Sciences Citation Index*; abstracts, such as the Anbar Marketing and Distribution Abstracts and the *International Abstracts in Operations Research*; research registers, such as the *BLLD Announcement Bulletin*, which as well as listing reports and translations produced by British government organizations, industry and academic institutions, also lists most doctoral theses produced at British universities. Finally, some specialist libraries are listed such as the members' reference library of the Institute of Chartered Accountants in England and Wales and the Production Engineering Research Association Library.

In summary, in order to make a start on a research topic it is necessary to identify the broad area in which the work will be conducted and then to focus down into a manageable topic. The next step is to make a plan by which stages in the research will be achieved. Alongside these early activities it will be necessary to search the literature relating to the field under study to look for gaps in the broad area and to secure an early appreciation of work already completed or under way.

We may now turn to the primary focus of this book: the approaches to management research, their choice and justification.

Suggested further reading

There are a number of useful texts covering the ideas in this chapter. Details of publishers, etc., are given in the References at the end of the book.

At a fairly elementary level and designed primarily for education and social science students is J. Bell's *Doing Your Research Project*. The first section, 'Preparing the Ground', is particularly helpful and covers such issues as planning, and reviewing and keeping records of the literature.

Similarly, K. Howard and J. A. Sharp's *The Management of a Student Research Project* is especially helpful in introducing systematic techniques to many aspects of getting research projects underway. It is particularly helpful as its examples are drawn mainly from management research.

Focused specifically on Ph.D. research, and again drawing its examples mainly from management and business, is E. M. Phillips and D. S. Pugh's *How to Get A PhD*. It is written largely as advice to the student and is particularly helpful on time management, managing the supervisor and the procedural tasks necessary for successful completion.

On the specialized matter of topic selection reference may usefully be made to J. P. Campbell, R. L. Daft and C. L. Hulin's *What to Study: Generating and Developing Research Questions*. Although taking most of its examples from psychology, this book may be readily applied to the selection of topics in any field.

Finally, a very comprehensive book that takes literature reviewing to a fine art is H. M. Cooper's *Integrating Research: A Guide for Literature Reviews*. While the book is concerned with integrative literature reviews in the broad social sciences it should also prove helpful to the management researcher. It uses a phase model of the research process to discuss different aspects of literature reviewing. Students should read the introduction at least, and then further chapters according to needs.

3
The Role of Theory in Research Methods

Theory and practice

Although we might not be immediately aware of it, our everyday lives are fundamentally interwoven with theory. One important aspect of this 'theory-dependent' character relates to the way in which the various practical activities in which we routinely engage, might be seen as involving regular attempts to create, apply and evaluate theory.

Our use of the term 'theory-dependent' must not be confused with the term 'theory-laden'. Although the two are related, the latter specifically refers to the way in which the prior theories and values of the observer influence what he or she 'sees'; that is, as Hanson (1958, p. 7) claims, 'there is more to seeing than meets the eyeball'. Thus the issue of how observation is 'theory-laden' raises the problem that there is no independent or neutral point from which an observer might occupy and objectively observe the world and thus all knowledge is knowledge from particular points of view or paradigms (see Burrell and Morgan, 1979). The methodological implications of the 'theory-laden' nature of observation are considered later; meanwhile, we shall use the term 'theory-dependent' to refer to the way in which human practical activities entail the application of theory in various ways.

To many readers, particularly those who might perceive themselves as 'practical people', this might seem an absurd assertion. Often such a view is expressed in the lament of vocationally orientated management and business students, to which we referred in Chapter 1, that particular courses are too 'theoretical' or 'academic' and hence irrelevant to the 'real' world of their chosen careers. Intriguingly this lament resonates with the archaic Platonic–Aristotelian view that theoretical knowledge was knowledge acquired for its own sake, rather than for some use.

Both Plato and Aristotle severed theory from practice in the sense that they distinguished between *episteme* (genuine theoretical knowledge that was an end in itself) and *doxa* (opinions or beliefs suitable only for the conduct of practical affairs). For many commentators such a view tended to endow a passivity and submissiveness on the part of people to nature's vagaries. However, to some extent this view of knowledge and science lost its dominance during the seventeenth and eighteenth centuries with the arrival of a new version of the scientific enterprise articulated by people such as Francis Bacon (Tiles, 1987). This emphasized the necessity for science to provide knowledge and theory for the control of nature through the discovery of physical regularities which allowed for the prediction of, intervention into and manipulation of nature.

Moreover, as we shall try to demonstrate, the conception of theory as being divorced from practice is grounded in a misunderstanding of the nature and purposes of theory.

During our everyday lives we all regularly attempt to understand the events that occur around us. For instance, in regard to the social behaviour of the people with whom we have regular contact, whether colleagues at work or friends and neighbours, we routinely have expectations about the way they will behave in particular circumstances. These expectations are closely tied to explanations of why they behave in the ways that they do. These expectations and explanations might concern rather mundane events such as a friend's change in mood or the behaviour of particular groups of colleagues at work, or even more personally distant events such as the performance of the national cricket team or the apparent nationwide increase in the incidence of particular types of criminal behaviour. Regardless of the particular focus of these expectations and explanations, when the former are not fulfilled or when the latter appear to be wrong, we will often reflect upon recent events and experiences and thereby begin to generate new webs of explanations and expectations that help us understand and cope with the events that impinge upon us (Law and Lodge, 1984, p. 125). This process might result in our changing the way in which we do things, such as how we relate to friends or communicate with colleagues at work.

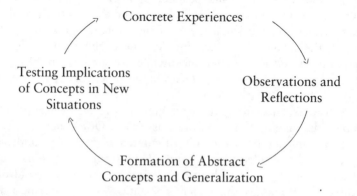

Figure 3.1   Kolb's experiential learning cycle

(Kolb, Rubin and McIntyre, Organization Psychology: An Experiential Approach. Reprinted by permission of Prentice-Hall Inc., Englewood Cliffs, NJ.1979 p. 38)

For Kolb, Rubin and McIntyre (1979), although their terminology is somewhat different, the above processes are linked to how human beings learn and might be diagramatically represented by the model in Figure 3.1.

According to Kolb, learning might start with the experience of an event or stimulus, which the individual then reflects upon in trying to make sense of it. This might lead to the generation of explanations of how or why something happened the way it did – explanations that can then be used to form an abstract rule or guiding principle that can be extrapolated (or generalized) to new events and stimuli of a similar type to that already experienced. Indeed, for Kolb, learning can start at this point where such a rule is merely received from others by the learner, along with its web of explanations and expectations, and is subsequently applied by that learner and thereby tested out. In either case, whether the rule is received or generated out of the prior experience and reflection, its testing in new situations creates new experiences which enable consequent reflection, observation and ultimately new rules. Kolb, Rubin and McIntyre (1979) suggest that particular individuals might emphasize particular elements of the learning cycle due to the presence of particular predilections into which they have been socialized.

For our purposes here, what is very significant about the processes described above is that they might be seen as attempts at constructing and evaluating explanatory statements, or theories, about what is going on around us. As Friedman (1953) puts it, such theories might be seen as 'filing systems' which allow observations to be used for predicting (i.e. they create expectations) and explaining events. For instance, consider the following statements/views.

1. The notion that a friend's evident irritability is due to his or her inability to get sufficient sleep the previous night.
2. The proposition that capital punishment deters would-be murderers.
3. The claim that the demise of English test match cricket is due to too many one day matches being played in county cricket.
4. The idea that improved training provision will create a more productive, reliable and satisfied workforce.

These four statements are all theories. They are all characterized by an attempt at explaining observations and, from those explanations, predictions or expectations might be generated. In this they reveal an important aspect of a theory – that it can be used to guide our practical actions, e.g. if we do A then B will happen, if we don't do A then C will happen. Taking theory 4 above, we could thus claim that if we improve a workforce's training we should expect an increase in employee productivity, reliability and satisfaction. By actually attempting to do this, and then by observing what happens, we can evaluate the accuracy of that theory; an outcome of that evaluation may be a retrospective change in the nature of theory 4 so as to make it more accurate.

Indeed, it is this latter process of the evaluation and change of theory, which is so often haphazard and imprecise, that for some commentators (e.g. Kidder and Judd, 1986, p. 5) separates science from common sense. Basically, it is claimed that 'science' entails deliberate and rigorous searches for bias and invalidity.

Now, so as to elaborate upon the above, it is necessary to consider more closely what a theory is and attempts to do. Although the terms 'theory' and 'hypothesis' are often used interchangeably, in its narrowest sense a theory is a network of hypotheses advanced so as to conceptualize and explain a particular social or natural phenomenon. In this, each hypothesis presents an assertion about the relationship between two or more concepts in an explanatory fashion. Concepts are the building blocks of theories and hypotheses in that they are 'abstract ideas which are used to classify together things sharing one or more common properties' (Krausz and Miller, 1974, p. 4).

For instance, in theory 4, or more accurately hypothesis 4, above 'improved training', 'productive', 'reliable' and 'satisfied' are all concepts. Moreover, we can see that theory 4 links together these concepts in an explanatory way. Such explanations are usually causal – that is, they state that one aspect of our world causes, or leads to another (see Pratt, 1978, pp. 65–7 for an elaboration of what is meant by 'cause' and its importance); that A Causes or leads to B i.e. (in theory 4) improved training causes or leads to a more productive, reliable and satisfied workforce.

An alternative example might be a hypothetical assertion that:

1. A participative management style causes or leads to job satisfaction among the manager's subordinates.
2. Job satisfaction causes or leads to increased productivity.

From 1 and 2 we might infer that:

3. A participative management style causes or leads to increased productivity among the manager's subordinates.

Obviously this theory would normally state the underlying reasoning behind the postulated associations between management style, job satisfaction and productivity. Although this example is simple, hypotheses can be much more complex, not only in terms of being interlinked with other hypotheses, but also by bringing in qualifying concepts that limit the causal relationship to particular classes of phenomena, e.g. A causes B only in conditions of C.

For instance, we could rewrite our initial hypothesis that a participative management style causes job satisfaction among subordinates by limiting its applicability to conditions where subordinates are motivated primarily by the desire for intrinsic rewards. By implication, where those conditions do not apply, neither does the hypothesis or eventual theory.

In trying to understand and explain the social and natural phenomena that surround us, and in our attempts at making decisions about what to do in particular circumstances, nobody escapes making or assuming these kinds of theoretical linkages. Every intentional act can be seen as an attempt to produce some desired state of affairs. This implies the belief on the part of the actor that a causal relationship exists between his or her decision, or act, and the state of affairs he or she desires. In this sense much of our everyday social lives and our work activities are in essence theory dependent activities. Now this clearly illustrates the conjectural and practical aspects of theory, since people act in accordance with their expectations, or prejudices, as to what will happen in particular circumstances – conjectures often derived from impressions regarding what has previously happened in similar circumstances. Thus, even the most mundane activity, such as walking down a street, might be considered in terms of an actor applying theoretical assertions, virtually without thinking about them in a conscious fashion, that are borne out by being able to accomplish that activity. Often it is only when we become aware that our expectations, that are grounded in such tacit or taken-for-granted knowledge, have not been met (perhaps due to the intervention of some capricious circumstances) that we begin consciously to re-evaluate the webs of causal relationships that have previously been used to orientate our action. Out of this re-evaluation we begin to generate a new theory to account for the previously unconsidered anomalies. So, to paraphrase Douglas (1970, pp. 80–103), such tacit knowledge is ordered and reordered according to the ebb and flow of situations.

So it is evident that theories are a means by which we generate expectations about the world; often they are derived from what we have perceived to have happened before and thus they influence (tacitly or otherwise) how we set about future interactions with our world(s). Moreover, it is also evident that if we have the expectation that by doing A, B will happen, then by manipulating the occurrence of A we can begin to predict and influence the occurrence of B. In other words, theory is clearly enmeshed in practice since explanation enables prediction which in turn enables control.

Indeed, one could argue that science has to some degree enabled the explanation and prediction of aspects of nature and thereby has allowed for human beings to exercise increasing control over nature. The advances in medicine, engineering and agriculture, for example, can all be considered in this light.

However, our concern in this review is with a substantive domain, management, that is essentially dependent upon the social sciences (see Lupton, 1971) in that its concern is primarily with the macro/micro behaviour and activities of human beings. Moreover, if we were to agree with commentators as varied as Braverman (1974, p. 68), Mant (1977) or Stewart (1982) there appears to be an inextricable relationship between management and the control of the behaviour of subordinates so as to ensure that the latter accomplish particular tasks. If this is so, the importance of theory so as to enable such a control process is only too evident: As Pugh (1971, p. 9) claims, every managerial act rests upon 'assumptions about what has happened and conjectures about what will happen; that is to say it rests on theory'.

As we have implied above, managers in their everyday activities rely upon both theories deriving from their 'common sense' and theories deriving from social science research. Although, as we shall see, the differences between the two are subtle and complex, many social scientists would ostensibly claim that the differences relate primarily to the extent to which social science research incorporates the overt and rigorous search for bias (Cook, 1983, p. 82), while common sense does not. For instance, Kidder and Judd (1986) claim that

social scientists look for biases and pitfalls in the processes used to support and validate hypotheses and submit their conclusions to the scrutiny
of other scientists who attempt to find biases that were overlooked. The
casual observer or ordinary knower often gathers evidence in support of
hypotheses without being aware of or worried about the biases inherent in
the process.

(op. cit., p. 18)

The danger in uncritically and unreflectively acting upon commonsense theories and hypotheses of the casual observer may be that one entraps oneself in
the current 'traditions' or 'fads' dominant among the social groups to which
we belong, at work or elsewhere. Although these traditions may at first sight
appear plausible, the potential for 'groupthink', so vividly described by Janis
(1972), is only too clear.

These issues provide a very useful starting point for considering the processes by which social science theories are constructed, evaluated and justified.
In other words, what are the sources of such theories and hypotheses, and how
do we set about judging rigorously, whether or not these theories and hypotheses are true?

Different answers to these questions enable us to distinguish between different social science research methods: that is, we can differentiate between
research methods that are deductive and those that are inductive.

Deduction

A deductive research method entails the development of a conceptual and
theoretical structure prior to its testing through empirical observation. As the
reader may realize, deduction in this sense corresponds to the left hand side of
Kolb's experiential learning cycle (see Figure 3.1) since it begins with abstract
conceptualization and then moves on to testing through the application of
theory so as to create new experiences or observations.

To many researchers working within the deductive tradition, the source of
one's theory is of little significance (Popper, 1967, pp. 130–43) – it is the
creative element in the process of science that is essentially unanalysable. Instead what is important is the logic of deduction and the operationalization
process, and how this involves the consequent testing of the theory by its
confrontation with the empirical world. Essentially the process of deduction
might be divided into the following stages.

1. The researcher decides which concepts represent important aspects of the
   theory or problem under investigation. As we have seen, concepts are abstractions that allow us to select and order our impressions of the world by
   enabling us to identify similarities and differences, e.g. 'efficient', 'social
   class', 'authoritarian', 'satisfied', and so on.

   The theory, or hypothesis, of interest links two or more concepts together
   in a causal chain – a set of untested assertions about the relationship between the concepts.

However, since concepts are abstract they are not readily observable, and therefore the asserted relationships between concepts provided by the theory are not open to empirical testing until these abstractions are translated into observables or indicators – that is, they have to be operationalized.

2. Through the operationalization of a concept it becomes defined in such a way that rules are laid down for making observations and determining when an instance of the concept has empirically occurred. For instance, take the concept 'managerial level' – something that is regularly used by some researchers to identify similarities and differences between the people with whom we come into contact, e.g. junior managers, middle managers and senior managers. But when people use this concept to categorize others, they often do so in vague and varied ways. For instance, the term 'middle manager' used by one person may mean something very different when used by another. They may appear to be talking about the same things when in fact they are not: e.g. one person might mean people in a certain income bracket, someone else may identify 'middle manager' with accent or educational background, but not income. Essentially, what these people are doing is operationalizing a concept in different ways hence creating different meanings.

Therefore by creating rules for making observations we are making a clear definition of what it is we are going to observe. In this we create indicators, or measures, which represent empirically observable instances or occurrences of the concepts under investigation. That is, we overtly link the abstract concept to something that is observable and whose variation is measurable. The linking rules, that is, the rules about when and where an observable instance of the concept has empirically occurred, are called operationalizations (see Figure 3.2). The point of these rules is that, by using the same indicators of a concept, and by standardizing the recording

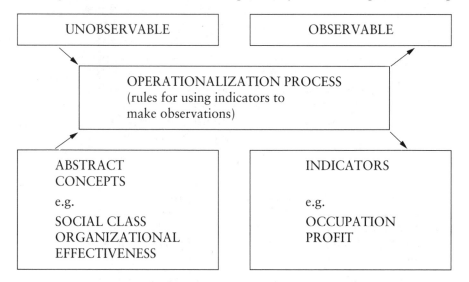

Figure 3.2   Operationalizing concepts

of the results of any observation, it should be possible to have a 'reliable' measure of the relevant concept.

There is a great deal of choice regarding how we operationalize concepts such as 'managerial level' or 'organizational efficiency' and it may be instructive at this point to try Exercise 3.1.

3. The process of operationalization enables the construction of clear and specific instructions about what and how to observe. This enables the testing of hypotheses and theories by confronting them with the empirical data, which is then collected. In this testing, priority is given to what are considered directly observable phenomena and behaviour: things, events or activities which are publicly observable and hence can be corroborated and agreed upon by other observers. This emphasis upon the control of potential bias through replication by others has thus led to attempts to create standardized procedures for undertaking observation that can be followed exactly by those other researchers. This has in turn created the tendency in this approach to dismiss the analysis of the subjective or intangible since these kinds of phenomena, it is often claimed, cannot be directly observed in an unproblematic fashion and hence any findings cannot be corroborated through the replication of the research by other researchers.

4. The outcome of the above is the process of testing, by which the assertions put forward by the theory or hypothesis are compared with the 'facts' collected by observation. Often, within the deductive tradition, once tested and corroborated the theory is assumed to be established as a valid explanation. Those explanations are often termed 'covering-law explanations' in that the observations or variables to be explained are covered by the assertions about those phenomena contained within the theory. However, since these covering-law explanations posit regular relationships between those variables, which hold across all circumstances, they not only explain past observations but also predict what future observations ought to be like. Take the example: 'water boils when heated to 100° centigrade, at sea level, in an open vessel'. This covering-law not only explains what has happened when water is heated to 100° centigrade in such circumstances, it also predicts what will happen if water is subjected to those conditions. However, in practice it is the statistical version of the covering-law, whereby the relationships asserted by the theory have only some degree of probability of obtaining across all circumstances, that

---

Exercise 3.1

1. Identify some alternative ways of operationalizing managerial level and organizational effectiveness with regard to the findings of research.
2. What do you think happens when we operationalize concepts in different ways?

What might this imply about deductive research methodology?

has generally been adopted by social scientists working within this deductive tradition.

We have used the term 'corroboration' (in 4 above) in a fairly unproblematic fashion; but what is possible in, and what is meant by, corroboration, is open to some dispute. Here we must turn to some of the debates that have taken place, and are continuing, in that branch of philosophy that has a concern with science: the 'philosophy of science'. What we are alluding to here has often been called 'Hume's problem of induction'. This problem arises because the testing of a theory inevitably involves a finite number of observations; and even if every observation that is made confirms the assertions put forward by a theory, logically we can never be certain whether some future observations might demonstrate instances in which the theory does not hold. It was Karl Popper, in perhaps one of his more famous contributions to the philosophy of science, who attempted to avoid the difficulties apparent in attempting to verify, or prove, a theory by a finite number of observations. Popper eschews 'verificationism', in which scientists attempt to prove or justify their theories, by proposing the maxim of 'falsificationism', in which scientists must attempt to refute their theories. At the risk of oversimplifying, what Popper (1967; 1972a; 1972b) proposes is that no theory can ever be proved by a finite number of observations; no matter how many confirmatory instances not yet observed which demonstrate the falsity of the theory. Take an example from Popper – that all swans are white; to Europeans this seemed self-evident, confirmed by millions of observations, until they explored the Australian continent. A further example of the potential problems created by 'induction' is provided by the statement 'one plus one equals two'. Again this appears self-evident, something that has been verified or confirmed by so many observations it would be impossible to count them. But according to the maxim of Popperian falsificationism, despite these numerous (but finite) confirmatory observations, we cannot be sure that some future instance might demonstrate its falsity, or limit its applicability. Indeed, such a consideration is to some extent borne out by the observations made in sub-atomic physics, that when two sub-atomic particles collide, their resultant fusion creates a mass that is sometimes more, or less, than their combined masses (Capra, 1975).

So, to summarize, Popper argues that while theories can never be proved true, they can be falsified, since only one contradictory observation is required. For Popper, therefore the defining features of scientific theories are:

1. they are capable of empirical testing;
2. scientists should not try to find confirming instances of their theories but, rather, should make rigorous attempts at falsifying them;
3. science advances as falsified propositions and theories fall away leaving a core of theory which has not, as yet, been disproved.

For Popper, knowledge grows through the above processes whereby error is removed. It follows that a critical attitude is a fundamental distinguishing feature of both science and rationality. Indeed, for Popper (1967, p. 50), a

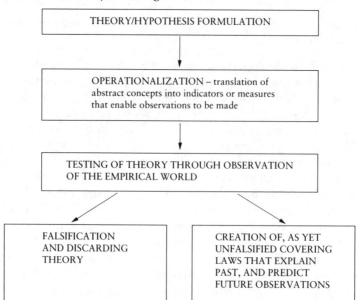

Figure 3.3   The process of deduction

dogmatic attitude 'is clearly related to the tendency to verify our laws and schemata by seeking to apply them and confirm them, even to the point of neglecting refutations, whereas the critical attitude is one of readiness to change them – to test them; to refute them; to falsify them, if possible'. The deductive approach is summarized in Figure 3.3.

The deductive tradition in the social sciences (although, as we shall show later, in Chapter 9, it is by no means unproblematic) clearly specifies what is involved in being 'scientific knowledge'. Often the approach illustrated in Figure 3.3 is called the 'hypothetico-deductive method'. It emphasizes that what is important in 'science' is not the sources of the theories and hypotheses that the scientist starts out with, rather it is the process by which those ideas are tested and justified that is crucial. Generally, the hypothetico-deductive approach to research is intimately bound up with what is often termed 'positivism'. Three of the main characteristics of positivism (there are others, which we shall consider later, that are elaborated in Keat and Urry, 1975, chapter 4) are:

1. the view that, for the social sciences to advance, they must follow the hypothetico-deductive methodology used, with such evident success, by natural scientists (e.g. physicists) – in a nutshell, the experimental method;
2. the knowledge produced and the explanations used in social science should be the same as those proffered by the natural sciences, – e.g. that A causes B;
3. the above entails social scientists treating their subject matter, the social world, as if it were the same as the natural world of the natural scientist.

It is from objections to the implications and assumptions of such a conception of social science that particular inductive approaches to research arise.

Induction

The logical ordering of induction is the reverse of deduction as it involves moving from the 'plane' of observation of the empirical world to the construction of explanations and theories about what has been observed. In this sense, induction relates to the right hand side of Kolb's learning cycle (Figure 3.1), i.e. learning by reflecting upon particular past experiences and through the formulation of abstract concepts, theories and generalizations that explain past, and predict future, experience. In sharp contrast to the deductive tradition, in which a conceptual and theoretical structure is developed prior to empirical research, theory is the outcome of induction.

The debates and rivalry between supporters of induction and supporters of deduction, in both the natural and social sciences, have a long history (for a useful overview, see Ryan, 1970, chapter 2). However, the modern justification for taking an inductive approach in the social sciences tends to revolve around two related arguments.

First, for many researchers working within the inductive tradition, explanations of social phenomena are relatively worthless unless they are grounded in observation and experience. Perhaps the most famous rendition of this view is provided by Glaser and Strauss (1967) in their book *The Discovery of Grounded Theory*. In this they argue that in contrast to the speculative and a priori nature of deductive theory, theory that inductively develops out of systematic empirical research is more likely to fit the data and thus is more likely to be useful, plausible and accessible.

The second, and related, rationale articulated in support of an inductive approach arises more overtly out of a critique of some of the philosophical assumptions embraced by positivism. It is to this critique that we shall now turn.

As we have seen, one of the main themes of positivism and of much of the deductive tradition in the social sciences is a conception of scientific method constructed from what is assumed to be the approach in the natural sciences, particularly physics. This entails the construction of covering-laws that explain past and predict future observations, through causal analysis and hypothesis testing. The format of this explanation and prediction is:

A causes B

or

Variation in A causes variation in B

that is

Stimulus A causes Response B

Specifically, it is this form of explanation and prediction that provides the initial point of departure for the ensuing critique that justifies much of inductivisim in the social sciences.

At the risk of oversimplifying, many supporters of induction in the social sciences reject the causal model illustrated above because they consider that this kind of explanation is inappropriate. Although it may be adequate for the subject matter of the natural sciences, it is not adequate for the social sciences.

This is because there are fundamental differences between the subject matter of the social sciences (human beings) and the subject matter of the natural sciences (animals and physical objects) from which the covering-law model came.

This position is illustrated by Laing (1967, p. 53), who points out the error of blindly following the approach of the natural sciences in the study of the social world. 'The error fundamentally is the failure to realise that there is an ontological discontinuity between human beings and it-beings . . . Persons are distinguished from things in that persons experience the world, whereas things behave in the world.'

Here Laing is drawing attention to the following issues.

1. Human action has an internal logic of its own which must be understood in order to make action intelligible. It is the aim of social science to understand this internal logic.
2. The subject matter of the natural sciences does not have this subjective comprehension of its own behaviour – it does not have an internal logic which the scientist must tap in order to understand its behaviour. Therefore the natural scientist can legitimately, and indeed has to, impose an external logic upon the behaviour of his or her subject matter in order to explain it. But such methodology is inappropriate and does not explain the actions of human beings, due to their subjectivity. Thus the behaviour of a billiard ball might be adequately understood in terms of necessary responses caused by particular sets of stimuli in certain conditions; but the actions of the billiards players can be adequately explained only through reference to their subjective motives and intentions; their interpretation of the situation and their knowledge of the rules of the game.
3. Therefore, the social world cannot be understood in terms of causal relationships that do not take account of the situation that human actions are based upon the actor's interpretation of events, his or her social meanings, intentions, motives, attitudes and beliefs; i.e. human action is explainable only by understanding this subjective quality. Therefore human action is seen as purposive and becomes intelligible only when we gain access to that subjective dimension.
4. It follows that research in the social sciences must entail emic analyses, in which explanations of human action derive from the meanings and interpretations of those conscious actors who are being studied. Thus the etic analyses embraced by deduction, in which an external frame of reference is imposed upon the behaviour of phenomena, are inappropriate where the phenomena in question have subjective capabilities – it is this internal dimension that is the key to explanation in the social sciences.

Inductivists therefore reject the stimulus–response model of human behaviour that is built into the methodological arguments of positivism. 'Stimulus causes response' is rejected in favour of:

(a) stimulus $\longrightarrow$ experience and interpretation $\longrightarrow$ response, *or*
(b) interpretation and meaning $\longrightarrow$ action.

In (a) above, the actor's subjectivity is taken to be an 'intervening variable' that mediates between the stimuli coming from external social reality and subsequent human responses expressed as behaviour or action. In (b), however, the actor's subjectivity is accorded greater 'formative or creative' power in its own right. Thus the interpretation of reality, upon which actions are based, is not merely the medium through which external stimuli act (as in (b)). Rather, it has a projective quality in the sense that such subjective processes create the reality in which action arises (see Berger and Luckmann, 1967), and hence the conception that subjectivity mediates external stimuli becomes rather meaningless. All there is is that subjectivity.

Although these differences have resulted in somewhat different methodological traditions, both (a) and (b) above share a commitment to conceiving human action as arising out of actors' subjectivity. Thus the possession by human beings of a mind has freed them from the stimulus–response relationships that dominate the behaviour of 'natural phenomena' (see Mead, 1934). Obviously, this view has created particular methodological commitments.

1. It creates serious objections to the positivist contention that social phenomena might be treated as being analogous to the 'it-beings' or 'things' of nature and thereby are amenable to a similar type of causal analysis in which the subjective or intentional dimension is lost. Instead, it is postulated that the difference between the social and the natural world is

   that the latter does not constitute itself as 'meaningful': the meanings it has are produced by men in the course of their practical life, and as a consequence of their endeavours to explain it for themselves. Social life – of which these endeavours are part – on the one hand, is produced by its component actors, precisely in terms of their active constitution and re-constitution of frames of meaning whereby they organise their experience.

   (Giddens, 1976, p. 79)

2. These considerations create the need for social scientists, to explain human behaviour adequately, to develop a sympathetic understanding of the frames of reference and meaning out of which that behaviour arises. This sympathetic understanding is sometimes called *'verstehen'*, and it entails 'fidelity to the phenomena under study' (Hammersley and Atkinson, 1983, p. 7).

3. The methodological implications of this perspective entail the avoidance of the highly structural approaches of deduction; these, it is usually argued, prevent and ignore the penetration of actors' subjectivity. This happens because the deductive researcher, prior to conducting empirical research, formulates a theoretical model of the behaviour of interest, which is then tested. Hence they impose an external logic upon a phenomenon which has an internal logic of its own. It is precisely the discovery of this internal logic, through empirical research, that is the concern of many supporters of induction in the social sciences. To achieve this, what is recommended are unstructured approaches to research that ostensibly allow for access to human subjectivity, without creating distortion, in its natural or everyday setting.

4. Naturally the prescriptions described above have caused the positivist counter-argument that because this kind of inductive research, is unstructured, it is unreliable since it is not replicable and therefore bias cannot be ruled out. Indeed, many positivists regard the 'intuitive or empathic grasp of consciousness' as merely a possible source of hypotheses about human conduct and not a method for social science research in its own right (Giddens, 1976, p. 19).

Research methods compared

As a heuristic device, it is possible to construct a continuum of research methods that allows us to differentiate between different methods in terms of the various logics they bring to bear in conducting research. That is, we can discriminate between different methods in terms of their relative emphasis upon deduction or induction, their degree of structure, the kinds of data they generate and the forms of explanation they create. At each extreme of the continuum we can distinguish what are known as nomothetic and ideographic methodologies.

Nomothetic methodologies (Burrell and Morgan, 1979, pp. 6–7) have an emphasis on the importance of basing research upon systematic protocol and technique. This is epitomized in the approach and methods employed in the natural sciences, which focus upon the process of testing hypotheses in accordance with the standards of scientific rigour. Standardized research instruments of all kinds are prominent among these methodologies. Emphasis is therefore, placed upon covering–law explanations and deduction, using quantified operationalizations of concepts in which the element of motive/purpose/meaning is lost, because of the need for precise models and hypotheses for testing.

Table 3.1   A Comparison of nomothetic and ideographic methods

Nomothetic methods emphasize		Ideographic methods emphasize
1. Deduction	*vs*	Induction
2. Explanation via analysis of causal relationships and explanation by covering-laws (etic)	*vs*	Explanation of subjective meaning systems and explanation by understanding (emic)
3. Generation and use of quantitative data	*vs*	generation and use of qualitative data
4. Use of various controls, physical or statistical, so as to allow the testing of hypotheses	*vs*	Commitment to research in everyday settings, to allow access to, and minimize reactivity among the subjects of research
5. Highly structured research methodology to ensure replicability of 1, 2, 3 and 4	*vs*	Minimum structure to ensure 2, 3 and 4 (and as a result of 1)

Laboratory experiments, Quasi experiments, Surveys, Action Research, Ethnography

Ideographic methodologies (Burrell and Morgan, 1979 pp.6–7), on the other hand, emphasize the analysis of subjective accounts that one generates by 'getting inside' situations and involving oneself in the everyday flow of life. There is an emphasis upon theory grounded in such empirical observations which takes account of subjects' meaning and interpretational systems in order to gain explanation by understanding.

Any method adopts a position on a continuum according to its relative emphasis upon the above characteristics shown in Table 3.1.

It is to the various different methods (laboratory, quasi-experiments, surveys, action research and ethnography), their various commitments and characteristics, together with their use in management research, that we turn in the following chapters. First, however, we consider experimental research design.

Suggested further reading

The following will be particularly useful in elaborating some of our points: Full bibliographical information appears in References, at the end of the book.

H. Blumer's 'What is wrong with social theory' provides an interesting consideration of the role and nature of theory in social science, as does T. Lupton's *Management and the Social Sciences* with specific reference to management. Also useful for its focus on the world of the manager is P. Checkland's *Systems Thinking, Systems Practice*. Checkland himself trained as a physical scientist, reviews the systems movement as a scientific endeavour to tackle the ill-structured problems of the managerial world. He comes to the conclusion that 'hard systems' engineering needs to be modified to something more appropriate which he calls 'soft systems' methodology. We have found the book to be particularly useful in helping students from a background in the physical or natural sciences to bridge the gap between 'hard' and 'soft' systems approaches to management research.

W. Wallace's *The Logic of Science in Sociology* elaborates an overview of the various elements in scientific research with particular reference to issues of induction and deduction. M. Lessnoff's *The Structure of Social Science* gives a detailed survey of many of the philosophical issues important in social science research, with an interesting focus upon the relevance of a natural science 'model' for research in the social sciences.

4
Experimental Research Design

The structuring process

The design of empirical research at the deductive end of the continuum of research methods outlined in Chapter 3 attempts to provide a blueprint that enables the researcher to structure a research problem in such a way that the outcome is the production of valid, objective and replicable answers. This initial structuring process entails four basic steps.

1. The first step is to delineate carefully the questions or problems the research is attempting to tackle. In this it is important to identify the particular phenomenon or factor whose variation we are trying to explain or understand: that is, we must identify what is known as the 'theoretically dependent variable'.
2. The second step involves identifying the phenomena or factors whose variation, according to the theory or hypothesis we are testing, explains or causes changes in our dependent variable. These causal or explanatory variables are usually termed the 'theoretically independent variables', and are the phenomena whose influence upon the dependent variable we are specifically interested in investigating.
3. In order to monitor any variation in the dependent and independent variables it is also necessary to operationalize them. This not only allows for the observation and measurement of any variation in the dependent and independent variables but also enables the researcher purposively to vary or manipulate the incidence of the latter. As we shall see, the ability to do this is a vital component of particular types of research design.
4. The final step deals with the issue that any observed variation in the dependent variable might not necessarily be an outcome of the action of the independent variable(s). So it follows that the fourth step in research design is to try to neutralize, or control for, the effects upon the dependent variable of what are usually called 'extraneous variables'.

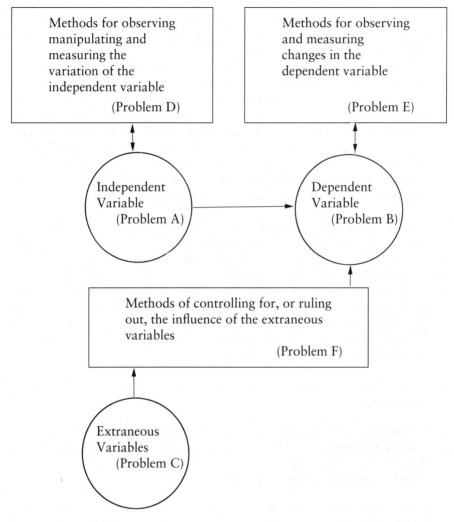

Figure 4.1   The problems for research design in deductive research

Extraneous variables (see Figure 4.1) other than those included in the research design as independent variable(s) are phenomena that might cause some of the variation observed in the dependent variable and thus provide alternative explanations of that observed variability; that is, they constitute rival hypotheses to the one(s) being put forward in our specification and operationalization of the independent variable(s). If the possible influence of these extraneous variables is not neutralized by some means, they might confound our interpretation of any observed association between the nominated dependent and independent variables. If through the research design we fail to control for the effects of extraneous variables, the internal validity

(Campbell and Stanley, 1963) of any findings is threatened. In other words, we could not be certain whether the independent variable *did* cause the observed changes in the dependent variable.

So it is vital in deductive hypothesis testing research, if we are to be able to make warranted statements about the relationship between the independent variables, both to identify any potentially extraneous variables and to develop a research design that neutralizes, rules out or controls for their confounding influence upon the dependent variable. Only when we have been successful in achieving this, and thereby have ruled out any rival hypotheses to those under test, can we claim internal validity for our research findings: only at that point can we make warranted statements about the association between independent and dependent variables.

These problems for research design at the deductive end of the continuum are represented in Figure 4.1. Although problems A to F in Figure 4.1 are all interrelated we can, for the sake of clarity, consider that problems A, B and C are concerned with identifying and defining the three types of variable and are essentially theoretical issues. Problems D, E and F are concerned with observing, manipulating, measuring and controlling variables and are essentially methodological issues. It is the way in which problems D, E and F are dealt with that leads to different kinds of deductive research design. At this point it will be helpful to try to do Exercise 4.1.

Exercise 4.1

You are interested in the contention that the educational attainment of MBA students is improved by the addition of mineral supplements to their daily diets. Design a way of investigating this proposition by following stages 1 to 3 below.

1. Identify the dependent and independent variables by constructing a researchable proposition, or hypothesis, about the relationship between the consumption of mineral supplements and MBA students' educational attainments.
2. Identify any other (i.e. extraneous) factors that might influence any observed variation in your designated dependent variable.
3. Deal with problems D, E and F (see Figure 4.1) by developing an appropriate research design.

If you did try to follow steps 1 to 3 in Exercise 4.1 you will probably have attempted to construct a research design that was in essence experimental. That is, you probably tried to vary the designated independent variable (the intake of mineral supplements) and monitor its effects upon the designated dependent variable (educational attainment), while trying to eliminate the effects of potential extraneous variables (e.g. age, IQ, etc.).

It is now necessary to proceed to consider experimental design in more detail by beginning with the 'true' or 'classical' experiment.

'True' or 'classical' experiments

Compared to the situation in substantive areas such as psychology, it appears that the true or classical experiment in management research is relatively unusual. Perhaps this is largely because in the true experiment the relevant behaviour of interest is not observed in its natural everyday setting. Rather, it is often only in laboratory conditions, where the researcher can exercise a great deal of control and manipulate the relevant variables, that the true experiment can take place. This creates not only numerous methodological strengths but also many problems, particularly with regard to the artificiality of the research setting.

Despite the apparent rarity of the true experiment in management research, however, and despite its inherently problematic nature, it is important for any researcher to be conversant with the logic that forms the basis of the 'true' experiment. This is because this very logic underpins many of the deductive research methodologies commonly used in management research, some aspects of which are considered in later chapters and which in essence take the logic of experimentation out of the laboratory.

The logic of the true experiment

The English philosopher, John Stuart Mill (1874), in his work *A System of Logic*, succinctly describes the experiment as the 'method of difference'. Indeed, as we shall attempt to show, the processes of manipulating, comparing and looking for differences are at the heart of experimental logic, whether it is expressed in the form of the true experiment or in the form of quasi-experiments.

As in all deductive approaches to research design the experimenter begins by developing a theoretical model of the phenomena of interest by identifying the independent, dependent and extraneous variables. Having operationalized those variables the model then enables the experimenter to produce predictions which may then be tested by confronting them with 'reality' in a true experiment. For instance, the prediction that would have been tested in the previous Exercise 4.1 would be that the intake of mineral supplements causes an increase in educational attainment. However, to test such a prediction through the design of a true experiment the following conditions must be met.

1. The experimenter must be able to manipulate the occurrence and non-occurrence of the independent variable through his or her direct intervention (e.g. the intake of mineral supplements).
2. The experimenter must be able to identify and measure any subsequent changes in the dependent variable (e.g. variation in educational achievement).

3. The experimenter must be able to control the effects of any extraneous variables upon the dependent variable (e.g. age, IQ, etc.).

In accomplishing 1 and 3 above we can distinguish one of the best known hallmarks of the true experiment: the creation of what are called 'control groups' and 'experimental groups'.

An experimental group is composed of subjects who experience the effects of the independent variable (often called the 'experimental treatment'). Any changes in the designated dependent variable are then monitored and measured.

A control group is composed of subjects who have not undergone the experimental treatment and who are compared with those who have been subjected to that independent variable. Any differences between the two groups, in terms of that independent variable, are then identified and noted.

Therefore in our example, one (experimental) group of MBA students have mineral supplements and any changes in their educational attainment are then measured. Another (control) group of MBA students do not have any mineral supplements. Any changes in their educational attainment are also measured. The educational attainment of each group is then compared and any differences identified.

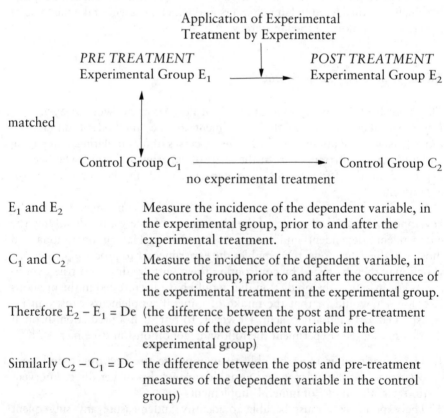

Figure 4.2   Experimental protocol and procedure

The idea behind this procedure is that if the experimental and control groups have been matched so that they are exactly the same, save for the incidence of the independent variable, any differences between the two groups after the experimental treatment must be due to the action of that treatment. Control and experimental groups are therefore used to ensure the elimination of the effects of as many extraneous variables as possible so that the only difference between them is the independent variable. It logically follows that any ensuing difference between them in respect of the dependent variable must be due to the effects of the independent variable. In this way it is possible to test the predictions posed by the original theoretical model. This whole procedure is illustrated in Figure 4.2.

Any difference between De and Dc (as defined in Figure 4.2) must be due to the manipulation effects of the independent variable. The nature of this difference, or indeed lack of it, then casts light upon the accuracy of the original predictions from the theoretical model.

The process of matching experimental and control groups

As is illustrated by Figure 4.2, the process of matching experimental and control groups prior to any 'treatment' is vital in the control of extraneous variables and allows for some confidence regarding the internal validity of any consequent findings. In the true experiment matching is usually achieved by one of two techniques.

Perhaps the most commonly used matching technique is randomization, or random assignment. Subjects are randomly assigned to control and experimental groups, therefore leaving it to chance that extraneous variables are equally distributed among the groups. Indeed, the assumption is that all variables, except the independent variable, will be randomly distributed and hence the control and experimental groups will be equivalent and thus comparable. The reasoning behind this assumption is that if subjects are allocated on a random basis their individual differences, wherein lie many potential extraneous variables, will also be randomly distributed together with their potentially confounding influences upon the dependent variable(s).

In our example, the procedure would be to allocate the MBA students randomly between a group that would have mineral supplements and a group that would not. The assumption would be that the extraneous variables, such as age, IQ, and so on, would also be randomly distributed. However, although randomization appears to allow for the creation of equivalent control and experimental groups, there is always the chance, particularly when dealing with small groups, that some bias is accidentally introduced so that a particular type of person predominates in one group and not the other. Although this possibility reduces as the size of the groups increases, there is no absolute guarantee in randomization that the groups created are equivalent. Perhaps it is this concern, that some important extraneous variable might be unevenly distributed accidentally, that has led some researchers to adopt an alternative procedure for matching control and experimental groups.

In using systematic controls the intent is again to create equivalent control and experimental groups, but in this case equivalence is specifically in terms of the extraneous variables that have been previously identified as potential sources of influence upon the independent variable. So an attempt is made to match subjects in the control and experimental groups on what appear to be characteristics and phenomena that might confound any results if they were not controlled for. Thus, in our example, a systematic attempt would be made to match the MBA students in the control and experimental groups according to characteristics that appear to have an influence on educational attainment (e.g. age). In identifying these characteristics, clearly the research would need to apply theory regarding educational attainment. Here a source of bias might creep in through a lack of knowledge about the influences upon educational attainment. A characteristic that influences educational attainment might be overlooked, not systematically controlled, and thus inadvertently create non-equivalent experimental and control groups by not being evenly distributed.

Both randomization and systematic controls are physical controls (i.e. subjects are physically allocated to experimental and control groups through the use of either procedure) aimed at ruling out rival explanations to those being advanced in the experimental treatment. Nevertheless, they both entail threats to the internal validity of any subsequent findings: some deriving from chance and bad luck, others from a lack of knowledge about possible extraneous influences upon the dependent variable. In principle, however, if the control and experimental groups are exactly matched, and consequently the only difference between them is the action of the independent variable(s), the internal validity of the true experiment is potentially very strong. Yet the problematic nature of matching must always cast some degree of doubt on whether or not any observed changes in the dependent variable are actually attributable to the experimenter's manipulation of the dependent variable. This potential source of bias must be a constant concern in the design and implementation of experiments; as we shall see, however, it is not the only one.

So far we have discussed biases that might arise from the inadvertent selection of non-equivalent experimental and control groups. However, other biases might arise during the course of the experiment.

Biases arising during the course of a true experiment

At the risk of oversimplifying, it is possible to distinguish three potential sources of bias that can and do arise during the course of a true experiment:

1. biases due to changes affecting the members of the experimental and control groups;
2. biases due to changes in the measurement processes;
3. biases due to the subjects' reaction to the processes and context of the experiment.

We shall now review each of these problematic areas in turn.

Changes affecting group members

This category of potential biases might threaten the validity of any experimental results. It refers to any unexpected and unintended changes, from the point of view of experimental design, that might affect members of the control and experimental groups during the course of the experiment and thereby influence or mediate the effects of the independent variable(s). In other words, such changes might create unforeseen extraneous variables. Any subsequent findings regarding the relationship between the dependent and independent variables must then be doubtful since they may be a result of the distorting influence of those uncontrolled extraneous variables. Unforeseen events and changes in the lives of subjects – varying, for example, from the psychological and physiological to the social, political and economic – may occur during the course of the experiment. These might affect how the subjects behave or perform and thus provide rival explanations to that preferred by the independent variable for any measured changes in the dependent variable. Essentially, the longer the time lapse between the pre-test and post-test measurements of the dependent variable the more likely it is that some of these events and changes may have occurred and their presence threaten the validity of any causal inference propounded by the unwitting experimenter.

So far, we have considered only changes in subjects created by processes happening outside the experimental context. Yet some inadvertent change might be created by the very procedures used by the researcher in his or her investigations. The processes of pre-testing and post-testing can themselves often cause a change in the dependent variable, thus obfuscating the experimenter's perception of the independent variables. Subjects may, for instance, become accustomed to, and more proficient at, the pre-test. Therefore any changes in their scores when it comes to post-testing might be attributed to their greater experience of that procedure, rather than to the influence of the experimental treatment. Indeed, in our example, the MBA students might well become accustomed to the educational attainment tests used in pre- and post-testing.

Many of these sources of bias may be resolved through better experimental design, particularly through the matching of control and experimental groups. However, an even greater problem for experimenters arises from changes occurring in subjects during the course of the experiment, as a reaction to the artificiality of the context and processes of experimental research – a reaction which better experimental design might exacerbate rather than resolve. These problems will be considered more closely after the next section.

Changes in the measurement processes

Generally, there are two main possible sources of change in the measurement process that can threaten the validity of any findings. The first is the withdrawal of subjects from either group during investigation, often called 'experimental mortality'. It becomes a significant problem when withdraws are such that researchers are no longer measuring and comparing like with like at the pre- and post-test analyses of the dependent variable. Indeed, this problem will be exacerbated when the 'drop-outs', whether from the experimental or control group, share some characteristic that differentiates them from subjects who continue to participate in the research. The danger is that the researchers might draw conclusions from incomplete sets of data and hence the validity of those conclusions may be doubtful.

The second source of changes in the measurement process relates to intended or unintended changes in the instrumentation that enables pre-test and post-test measurement of the independent variable. If, for whatever reason, changes occur in the procedures used in measuring the dependent variable, any observed differencs in that variable could be attributed to those changes rather than to any actual change in that variable. The different instrumentation may be inadvertently sampling and measuring different phenomena and thus the researcher is not observing the same things with his or her pre-test and post-test measurements; is no longer comparing like with like.

The potential biases discussed in the previous two sections can pose significant problems in experimental design. Moreover, they are important elements for consideration in evaluating the robustness of any experimental research findings. But it is important to emphasize that they can be resolved largely through the careful design and maintenance of experimental procedures, particularly in the measurement of variables and the matching of control and experimental groups. In other words, the issues discussed above do not create inevitable or inherent biases in experimental design. Moreover, carefully designed and implemented experiments have several major strengths.

Experiments are highly structured and entail a priori delineation of the theory under test and the explicit construction and statement of the hypotheses that will be tested. In addition, since the methods for operationalizing, measuring and manipulating variables will be specified, other researchers can easily replicate experiments to check any findings. Furthermore, the use of control and experimental groups, together with the manipulation of one or more independent variables, enables researchers to control for, and rule out, the influence of extraneous variables. This high degree of (physical) control allows researchers to demonstrate and evaluate the independent variable(s)' causal effects upon the dependent variable through their manipulation of the conditions experienced by subjects. So the control afforded by the true experiment can provide some degree of certainty as to whether or not the independent variables *did* cause any observed changes in the dependent variable; that is the internal validity of the true experiment can be seen to be relatively strong.

However, while the high degree of structure and control provided by the true experiment confers significant strengths, those very strengths are seen to create particular problems that have led some researchers to question the utility of the true experiment in management and social science research. Many of these problems appertain to the reactions of subjects to the artificiality of the true experiment; an artificiality created by that same structure. So, as we address the issue of biases arising out of subjects' reactions to the processes and context of the true experiment, we confront weaknesses that stem from that very design which endows experimental research with particular strengths. Indeed, we confront what are perhaps irresolvable sources of bias inherent in the design of true experiments.

Subjects' reaction to the processes and context of the experiment

There are several complex and interrelated aspects to this issue of reactivity that need to be considered here. Some of these issues relate to the processes by which subjects comprehend, interpret and attach meaning to the stimuli that constitute the experimental treatment or independent variable(s). The problem is whether or not subjects, during these sense-making activities, attach the same meanings to those stimuli as do fellow subjects and researchers. Do they experience the same phenomena or, because interpretation can vary, do they attach different meanings to those ostensibly shared events and thus experience different phenomena and stimuli? Obviously the internal validity of experiments depends upon the assumption that subjects experience the same stimuli that constitute the independent variable(s).

A second aspect of this problem relates to the social interaction that often occurs between an experimenter and subjects. As we try to illustrate, sometimes an experimenter might unintentionally influence events and thus distort or mediate the effects of the independent variable upon subjects' behaviour by his or her very presence in the research context, and by any subsequent interaction with subjects. Again, if this occurs, and if this is unavoidable in this type of experimental research, it creates a major threat to the validity of the experiment.

Finally, we must also consider the broader issue of the artificiality of the context in which a true experiment takes place. Since such research occurs only through the contrivance of a researcher in what amounts to a laboratory setting, its context is artificial, from the subjects' point of view. The situation in which a true experiment takes place is markedly different from and outside the normal, everyday situation in which subjects perform the acts that are the focus of the experimental design. This leads to the question whether or not it is possible for researchers to generalize or extrapolate their findings from the artificial situation of a laboratory to the everyday and mundane situations in which people normally behave: in essence, are such findings limited to the laboratory context in which the research took place?

The issues delineated above pose a potentially devastating critique of the use of the true experiment in social science and management research. In the natural or physical sciences these issues are not as significant since inanimate phenomena, such as molecules of water, are unaware of the context of the experimental research, the procedure in use or the behaviour of a chemist or physicist. But human beings patently would be aware of these aspects. Therefore it is necessary to look at these matters more closely by considering an example of an influential experiment in management research. Here we include some of the problems confronted by the researchers and the way in which they attempted to deal with them.

The Hawthorne studies

In 1924, at the Hawthorne Plant of the Western Electric Company in Chicago, there began a series of experiments aimed at investigating the relationship between different kinds of physical working conditions, such as illumination, temperature, humidity and the frequency of rest pauses, and the productivity of employees (Roethlisberger and Dickson, 1939). Underlying this approach was the assertion that, for instance, there would be an ideal level of illumination or temperature at which productivity would be maximized. Therefore physical working conditions, such as the degree of brightness of illumination, were taken to be independent variables, which were experimentally manipulated and their effects upon the dependent variable, employee output, monitored.

Two groups of employees, matched in terms of their productivity, were selected and isolated from the rest of the workforce by placing them in what amounted to laboratory conditions in different parts of the plant. So, included in the initial research design was a control group of employees who were not subjected to the experimental treatments and whose output was also monitored.

The findings were rather unexpected and confusing. For example, output in the experimental group increased regardless of how illumination was manipulated. Even when lighting was dimmed to a flicker, output still increased! Output in the control group also steadily increased despite the absence of experimental manipulation of the physical working conditions.

The researchers then conducted a series of experiments in the relay assembly test room, to provide a more detailed investigation of the effects of different physical conditions upon employee productivity. These experiments again entailed segregating a group of employees (whose output had previously been secretly measured) from other workers and manipulating their working conditions while monitoring their output. No matter what the researchers did – even lengthening the working day and reducing rest periods – there appeared to be little effect upon an upward trend in productivity.

These events caused the researchers to conclude that they were not investigating simply the effects of changing physical working conditions upon productivity. They were also inadvertently researching employee attitudes, values and norms, which were mediating the effects of the experimental treatments. These conclusions, and the later research which developed from such findings, have been credited with raising important issues regarding motivation and the role of the 'informal' organization (Schein, 1970). Methodologically, they are important here for demonstrating some of the problems associated with the true experiment, not the least of which has since become known as the 'Hawthorne effect'. Before turning to the 'Hawthorne effect' it is useful to consider some weaknesses evident in this research which could have been avoided through more careful design of the experiments.

1. Although the illumination experiments entailed the use of experimental and control groups, the researchers failed to match these groups by using

randomization or systematic controls. It follows that the researchers were unlikely to be comparing like with like, and this was exacerbated by their failure to isolate the control and experimental groups under identical conditions. These particular threats to the internal validity of the experiments were heightened in their later research when, in the relay assembly test room experiments, the researchers inexplicably failed to use a control group to control extraneous variables.

2. External events affected how subjects behaved occurred during the course of some of the experiments. For instance, the depression of the early 1930s caused the female subjects participating in the relay assembly test room experiments to express anxiety regarding their job security, and eventually halted that experiment (Rose, 1975 p. 108). Yet the effects of these events were not fully or competently assessed and, due to the lack of a control group, constituted yet another threat to the internal validity of the research.

3. Experimental mortality occurred during the relay assembly test room research due to the actions of the experimenters. At an early stage two operators were replaced for being 'uncooperative'. This characteristic seems to have clearly differentiated them from other participants and poses the danger that by replacing them the researchers began to draw conclusions from biased data sources.

4. This last issue implicitly raises the question how representative were the personnel involved in the experiments of the Hawthorne workforce, or indeed of employees generally. The initial relay assembly test room experiments involved only six female personnel, yet the Hawthorne workforce totalled some 40,000. This issue of representativeness, or population validity, can be a major problem for experimental research.

True experiments by their very nature can only involve relatively small numbers of people. This poses the problem of how any findings can be generalized to the wider population when they are derived from such a small database. This matter might not appear to be a problem for experimental research in the natural and physical sciences, whose subject matter is assumed to be homogeneous (e.g. one molecule of water is considered to display the same characteristics and behaviour as any other molecule of water). Such an assumption is not possible, however, when research concerns human beings – who are so evidently heterogeneous.

In principle this problem of population validity can be partly resolved by the prior random sampling of people from a particular population (e.g. the Hawthorne workforce) and then assigning them to the experimental and control groups. Any results can then be extrapolated from the original population from which the sample of subjects was drawn. Thus, as with other problems so far discussed regarding the Hawthorne experiments, better design and maintenance of experimental procedures might have resolved them and allowed the researchers to avoid arriving at what seem to be spurious conclusions.

The Hawthorne effect

The behaviour of the subjects, in apparent response to the experimental treatments administered during the illumination and relay assembly investigations that so surprised the Hawthorne researchers, has since been explained by what has been termed the 'Hawthorne effect'. This phenomenon refers to the way in which the novelty of experiencing a new situation, together with their sense of being a special group that had become the focus of attention, influencd the participants' response to their situation. It may therefore be argued that the observed increases in output, in the various control and experimental groups, were a product of the experimental situation itself. That is to say they were artifacts, created by these conditions, which in effect were mediating and obscuring the underlying relationship between the independent and dependent variables. Strangely, this phenomenon had been observed earlier and noted by Myers in a similar context. Myers (1924, p. 28, quoted in Rose, 1975, p. 96) claimed that 'sometimes the mere presence of the Institute's investigators and the interest they have shown in employees' work has served to send output up before any changes have been introduced'.

Generally, this phenomenon of the Hawthorne effect, often called 'experimental artifacts', might usefully be subdivided into three related areas: indexicality, experimenter effects, and subjects' mediation through interpretation. We elaborate each in turn and then consider their methodological implications.

1. *Indexicality*   This refers to the way that people vary their behaviour according to the situation in which they find themselves. Our own everyday experience tells us that as we move from social context to social context we modify and try to control how we behave in terms of our understanding of the situation and our impressions of the people with whom we interact (Goffman, 1969; Douglas, 1976). For instance, it would be unlikely for someone to behave in the same way and use the same speech codes in a meeting at work as when drinking with friends at their 'local'. So it would appear that how we behave, and the impressions we 'give off' to others in a specific social context, are intimately bound to that context since it greatly influences their production.

   Accordingly, a true experiment taking place in laboratory conditions is as much a social situation as drinking with friends in a pub. Therefore, can any behaviours elicited during the course of a laboratory experiment be understood in isolation from the social context which has been contrived to produce it? Perhaps the Hawthorne experiments illustrate how such behaviour is indeed 'bounded' by, and intelligible only in terms of, that social context.

   The problem this poses for the true experiment is whether or not the behaviour observed in an experimental situation will be repeated in a subject's natural or everyday surroundings. This raises the question whether or not the results of experiments are mere artifacts of the research procedures used, and the social situation thereby contrived, which can be extrapolated to social contexts beyond that surrounding the experiment.

2. *Experimenter effects* This matter is closely linked to the problem of indexicality. It refers to the way in which a particular experimenter may inadvertently influence the behaviour of different subjects, or the varying effect that different experimenters may have upon the same subject. As we have seen, the way people behave in a social situation is often influenced by how they perceive the other people present in that situation. In an experiment probably the most significant 'other' will be the experimenter. Therefore the personal qualities attributed to the experimenter by subjects, together with any intended or unintended cues the experimenter gives about how subjects should behave, might all influence the way in which subjects conduct themselves in the experimental setting. Indeed, subjects' awareness that they are participating in an experiment might heighten their sensitivity to any cues deriving from the experimenter or the setting regarding appropriate expected behaviour (Rosenthal, 1966; Rosenthal and Rosnow, 1975). These predilections might be heightened by subjects' anxiety about how they will appear to the researchers to the extent that they will try to give the 'correct' responses to any stimuli (Rosenberg, 1968). All these factors add to the stimuli being administered in the experimental setting, thus making the interpretation of any subsequent data problematic.

3. *Subjects' mediation through interpretation* A further significant problem for experimental research derives from the situation that it is not necessarily possible to assume that a particular independent variable is experienced as the same thing or event by different subjects. Human beings are not passive creatures who automatically respond to the stimulus of any particular independent variable. Rather, people perceive and interpret and thereby attach meaning to the various stimuli they might experience in a particular environment. They then act in accordance with those understandings and meanings, which might vary from person to person and which may be related to the social context in which the stimuli are experienced. Therefore independent variables, such as illumination in the Hawthorne experiments, cannot be considered as acting independently of the meanings and interpretations given to them by subjects; for it is those processes which form the basis of any subsequent behaviour. As Shotter,(1975) has argued, much experimental research treats subjects as if they were analogous to an unthinking inanimate entity, such as an atom, at the mercy of stimuli administered by the experimenter. For Shotter this is a distorted image of a human being, who is in fact a free agent capable of making choices based upon his or her subjective interpretation of the situation. Indeed, these interpretative processes might be seen as rival explanations – to those constituted by the independent variable – of any subsequent behaviour observed in an experimental setting. As such they constitute a significant threat to the internal validity of any research findings.

The experimental artifacts analysed above and their threats to the internal validity of the true experiment are illustrated in Figure 4.3.

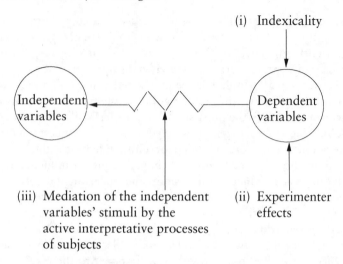

Figure 4.3   The Threats to the Internal Validity of the True Experiment

The problems created by experimental artifacts illustrate the paradox of the true experiment. By manipulating the independent variables while controlling extraneous variables, through the use of control and experimental groups, researchers appear to be able to conclude with some certainty that particular independent variables cause particular changes in particular independent variables. At first sight the internal validity of the true experiment appears to be very strong. However, the need for structure and artificiality, so necessary for enabling manipulation and control, in itself creates a set of what might be seen as further extraneous variables. These in effect constitute rival hypotheses to the one(s) being tested by the original research design.

These experimental artifacts, illustrated in Figure 4.3, are not a problem in the natural or physical sciences. The subject matter of those sciences does not have the subjective capacities that human beings so patently possess. It is the presence of subjectivity in human beings and their consequent variable reactivity to the artificiality and manipulation of the true experiment that casts doubt upon the internal validity of this type of research design. Furthermore, the artificiality of the experiment, since its context is divorced from the normal lives of subjects, makes it doubtful whether or not findings could be extrapolated to everyday behavioural situations: that is, the ecological validity of the true experiment appears to be low.

Alternatives to the true experiment

The weaknesses of the true experiment that we have reviewed here have caused researchers in the various branches of the social sciences to try to develop alternative research designs that avoid these problems yet maintain the logic of experimentation, in which lie many potential strengths. Thus many researchers have tried to take the logic of the experiment out 'into the field', thereby avoiding the artificiality of the laboratory by investigating social phenomena in their natural everyday context. The lack of ecological validity and the various threats to internal validity, inherent in the true experiment are not, however, the only reason for this 'flight'. For instance, in conducting an experiment the researcher is purposively inducing changes among the subjects of the research. Depending on the nature of these changes, and the moral code of the researcher, ethical problems may ensue. Indeed, for many areas of research it is considered to be unethical to manipulate certain kinds of variables since they might promote changes that might be detrimental to the well-being of subjects (H. W. Smith, 1975, pp.3–17). Alternatively, some research problems are quite simply not amenable to investigation through a true experiment, particularly those concerning macro issues.

Thus whatever the reason – pragmatic, ethical or methodological – many researchers have been concerned to try to preserve aspects of the logic of the true experiment that might enable the control of extraneous variables, while undertaking research outside the confines of laboratory conditions. These endeavours, expressed as quasi-experimentation and action research, are the subjects of the next chapter.

Suggested further reading

As we have already pointed out, the use of the true experiment in management research is relatively rare. So we suggest that accounts of where it has been used, such as F. J. Roethlisberger and W. J. Dickson's account of the Hawthorne studies, in *Management and the Worker*, are particularly worthwhile (see also M. Rose's *Industrial Behaviour: Theoretical Developments since Taylor*). Meanwhile, there is a large body of literature and accounts of experimental research primarily orientated towards social psychology. However, much of this is relevant to management, particularly studies of decision making. Examples are S. E. Asch's 'Effects of group pressures upon the modification and distortion of judgements' and S. Milgram's 'Behavioural study of obedience'.

Both J. Shotter's *Images of Man in Psychological Research* and A. Gauld and J. Shotter's *Human Action and the Psychological Investigation* provide reviews and evaluations of the philosophical assumptions regarding human beings that underpin experimentally based research in social science and proceed to consider alternative methodologies.

Finally, H. W. Smith's *Strategies of Social Research: The Methodological Imagination* provides an incisive review of some ethical issues in experimental research, as also does H. C. Kelman's 'Human use of human subjects: the problem of deception in social psychological experiments', with particular reference to the ethical dilemmas raised by the deception of subjects in experimental research designs.

(Full bibliographical details of these works are in the References, at the end of the book.)

5
Quasi-Experiments and Action Research

We introduce this chapter by first contrasting quasi-experiments, action research, and experimental approaches. We then briefly review the historical development of action research and define its meaning and methodology by reference to examples. Finally, the appropriateness of action research to those undertaking research in business and management is considered together with its methodological and ethical justification.

Experiments, quasi-experiments and action research compared

As we attempted to demonstrate in Chapter 3 the 'true' or 'classical' experiment enables a researcher to test theories and hypotheses systematically since it has the following characteristics:

1. The experimenter is able to allocate subjects to control and experimental groups in a systematic or random manner.
2. He or she is then able to manipulate the incidence of one or more independent variables and observe any consequent changes in the dependent variable(s).
3. Because of these characteristics a true experiment occurs through the direct intervention of the experimenter and is usually possible only under laboratory conditions.

Although the ability to manipulate independent variables and to control extraneous variables through this highly structured research design has many strengths we have pointed to the way these strengths also create severe problems. This is due mainly to the inevitable artificiality of the context in which the research takes place.

Many researchers have therefore sought to preserve much of the logic underpinning the true experiment while avoiding the difficulties that arise from the artificiality of the laboratory context. They have attempted to achieve this by taking this guiding logic out of the laboratory and applying it to the investigation of an environment that existed, or events that have occurred naturally, without the investigator's direct intervention (Campbell and Stanley, 1963: Campbell, 1969). By adopting this approach the researcher begins to lose some of the attributes of the true experiment, particularly those deriving from the ability to allocate subjects to experimental and control groups randomly or systematically. Meanwhile, the attempt is made to avoid problems arising from the artificiality of the context and processes of the true experiment.

In this sense the researcher is gaining naturalism or ecological validity as subjects are investigated in their normal everyday environments. However, this strength is acquired only at the expense of trading off control over certain extraneous variables – a reduction in aspects of the internal validity of findings.

Such attempts at approximating the logic of the true experiment outside the confines of the laboratory in a natural, or field, setting have generally been dubbed 'quasi-experiments'.

Quasi-experiments

As in the case of the true experiment, the prime aim of the quasi-experiment is to analyse causal relationships between independent and dependent variables. However, in a quasi-experiment, since it does not take place in a laboratory and since its focus is on real-life, naturally occurring events, subjects cannot be randomly or systematically allocated to experimental and control groups. This does not mean that control and experimental groups are not used; rather, control and experimental groups are identified in the field in terms of whether or not they have experienced the notional experimental treatment(s) or independent variable(s).

As such the identified control and experimental groups are naturally occurring populations; and thus, many aspects of being able to match them exactly so as to compare like with like are not possible. Inevitably, some degree of control over extraneous variables, relative to that possible in the laboratory, is lost due to this lack of equivalence between groups. So instead of attempting to manipulate the incidence of the independent variable by selecting equivalent control and experimental groups and then administering an experimental treatment, the researcher attempts to identify people who have naturally experienced the notional experimental treatment. The attempt is then made to compare their consequent behaviour with as similar a group as possible who have not experienced that event or phenomenon.

To summarize, a quasi-experimental approach is often adopted because:

1. it avoids the artificiality of the context in which a true experiment takes place;
2. it allows research to be conducted in the actual settings to which any research findings must be extrapolated;
3. it is often adopted by researchers when they wish to investigate causal relationships in situations where manipulation of the independent variable and/or the systematic assignation of subjects to control and experimental groups is not ethically or practically feasible.

Given these characteristics, quasi-experimentation seems to be a particularly useful approach to research designs aimed at evaluating various types of social policy innovations or reforms. This application has been considered by

Campbell (1969) and it is useful to summarize one of his investigations that concisely illustrates the application of quasi-experimental logic.

Campbell and Ross (1968) discuss the application of quasi-experimental design to the investigation of the effects upon fatality rates of the 1955 'Connecticut Crackdown on Speeding'. In this they attempted to examine the effects of the police crackdown on speeding in Connecticut (the independent variable) upon the fatality rates on Connecticut roads (the dependent variable).

To determine the nature of this relationship Campbell and Ross needed to gather data pertaining to the rate of fatalities upon Connecticut roads prior to and after the crackdown. In essence they needed to measure the incidence of the dependent variable prior to and after the experimental treatment:

Data pertaining to fatality rates on Connecticut roads prior to 1955 $\longrightarrow$ Crackdown $\longrightarrow$ Data pertaining to fatality rates on Connecticut roads, 1955 and after.

But this simple 'interrupted time series design', in which any changes in fatality rates before and after 1955 appear to provide evidence regarding the effects of the crackdown, fails to rule out other rival explanations. As Campbell and Ross (1968) point out, the resultant patterns could have been caused by a host of extraneous variables (e.g. the weather).

So in order to rule out some of the potential rival explanations and thus improve our understanding of the effects of the crackdown upon fatality rates it was necessary to identify States which could serve as control groups and so provide comparative data regarding extraneous factors, as well as data pertaining to fatality rates. Clearly, these States had not experienced a crackdown on speeding and although not exactly equivalent to Connecticut in other respects could act analogously as control groups. Thus the research design adopted by Campbell and Ross entailed what is often called a 'multiple time series' quasi-experimental design in which data was collected from comparable, though not equivalent, 'subjects'.

E1 (fatality rates on Connecticut roads prior to 1955) $\longrightarrow$ 'Experimental treatment' (police crackdown) $\longrightarrow$ E2 (fatality rates on Connecticut roads, 1955 and after).

C1 (fatality rates in four comparable States prior to 1955) $\longrightarrow$ No 'experimental treatment' $\longrightarrow$ C2 (fatality rates in four comparable states, 1955 and after).

Consequently, a comparison of the differences between C2 and C1 and between E2 and E1 might better reveal the effects of the crackdown as compared with the simple interrupted time series design.

Therefore, in the case of the quasi-experiment there is a lack of manipulative control over the independent variable(s) and a lack of equivalence between experimental and control groups. This inevitably results in a loss of control over extraneous variables and consequently raises doubts around the internal validity of any research findings.

Nevertheless, the quasi-experiment does attempt to follow the 'logic of difference' by comparing the natural incidence and non incidence of the notional experimental treatment(s) in real-life situations. Indeed, it is this naturalism that not only confers upon the quasi-experiment the ecological validity so lacking in the true experiment but also allows for the experimental investigation of areas in which it would be ethically, logically and politically problematic to conduct a true experiment.

Action research

Particularly in management research, a valuable variant of the quasi-experiment is action research. We explore definitions of action research in a little more detail below but for the purpose of contrasting action research with quasi-experiments the approach to research design involves a planned intervention by a researcher, or more often a consultant, into some naturally occurring events. The effects of that intervention are then monitored and evaluated with the aim of discerning whether or not that action has produced the expected consequences. In other words, the researcher acts upon his or her beliefs or theories.

From their intervention and subsequent evaluation action researchers intend not only to contribute to existing knowledge but also to help resolve some of the practical concerns of the people, or clients, who are trying to deal with a problematic situation.

In this approach, therefore, the researcher's intervention, whether it be in a consulting context or not, is an intrinsic part of the research design. Generally, the intervention may be perceived as analogous to the independent variable(s) of the true and quasi-experiment, with its consequences being treated as dependent variables whose change is monitored and evaluated.

Action research will often entail the use of control groups so as to allow elucidation of cause and effect through the control of extraneous variables. However, the context of action research and the possible commitments of the action researcher may make the use of control groups very difficult.

Primarily, the practicalities of the situation being studied may preclude the identification of possible control groups. Moreover, given that the context is a naturally occurring situation, the possibility of matching control and experimental groups through the systematic or random allocation of subjects is inevitably problematic.

Finally, even if it were possible to allocate subjects to equivalent groups for comparative purposes, the action researcher might be in danger of destroying the very naturalism it is intended to study. A summary comparison of experiments, quasi-experiments and action research is given in Table 5.1. The problems and tensions inherent in action research are well illustrated by some examples of its use in management research, to which we now turn.

The development of action research

Although action research has been undertaken for decades the first conscious use of the expression is generally attributed to Kurt Lewin in the 1940s (Lewin,

Table 5.1   A comparison of true experiments, quasi-experiments and action research

True experiments	Quasi-experiments	Action research
Entail the analysis of the direct intervention of the researcher	Entail the analysis of events that have naturally occurred without the intervention of the researcher, i.e. after the fact	Entails the analysis of the direct interventions of the researcher
Incidence of the independent variable due to the manipulations of the researcher	Incidence of the independent variable occurs naturally	Incidence of the independent variable is constituted by the actions of the researcher
Entail pre- and post-treatment, measurement and comparison of the dependent variable in both the experimental and the control groups	Entail pre- and post-treatment, measurement and comparison of the dependent variable in both the experimental and the control groups	Entails pre-and post-treatment, mesaurement and comparison of the dependent variable in the experimental group. Availability of an equivalent or non-equivalent control group problematic according to the context of the research
Entail physical control over extraneous variables through assignation of subjects to equivalent experimental and control groups	Since analysis entails naturally occurring events, prior assignation of subjects to control and experimental groups problematic. Instead, control and experimental groups are identified in terms of the incidence of the independent variable and cannot be exactly matched	As the incidence of the independent variable is constituted by the actions of the researcher prior identification of control and experimental groups is sometimes possible. However, their full equivalence problematic since such groups are usually naturally occurring
Strengths		
High internal validity	High ecological validity. Avoids problems associated with experimental artefacts; can have high population validity	Can be very high in ecological validity. Can avoid problems associated with experimental artefacts
Weaknesses		
Low ecological validity; often population validity is limited	Loss of control over extraneous variables	Population validity limited to those subjects involved; loss of control over extraneous variables

1946). Lewin, a social psychologist, was concerned to apply social science knowledge to solve social problems such as conflict between groups and the need to change eating habits in wartime. Others closely followed applying the approach, for example, to community relations issues, leadership training and resistance to change in manufacturing plants.

Lewin does not seem to have used any comprehensive definition of the term but he nevertheless refers to research programmes within organizations whose progress is guided the needs of the organizations, and frequently uses the expression 'problem centred research'. The main feature of action research, according to Lewin, was that it should be focused on problems and that it should lead to some kind of action and research on the effects of that action by understanding the dynamic nature of change and studying it under controlled conditions as it took place.

Lewin also stressed the limitations of studying complex social events in a laboratory and the artificiality of isolating single behavioural elements from what was an integrated and complex system. He also conceptualized the tensions between social science and practice, for example by the use of his still widely practised notion of change processes being in a quasi-stationary state maintained by a balance of driving and restraining forces. A clue to a means of bringing about a desired change was then to choose to unbalance the forces by reducing some of the restraining forces rather than by increasing the driving forces. Such process generalizations were, he believed, applicable to any change problem and capable of being added to theory development in action research.

At roughly the same time, and virtually unconnected with these developments in North America, there was significant growth of action research in the United Kingdom. As in North America, the roots of this growth were to be found in the Second World War, during which psychologists, anthropologists and psychiatrists of a psychoanalytic orientation came together in multi-disciplinary teams to work on a number of problems. During and just after the war a number of successful action research programmes were conducted in personnel selection and the treatment and rehabilitation of returning prisoners of war. This led to a body of research findings and a particular action research approach, well exemplified in the Glacier Metal study discussed below.

This work derived from wartime experience led to the formation of the Tavistock Institute of Human Relations, which was composed of people of various social science backgrounds but all with the objective of attempting to find ways of by which social science could contribute to finding solutions to some of the pressing social problems of the post-war period.

Although the term 'action research' was not specifically used by workers at the Tavistock Institute until the 1960s, almost all their work was problem-centred and was based on a long-term involvement with clients and their needs and with helping with the implementation and monitoring of changes.

The work was guided throughout by a strong orientation towards the study of the research process and in particular to the relationships that developed between researcher and client and the extent to which these helped or inhibited utilization of findings.

In more recent work psychoanalytic ideas have become less prominent, although the analogy of the psychoanalytic situation, where the client is confronted with the researcher's perception of what in reality is occurring, is still a feature of much of the work in this tradition.

In the management field probably the best-known early work in this tradition is by Jaques (1951), based on research in the Glacier Metal Company; Sofer (1961) in further education; Wilson (1961) in Unilever; and Trist *et al.*

(1963), working in the Durham coalfield. Topics included planned organizational change, the analysis of tasks in organizations and the relationship of the
organization to its environment, and the analysis of absenteeism, accidents and
alienation as symptoms of organizational malfunction.

In almost all cases the researchers included very full accounts of their fieldwork methods, especially the day-to-day interactions between researcher and
client, and the contexts in which the work was carried out as being major
influences on the change process.

Defining action research

The term 'action research' became fashionable and has given rise to a large
literature and many varied uses of the term. Here we use Rapoport's (1970, p.
499) definition: 'Action Research aims to contribute both to the practical concerns of people in an immediate problematic situation and to the goals of social
science by joint collaboration within a mutually acceptable ethical framework.'

Such a definition does, however, pose many questions – as Rapoport himself was well aware. The main difficulties arise from the inherent need for
close collaboration between the parties. Close collaboration between the
distinctive and very different cultures of the managerial and academic worlds
gives rise to issues about whether the aims of the work will be concerned
primarily with problem-solving for the particular organization, or with producing theoretical generalizations for the wider community (Gill, 1986).
These ambiguities are brought into focus when action research, consultancy
and theory building or 'basic' research are compared at each stage of the
research sequence (see Table 5.2).

At the entry stage of the action research process either the client or the
researcher may take the initiative in presenting the problem. In consultancy the
client most usually presents the problem, and in 'basic' research the researcher
generally asks for access to research a problem in which he or she is interested.
The essential difference between the action research mode and the others lies in
the former's close collaborative relationship, where there is mutual agreement
at each stage of the action research sequence.

Contracting is more than simply an issue concerned with regulating business
relationships as is often the case with consultancy; or to maintain at least a
sufficiently good relationship to preserve access to the organization, as is frequently the case with 'basic' research. Contracting in action research is generally described as 'psychological', as motives, goals and the *locus* of control, as
well as business arrangments, are carefully discussed and agreed.

Similarly, the diagnostic stage is ideally carried out jointly by action researcher
and client if the results of the investigation are to have the client organization's
commitment to the work and if outcomes are to have a fair chance of successful
implementation. The action researcher may introduce concepts to the client, for
example the notion of organizations as systems which may enable the client to
restructure his idosyncratic data on the consultant's systems model. This
joint endeavour generally leads to the increased commitment of both parties to

Table 5.2 Action research, consultancy and 'pure' research

Stages	Action research	Consultancy	'Pure' research
Entry	Client or researcher presents problem. Mutually agreed goals.	Client presents problems and defines goals.	Researcher presents problem and defines goals.
Contracting	Business and psychological contracting. Mutual control.	Business contract. Consultant controls client.	Researcher controls as expert. Keeps client happy. Minimal contracting.
Diagnosis	Joint diagnosis. Client data/researcher's concepts.	Consultant diagnosis. Often minimal. Sells package.	Researcher carries out expert diagnosis. Client provides data.
Action	Feedback. Dissonance. Joint action plan Client action with support. Published.	Consultant prescribes action. Not published.	Report often designed to impress client with how much researcher has learned and how competent he or she is. Published.
Evaluation	New problems emerge. Recycles. Generalizations emerge.	Rarely undertaken by neutrals.	Rarely undertaken.
Withdrawal	Client self-supporting.	Client dependent.	Client dependent.

Source: Gill, 1986, p. 103

the diagnosis. Alternatively, the client and researcher may jointly devise instruments, such as a questionnaire, by which to collect data.

The action stage of the action research sequence is primarily the province of the client, with action researcher's support, but the action plan is jointly agreed and the work is generally published.

Finally, the work is jointly reviewed, when fresh problems are likely to emerge, and the problem-solving sequence recycled.

Management students who approach their research work in this tradition will, even if working full time as a manager, probably be stereotyped as an academic – with all that may imply for the successful outcome of the work. Ethical and value dilemmas and problems of role ambiguity also arise from the very nature of action research. Implicit, too, in much of the literature on action research is its advocacy of the method as an alternative to positivist social science and the consequent need to justify the approach in methodological terms. We deal with these issues later in this chapter. First, some examples of the practice of action research in management are introduced.

Action research in practice

We consider here three examples of action research projects which were all undertaken to solve specific managerial problems and, at the same time, to generalize from the specific and to contribute to theory:

1. a project designed to help management at BP's Stanlow refinery to resolve some industrial relations issues on the construction site and simultaneously

to add to the general understanding of a number of industrial relations matters (Lumley, 1978);
2. the now classic study of the day-to-day problems experienced at the manufacturing plant of the Glacier Metal Company (Jaques, 1951);
3. a research investigation into the factors contributing to the growth of the small business which, at the same time, was designed to help those managing the small businesses which provided the data (Gill, 1985).

Industrial relations at a refinery construction site.

This project was undertaken in the late 1970s and had its origins in a research contract between the Stanlow refinery of Shell UK Ltd and Sheffield Polytechnic.

BP had embarked on a major expansion programme on its petro-chemicals complex on Merseyside involving a capital expenditure programme of £110 million over three years. This was expected to involve contractors on the production site with a peak labour force of more than 3,000.

The general experience from this and other large construction sites in the UK was of a high incidence of industrial relations unrest leading to expensive delays in completion times. BP was puzzled by the considerable differences between the behaviour of contractors' employees and that of its own more permanent refinery workforce on the same site. BP felt the need for some systematic research into the contractors' industrial relations behaviour as an aid to formulating policies to improve contractors' industrial relations and so reduce completion times. In particular, management were seeking predictors of contractors' industrial relations performance which would help them select contracting companies that would be relatively trouble free.

At the same time, the researcher intended to use the data for a parallel academic study he wished to present for publication and a doctorate, by making a specific substantive contribution not only to the nature of industrial relations on large construction sites but also to the resolution of some issues in the understanding of industrial relations as a field of study. He also wished to generalize about the practicability of a research strategy that had as its objective to satisfy simultaneously the needs of the client company and the academic community.

By definition most action research projects are pursued through the medium of a case study, and this was no exception, the work being confined to one large industrial construction site. This of course raised issues about the extent to which the findings were generalizable to other cases.

In all these respects, then, the project met the goals Rapoport defines for action research – but also raised many problematic issues. Three main pressures arose out of the dual role which is the lot of the action researcher.

One was the matter of independence and confidentiality of the work, for meaningful data could be collected only with the consent and support of contractors' managements, their employees and the trade unions. This in turn required the giving and acceptance of guarantees of anonymity, and in some cases confidentiality, of data. Furthermore, there was the matter of feedback of data and the uses to which this might be put. Accordingly, it was felt necessary to agree with the client, and a guarantee offered to other parties to the study, that the same written reports of findings would be made available to all the participants in the research. In addition, the client company as sponsor of the project would receive recommendations intended to be of help in reaching its objectives.

A second issue was that collaboration between researcher and client in defining the goals of the research might be at the expense of neutrality; while collaboration with contractors and unions, even if approved by the client would doubtless be impracticable in a sensitive, often low trust, situation.

The third pressure was that of time. The temporary nature of construction activity was likely to inhibit the effective implementation of changes arising from the work. The client company was naturally keen to see that empirical findings were presented quickly, and this was accentuated by the client's unforeseen curtailment of its planned expansion, resulting in an earlier than expected run-down in the construction programme. This accentuated the practical problem of theoretical understanding and development and in consequence led to the work being achieved in two phases: first, by presenting the client with a specific report on the problems as defined within its time scale; and then subsequently developing theoretical and generalizable propositions.

In reviewing the outcomes from the work the theoretical objectives were reasonably well met: a substantial contribution was made to the understanding of workplace industrial relations, especially those on large construction sites.

On the matter of generalization of findings from a single case it is clear that all findings needed to be qualified with the cautionary note that they applied only within the specific context; there was nevertheless clear evidence that they had wider applicability. Descriptive data from the site on, for example, the structural behaviours and characteristics of contracting firms led to the conclusion that they were fairly typical of those on large construction sites in the UK as a whole. Further, in the construction industry there is a large amount of inter-site and inter-firm mobility on the part of construction employees; so in general terms the Merseyside site seemed not untypical of all highly unionized sites in the UK. Moreover, the methods used in the case study, of seeking multiple determining conditions, meant that the explanatory mechanisms underlying relationships put forward could be fairly specifically described and it seemed reasonable that they would apply to other, similar environments. Nevertheless, some issues clearly needed to be tested against data from other cases but a start had been made in an exploratory study on which others might build.

However, when we come to consider the extent to which the work was implemented, and the degree to which client needs were met, the evidence is less conclusive. The findings from an intensive study, in which the researcher absorbed himself in the culture of the site, led to recommendations at both long-range strategic planning and operational levels. Some were implemented directly by the client but others were of course dependent on the influence the client could bring to bear on the other parties on the site.

It was also clear that a major potential utility of the investigation was the provision of a large pool of information which could be of help in diagnosing situations that might arise and in predicting the likely industrial relations consequences of proposed actions. The extent to which these recommendations were accepted and implemented was clearly affected by the problems posed by the short time scale of construction projects in relation to a research activity requiring the collection of large amounts of data and long periods spent on the site. By the time reports were presented, work on the site was beginning to run down and the implementation of many recommendations had to await the commencement of a major new construction phase.

Other factors negatively affected implementation. The refinery manager who had initiated the project retired and the dispersion of industrial relations and construction personnel to other locations effectively eliminated the possibility of useful discussions on the site. In particular, for these reasons, meetings proposed by the researchers to bring together client, contractors and unions did not take place.

Clearly in work of this nature there is a tension between the need to remain independent, particularly from a client who, as in this case , was financing the work, in order to collect sensitive data from the other parties; and the danger that too little client involvement might lessen commitment to the conclusions. This was especially so in the phases of design, data collection, analysis and interpretation. Moreover, action research designs that attempt to involve clients with approaches with which they are unfamiliar carry the risk that the researcher will be placed in the classic role of the detached academic, requiring him or her to work remotely, present findings and leave it to the client to decide whether or not the work will be implemented.

In this case a degree of independence was established at the cost of the client ascribing an expert role to the researcher and to a large extent withdrawing from close involvement in the conduct of the study. Although much of the work was utilized, closer involvement of the client in the research process, in the way this was achieved in the Glacier Metal case described below, may have greatly facilitated major changes based upon the study.

The changing culture of a factory

The research briefly reviewed here was undertaken in the Glacier Metal Company by a group from the Tavistock Institute of Human Relations led by Jaques, over three years from 1948 to 1950 (Jaques, 1951).

Glacier, primarily concerned with precision engineering, had a wide reputation for its social policies and for its modern, progressive management methods. The research design chosen for the project was for the researchers to take the initiative and seek a firm which would be willing to study and develop its methods for creating satisfactory group relations.

A relatively advanced company seemed particularly appropriate for a deep study into the day-to-day problems experienced by the factory in its attempts to find more satisfying ways of working consistent with the demands of a competitive industrial environment. It was assumed such a company would be less likely to be concerned with mere proceedural changes and more interested in the forces underlying them; and, being an innovator in its field, would be more likely to tolerate the stresses associated with unpredictable research activities.

It was appreciated that work with one company, and that untypical, might make broad generalizations difficult on the basis of one idiosyncratic case. At the same time, however, it was believed that the problems under study – the psychological and social roots of stresses in group relations – in one factory would have common underlying features with similar problems elsewhere.

So Glacier was approached, both for the reasons above, and also because an intermittent working contract over two years had already established that particularly favourable conditions already existed for adhering to a Tavistock principle that management, supervision and workforce should each independently agree to collaborate in any work undertaken. So, unlike the BP case, the Tavistock Institute was in a position to choose its client and to insist on preliminary conditions for commencing research work.

Three months were taken up in reaching agreement with all the parties before access was gained. The managing director and his immediate subordinates were approached first. Although, unusually, the managing director was as interested in research into the company as managing it, preliminary agreement was not automatic partly because several members of senior management felt that the managing director was already spending too much of his time in social experiments and that production might be adversely affected by such 'diversions'. However, the fact that the managing director was particularly keen on the project, and that the Institute would not agree to the work being imposed from above, eventually resulted in agreement to start.

The works' council, for its part, was generally antipathetic and sceptical of industrial psychologists and psychiatrists but agreed to meet a member of the Institute to discuss the proposal. It suggested a senior member of the Institute but this suggestion was rejected on the grounds that persuasion of this kind would run counter to the principle of obtaining genuine co-operation from the factory. Accordingly the works' council, after hearing the leader of the research team, and in particular his stipulation that independent agreement would be required from the workers' side, referred the matter for independent consideration to the works' committee, a body composed entirely of elected representatives of the Glacier workforce.

At this meeting detailed questions were asked about, for example, who had initiated the project and who was paying for it. These questions were readily answered. Tavistock had made the approach, one of the research coucils was paying for it and the Trades Union Congress was supportive. Other questions were more difficult to answer, such as the time scale for the work, how it would be accomplished and specifically what research methods would be employed. Underlying these questions of course lay natural fears about speeding up and rate cutting, fears associated particularly with some psychologist members of the research team. The answers to these questions were necessarily vague for there was by its very nature no clear specification for the work and it was expected that topics for study would be chosen jointly as the work progressed. Nevertheless, despite this unavoidable vagueness, these explanations were accepted, particularly when it was realized that the Institute did not wish to work either for management or shop floor but to define its client as the workforce as a whole.

The careful building up of the independence of the researcher role was justified on ethical and scientific grounds as avoiding becoming involved in conflict between groups in the factory and having conflicts projected on to the research team. Further, the research team wished to establish from the beginning that a part of the approach used would be the avoidance of capture of the team by any particular group.

Following the decision of the works' committee to go ahead, a project sub-committee of two management and three shop-floor representatives was established to work with the research team; its first task being to clarify issues concerning the control of the work. These discussions resulted in jointly agreed principles to include the reporting relationships of the research team and the ways in which research topics might be undertaken. It was agreed that the research team should be resposible to and report to the works' council and that any suggestions for the study of a topic should be effected only with the general approval of those likely to be affected by the results.

The attitude of the team was that it was not intending to solve all Glacier's problems, but hoped that it might find ways of achieving a smoother-running organization. Nothing would be done behind anyone's back and no matter would be discussed unless representatives of the group affected were present or agreed to the topic being raised.

In practice the team worked with any part of the factory at its request but would comment only on relationships within the immediate group and would not discuss matters relating to anyone not present. Indeed, so strictly did the team work in this respect that it limited relationships with members of the factory to formal contacts publicly sanctioned by the works' council. No personal relationships with Glacier employees either inside or outside working hours were entertained, except for the inevitable informal contacts occurring when, for example, eating in canteens. Even then care was taken to discuss only those aspects of the project which were public knowledge. Thus invitations to people's homes were refused as were invitations to play tennis on the factory's courts. After about a year the seriousness of the research team's intentions was appreciated and all such invitations gradually ceased.

This degree of formality was chosen, by analogy with clinical medicine, primarily to preserve the independence of the research team for only the formal channels of the works' council could be used in starting projects and consequently everyone knew, and had access to, what was under way at any point in time. Further, the team regarded it as inconsistent to have informal relationships with members of one group and at the same time to hold a publicly independent attitude when debates took place between groups without being regarded as having been captured by one of them.

Finally, care needed to be taken with an agreement regarding publication, a matter which may cause difficulty when undertaking research in organizations when the working lives of people are under scrutiny. Since individuals would be easily identifiable to anyone familiar with the company steps were taken to agree a publications policy early in the course of the work. It was agreed that any public statements about the project would be governed by the same policy as other public statements about the company. For its part, the Tavistock Institute undertook to make public comments only in collaboration with the company, or after due consultation.

The research quickly got under way once the detailed, time consuming preliminaries regarding independence had been negotiated and sufficient confidence had been developed in the research team; a confidence demonstrated by a number of sections of the factory offering collaboration on specific problems. Accordingly, projects began to be undertaken on, for example, relationships within the divisional managers meetings; payment systems in mass-production assembly plants; and, at the request of the works' council, an extensive study of difficulties in the operation of channels of communication down the executive line. Studies generally followed the same pattern in that papers were written and then validated by submitting them for rigorous analysis by the groups concerned.

Changes that occurred fairly quickly included the alteration of payment systems in one department. However, it was only after more than two years' research with a number of groups that changes affecting the factory as a whole occurred that had profound effects on the company's perception of its executive and consultative processes.

The survival and growth of the small company

This research originated in the context of the growing unemployment in the Yorkshire and Humberside region during the early 1980s. A small group of managers and academics from the region, meeting in 1980 as part of the activities of Sheffield City Polytechnic's (then) Regional Management Centre, believed unemployment to be fundamental to the region's growing difficulties. They believed that a more vigorous small firm sector, particularly small firms which might be helped to grow into larger companies, might make a major contribution to solving the problem.

Accordingly, it was decided to examine the underlying reasons for business failure, on the one hand, and survival and growth on the other. It was further decided to seek sponsorship from a reasonably independent source and to carry out the work in such a way that those small businesses agreeing to participate would derive benefit from the research.

The work was financed by the Foundation for Management Education and took place between 1982 and 1984; a period of growing unemployment and particularly low economic activity in the region (Gill, 1985).

The aims of the research were to discover the types of crises faced by infant businesses, how these crises were met, and the factors affecting growth and decline – particularly those which the business people themselves might influence. Further, it was the purpose to discover whether within the findings there were any indications as to the most appropriate ways of training those intending to start a small business and supporting them once in business. At the same time it was a major aim, in the course of carrying out the work, to help the small businesses to which we had access.

Access was gained to small businesses which had been started by people attending sixteen-week, full-time Start Your Own Business programmes sponsored by the then Manpower Services Commission and mounted by staff of the Yorkshire and Humberside Regional Management Centre.

These businesses were chosen primarily because it was expected that access would be facilitated through their earlier contact with polytechnic lecturers on the Start Your Own Business programmes with whom close relationships had been formed. Thanks to these mutually beneficial relationships, access was in fact much easier than had been anticipated in what has generally been regarded as an inaccessible research area. It was believed at the outset that many business people would be too busy to spend time being interviewed and that they would not in any case wish their business activities to be publicized. These fears were also not realized and, consequently, out of the thirty-two small businesses approached only one refused co-operation outright, although others soon proved difficult to pin down for meetings. By the summer of 1982 a sample of twenty-two small companies were collaborating, twenty-one of which were still trading when the project ended at the end of 1983.

Small companies were studied longitudinally over two years and case material built up on each through an interpersonal strategy; it being recognized that building a good relationship with each business person was essential if contact was to continue at intervals over two years and if the data gathered was to be of high quality. Further, as trust grew business people began to share confidential data and began to look for help with their business problems some aspects of which were both personal and sensitive.

Methodologically the suggestions of Bygrave (1989) for research into entrepreneurship are supported. That is in an emergent field we were less concerned with sophisticated statistical analyses and theoretical models and more with empirical models based upon longitudinal field research. In this way, through non-directive, semi-structured interviewing a series of cases was developed of each participating small business. Issues so investigated were company origins and background, the personal biographies of the business person, and in particular the progress, plans and problems of the business as they arose. It was decided to examine businesses longitudinally, rather than cross-sectionally at one point in time, as this method, among other advantages, enabled our aims to be more effectively achieved. Retrospection was employed to discover the earlier history of the business from its conception.

Longitudinal designs have been advocated by other researchers with an interest in bringing about change (e.g. Miller and Friesen, 1982; Vitalari, 1985; Galliers, 1985; Pettigrew, 1985a). Vitalari, for example, calling for more longitudinal designs in the study of computing environments, believes that they have significant advantages over data collected at one point in time. They permit the exploration of phenomena which develop over time such as learning and adaptation. Pettigrew, too, in his studies of organizational change in, for instance, ICI (Pettigrew, 1985b), believes that the relationship between organization structure and process needs to be studied in the context of historical change, a research approach he calls contextualism. In the case of the investigation into small businesses the principal researcher was not experienced in managing a small business and requests for specialist help were accordingly referred to experts in, for example, marketing, finance or business strategy. An action research role therefore slowly emerged and was facilitated by the primary research method employed of gathering data through carefully structured conversations with people whose job was of its very nature very isolated and lonely and which deprived them of helpful, non-evaluative feedback. The fact that the investigator was not a technical expert in small business was probably for the most part helpful as there was no temptation on his part to offer advice when in most cases the owner–managers were already aware of the solutions to their problems and simply needed a non-threatening listener to bounce ideas off. Credibility was thus maintained by non-directive listening so that, on the one hand, objectivity was not impaired by too close association, and yet access was gained to information which might otherwise have been withheld. By such means action was taken on a wide variety of day-to-day matters such as cash flow, the installation of labour-saving machinery and the severing of partnerships and staffing. Strategic clarification, and sometimes changes in business objectives – including diversification, expansion or contraction – occurred.

This project added to the stock of general theory on small business initiation, growth and decline and concurrently served to help small business people with their idiosyncratic problems. Its main findings, particularly the interpersonal research strategy of working closely with clients and offering 'active' listening, were later confirmed in another research project into the very different small business setting of a community endeavour to create employment through small business initiatives in a deprived, inner city area (Gill, 1988; Pedler *et al.*, 1990).

Action research and its methodological justification

There is an extensive literature of attempts to define action research and these various attempts reflect differences inherent in the methodological variations in approach.

Although Rapoport's (1970) definition subsumes most of the approaches it is necessary to refer to some of them as illustrative of ways of undertaking work which contributes both to theory and practice. It is also necessary to clarify some possible confusions in terminology.

Heller (1986) describes twelve different types of problem-solving on a continuum from a traditional 'science only' approach to what he terms 'client dominated quest'; or what in effect amounts for all practical purposes to consultancy. Within these extremes Heller distinguishes various forms of collaborative problem-solving between researcher and client differentiated by the type of diffusion channel, the methods of funding and the anticipated audience, all of which would be contained in Rapoport's definition as action research. Heller also makes a distinction between what he calls 'research action' and action research; a distinction depending on how much emphasis is placed on the fact finding or research phase. He defines work as action research when the fact finding phase plays a subsidiary role to implementation.

Similarly, Argyris, Putman and Smith (1985) distinguish 'action science' from action research on the grounds that they believe that action research has been regarded by social scientists as being primarily concerned with problem solving for clients and not necessarily with testing theory. Second, they believe that many action researchers conduct their empirical work using rigorous research methods which Argyris, Putman and Smith believe to be unhelpful to utilization and, accordingly, that action research needs to be replaced by the use of the distinguishing term 'action science'.

In much the same way Schein, (1987) tries to make explicit some of the assumptions and methodologies in what he terms the 'clinical perspective' by contrasting it with other approaches to data gathering and analysis, especially to the work of ethnographers. In the Preface we referred briefly to Schein's clinical perspective, by which he means those professionals who become involved in a helping role. This would include, for example, psychiatrists and organization development consultants and, more generally, those who work with human systems in a way we have defined as action research.

Schein contrasts the clinical perspective with ethnography by examining the phases of the research process and its scientific justification, as also does Argyris to justify his use of the term 'action science'. It is thus necessary at this point to examine their arguments in the course of justifying action research on methodological grounds.

Susman and Evered (1978) take much the same position as Argyris, Putman and Smith (1985). They believe the principal symptom of what they describe as the crisis in the field of organizational science to be that, as research methods and techniques have become more sophisticated they have also become increasingly less useful for resolving the practical problems faced by members of organizations.

Indeed, there is some research evidence for this point of view, in work undertaken by Van de Vall, Bolas and Kang (1976), who discovered that in more than 120 applied research projects surveyed in the Netherlands, of which forty were in industry, deductive, positivist methodologies were less likely to be implemented. This seemed to be because rigorous research designs in field settings were more likely to make managers defensive and dependent and to reject collaboration; solving the problem was the test of validity rather than high correlations and perfect causal models.

In contrasting clinical and diagnostic methods of inquiry Schein (1987) explores issues concerned with the fundamental relationship between client and researcher, the inquiry and intervention process and professional and ethical matters. Since these considerations are at the root of exploring and justifying action research we follow this structure.

One of the most crucial issues in contrasting action research and ethnography is that the client chooses the clinician while the ethnographer chooses the subject group to be studied. Clinicians enter an organization only if they are asked to do so and the initiative is always with the client. In contrast, ethnographers, as we shall see in Chapters 7 and 8, select an organization as a research site on the basis of their specific research interests, and accordingly need to find ways of gaining entry or taking advantage of situations as they arise. Thus in the three cases discussed above, the small businesses were entered opportunistically while BP, and to some extent the Glacier Metal Company, both invited researchers in. Nevertheless, Schein's distinction is not clear cut (as he is well aware), for as trust is built up, as in the case of the small business study, the roles of ethnographer and clinician become increasingly blurred. Indeed in the Glacier case one of the clear aims of the intervention was to offer help to the client in often sensitive situations from a position of independence from any particular interest group; a stance made more possible by the financial support of the research team by one of the research councils.

The clinician starts with a model Schein (1987) terms 'action research', which he defines as beginning with an assumption that one cannot understand a human system without trying to change it. As Schein points out, the notion of diagnosis preceding action in discrete stages is, of course, misleading, for change starts at the diagnostic stage – which itself begins as soon as the clinician enters the organization. While clinicians are supposed to change the system, then, ethnographers assume they are not in the change business but that their endeavour is to observe how the system works, aided in this objective by the effect on it of their intervention. Nevertheless, while the work of ethnographers is less direct than the clinician in effecting change it may be at least as powerful, as we have already suggested in the Preface by citing the work of ethnographers such as Lupton (1963), Goffman (1968) and Beynon (1973).

The psychological contract in the two situations also differs. The client expects to pay fees to the clinician, in exchange for which problems may be solved and the organization improved. The ethnographer, in contrast, expects to be given access to organizational settings with the proviso that there will be as little disruption as possible and that some feedback will ultimately be provided which might be of some value to the organization.

The ethnographer decides when there is enough research data to fulfil the research goals whereas the client decides when sufficient help has been provided by the clinician as he is paying the bills. Schein (1987) mentions that, while the ethnographer's job continues after the fieldwork has finished and data has to be analysed, normally the clinician's work terminates when he or she leaves the organization. This was not of course the case in the BP project, discussed above, which continued long after client needs were met and the work generalized to the point when it fulfilled our working definition of action research and enabled the researcher to publish his work.

Thus the clinician and ethnographer focus on different kinds of data based on the different conceptual models they bring to the situation. We now turn to the ways ethnographers and clinicians, or more broadly action researchers, validate their findings.

Susman and Evered (1978) attempt to legitimate action research as science by locating its foundation in philosophical viewpoints which differ from those used to legitimate positivist science. These are the notions of praxis, hermeneutics, existentialism, pragmatism, process philosophies and phenomenology.

The concept of praxis is concerned with the art of taking action in problematic situations in order to change them, and is guided by good judgement. Marx, for example, made praxis the central concept in his theories of alienation, economics and society.

Hermeneutics has probably been more influential in the social sciences in continental Europe than positivist approaches. In the social sciences the learning process implied by what is termed the hermeneutic cycle is not unlike Lewin's (1946) conception of the manner in which an initial holistic understanding of a social system is then used for understanding parts of the system and knowledge acquired by proceeding from the whole to the parts and back again. Whenever there are discrepancies between the parts and the whole a reconceptualization takes place. The action researcher is thus forewarned that his or her interpretation of the social system will never be exactly the same as that held by members of the system. This enables the researcher better to understand both his or her own preconceptions and those of the members of the system under study. It also allows the researcher some detachment and may suggest solutions not perceived by system members.

Action research also has much in common with existentialism, both arising out of concerns about the inadequacies of positivist science. Central to the existentialist viewpoint is the importance of human choice and human action; the possibility of choice is central to taking action and the necessity to choose is central to human development.

Pragmatists, instead of focusing on formal criteria to establish the truth of a statement, rather examine what are the practical consequences of adopting a particular position. Process philosophies for their part are concerned to make clear the view that organizations are in the process of continuous change.

Finally, phenomenologists insist on the primacy of immediate subjective experience as the basis for knowledge. Whether the focus is a person or a group the ends that each pursues to bring about a desired end state, as well as the values and norms that guide action, have no objective reality that can be empirically determined as required by positivist science. Nevertheless, such ends, values and norms have a phenomenological reality from the viewpoint of those taking action and being aware of them is essential to the action researcher in predicting and understanding the behaviour of those engaged. From a phenomenological perspective behaviour is understood by knowing the ends towards which the action is taken as well as sharing the same time scale and moral concerns.

Positivist science tends to regard the researcher as sole possessor of knowledge from which action will ensue and sole originator of action to be taken on an essentially passive world. By contrast, the action research process is essentially collaborative, synthesizing the contributions that both action researcher and client make to solving problems. The action researcher with theoretical ideas and broad practical experience may help clients make more sense of their practical knowledge and experience in situations in which they are trying to solve their particular problems.

It is argued that if the researcher is effective the hoped for outcome will come about because of the researcher's involvement, not from a detachment from the research process. Thus a key criterion for the success of the action research approach may lie in such behaviours as empathetic understanding, taking the role of the other and in specific research methods that are more collaborative, such as participant observation and non-directive interviewing (as was employed in the small business study discussed above).

Thus, action research would not be granted the status of a valid science on the basis of the covering-law model of explanation. The ultimate criterion is the perceived likelihood of chosen actions to produce desirable consequences for the organization. Action research is a kind of science with a different epistemology which produces a different kind of knowledge of use to the particular organization, in the course of which its members are developed to solve their future problems. Our epistemological review in later chapters, especially in Chapter 9, may be regarded as offering further legitimation of action research.

Ethical dilemmas in action research

Some years ago Rapoport (1970) referred to three dilemmas in action research, related to issues of goals, initiatives and ethics; the dilemmas being based in the tensions to which we have already referred between simultaneously contributing to the stock of scientific knowledge and to practical, specific organizational problems.

It is not surprising, therefore, that ethical dilemmas arise at all phases of most action research projects. First, there is the issue of the acceptability of the client to the researcher. Whether, for example, the action researcher should work for organizations such as tobacco companies, or for those known to be engaged in the manufacture of weapons was an issue posed in the pioneering work of the Tavistock Institute. Such difficulties were partly resolved by working in a values framework acceptable to both parties. So, for example, work between the Tavistock Institute and the Tobacco Research Council was made possible in this fashion. Tavistock was primarily interested in developing new mathematical models for multiple correlation analysis whereas the Tobacco Research Council wished to sell more tobacco. Both, however, shared an interest in individual responses to the stresses of life and the part played in it by tobacco, and this became a superordinate goal enabling the work to proceed. Another response to ethical dilemmas of this nature is to ensure multiple client support from trade unions and government as well as particular organizations.

Once work begins other ethical dilemmas may arise, for example confidentiality and the protection of respondents, and this may be especially awkward in action research projects because of their specific, and so easily identifiable, character. Though it might have been agreed that individuals or organizations would not be identifiable, in practice this might prove very difficult to ensure, for anyone familiar with the identity of the researcher might soon become aware of the identity of both individuals and the organization, to their possible detriment. In the case of the small business project mentioned earlier, some owner–managers were willing for their identities to be made known while others were not; as a consequence all their identities were concealed in publications. Frequently, this issue may arise in the cases of student dissertations, for example those having a marketing content of possible advantage to competitors. In such cases the work may need to be protected for a period and made immediately available only to assessors, so depriving the research community of the findings for a while.

Action research, then, is clearly an important approach to research in business and management, particularly given its declared aim of serving both the practical concerns of managers and simultaneously generalizing and adding to theory. Most researchers using this approach wish to do immediately useful work and at the same time to stand back from the specific so that their research may be more widely utilized. Indeed, this is the often stated requirement for student dissertations at master's level and beyond. These twin objectives may frequently be achieved by the resolution of a particular content problem in a specific case, and the investigation then widened to address more general issues, such as Lumley (1978) achieved in his research at the BP Stanlow refinery.

Alongside the solution of a specific problem, generalizations may be made about the methods used to address the problem; especially about the ways the relationship between client and action researcher developed during the course of the work, which of course is so crucial to smooth implementation. The interactions between client and researcher at each phase of the action research sequence may be a convenient way of structuring such an analysis especially if generalizations can be made about the contribution of the action research process to implementation, in the way described in Table 5.2.

Suggested further reading

D.T. Campbell and J. C. Stanley's *Experimental and Quasi-Experimental Designs for Research* is useful at a general level, linking action research, experiments and quasi-experiments.

There is a voluminous literature on action research. We have found the article by R. N. Rapoport, 'Three dilemmas in action research', particularly useful. In addition, the paper by A. Warmington, 'Action research: its methods and its implications', may usefully be consulted for its focus on managerial issues in action research.

E. H. Schein's *The Clinical Perspective in Fieldwork* usefully contrasts and clarifies the differences between action research and ethnography.

F. Heller's *The Use and Abuse of Social Science* addresses many of the issues in action research and provides some interesting business examples as also does C. Argyris, R. Putman and D. M. Smith's *Action Science*. The latter also deals in some depth with philosophical and methodological matters, especially so in Part 1.

(Full bibliographical details of the works mentioned in this section appear in the References, at the end of the book.)

6
Survey Research Design

Approaches to survey research

In this chapter we begin by outlining the main approaches to survey research methodology and their determinants; we then discuss examples drawn from business and management. Finally, we consider the essential practical steps entailed in undertaking surveys such as questionnaire format and issues in fieldwork.

In terms of the methodological continuum developed at the end of Chapter 3, survey research occupies a variable, intermediate position somewhere between ethnography and experimental research. This is because the form a survey takes differs considerably depending on the intentions and dispositions of the researcher. For instance, on some occasions, by taking the logic of experimentation out of the laboratory and into the field so as to assess causal relationships, a deductive orientation is emphasized. Such analytical survey approaches acknowledge their intermediate position and their connection with the logic of deductive inquiry by their emphasis on reliability in data collection and the statistical control of variables in place of the physical controls of the laboratory. In their attempts to overcome a major perceived weakness of experiments, there is emphasis on the generalizability of results. Thus sample size, data collection procedures, analysis and measurement are major concerns of survey researchers; many texts deal with these matters and some of the most useful will be cited later. Alternatively, the use of surveys to explore a substantive area, often using open-ended questions to collect data in an inductive form, merges the survey approach with styles of research which are more ethnographic in orientation. Indeed, much survey research may begin with an unstructured and exploratory investigation using overtly ethnographic methods. Thus theory is developed inductively to be tested later using a more structured questionnaire as part of the main study.

Other forms of survey are not necessarily concerned with the development and testing of theory, rather, the prime aim, just like a census, is to describe the characteristics of a specific population at a specific point in time, or at varying points in time for comparative purposes. It should of course also be noted at this preliminary stage that the point made succinctly by Bynner and Stribley (1978) and emphasized throughout this book, that qualitative and quantitative researchers have much to learn from one another, has force. On the one hand, those engaged in experimental research, as well as many survey researchers, may profitably use imaginative insights in the exploration of data as well as in the testing of hypotheses; and on the other ethnographers may need to be more aware of the analytical aspects of their research when inductively generated hypotheses may need to be rigorously tested and refined through a more structured methodology. This point is also made, for example, by Campbell and Fiske (1959) and Jick (1979a), and in practice is interestingly employed in Gladwin's (1989) method of ethnographic decision-tree modelling as a means of researching decision-making.

Planning survey research

How the researcher initially sets about conceptualizing and structuring a problem, so that it is amenable to investigation, is largely determined by the researcher's aims.

For instance, it is important first to be clear whether the intention is to test a theory deductively by elucidating cause and effect relationships among a set of phenomena, or whether the aim is to assess the attributes of a population of subjects. A consideration of these issues determines the type of survey research to be undertaken, whether analytic or descriptive. It thereby points to particular research design problems and issues that need to be addressed prior to any attempt at data collection (Figure 6.1).

Analytic surveys

As we have seen, analytic or explanatory surveys attempt to test a theory by taking the logic of the experiment out of the laboratory and into the field, for example to determine the relationship between accounting control systems and business strategy (Simons, 1987). Hence, in conceptualizing and structuring the research there needs to be an emphasis on specifying the independent, dependent and extraneous variables. This process must be undertaken with due attention to any existing research, theory and literature relevant to the problem as will be evident from the examples cited later in this chapter.

A thorough review of this literature is essential at this stage since it helps the researcher elaborate the various possible relationships that might exist between, and impinge upon, the phenomena whose empirical variation is of prime concern. Indeed this prior review of the relevant literature is vital to a successful and internally valid analytical survey since it enables the researcher to identify any potentially extraneous variables whose influence must be controlled.

The control of variables in analytic surveys is not achieved through the use of physical controls, by allocating subjects to control and experimental groups

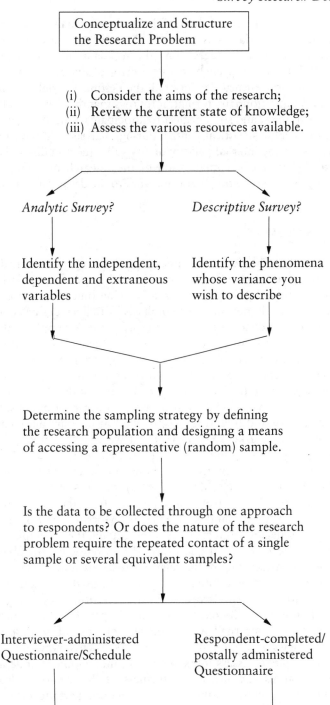

Conceptualize and Structure
the Research Problem

(i)   Consider the aims of the research;
(ii) Review the current state of knowledge;
(iii) Assess the various resources available.

Analytic Survey?   *Descriptive Survey?*

Identify the independent,   Identify the phenomena
dependent and extraneous   whose variance you
variables   wish to describe

Determine the sampling strategy by defining
the research population and designing a means
of accessing a representative (random) sample.

Is the data to be collected through one approach
to respondents? Or does the nature of the research
problem require the repeated contact of a single
sample or several equivalent samples?

Interviewer-administered   Respondent-completed/
Questionnaire/Schedule   postally administered
                               Questionnaire

Figure 6.1   Planning a survey – a summary

as is the case with experimental research. Rather, in analytic surveys the control of extraneous variables is achieved through the use of statistical techniques, such as multiple regression, during data analyses (Ahlgren and Walberg, 1979). This approach to the control of extraneous variables thus necessitates the prior measurememt of all the pertinent variables through their inclusion in the questionnaire format. It follows that the failure to identify such extraneous variables, and so to neglect to anticipate the need to gather data on them so as to enable statistical control during analysis, will have unfortunate consequences for the internal validity of any subsequent findings. These issues thus make the prior conceptualization of the research problem, aided by a careful analysis of the existing literature, vital to the design of analytic surveys.

Descriptive surveys

In contrast to the analytic survey, a descriptive survey is concerned primarily with addressing the particular characteristics of a specific population of subjects, either at a fixed point in time or at varying times for comparative purposes. As such they do not share the emphasis in analytic designs upon control but they do share a concern to secure a representative sample of the relevant population. This is to ensure that any subsequent assessment of the attributes of that population are accurate and the findings are generalizable – in other words, they have population validity. However, this is not to say that descriptive surveys are atheoretical and that prior reviews of the literature are not as important as in the case of an analytical survey. Rather, prior consideration of the relevant theory and literature may be vital in determining what kinds of questions need to be asked. For instance, if we were attempting to describe what it is that motivates employees in a particular context it would be vital to consider which theory of motivation should guide this task. If we were to adopt a Maslovian approach (Maslow, 1943) the types of questions we would ask would be very different from those deriving from the use of, for instance, expectancy theory (Lawler and Rhode, 1976). Moreover, it would be important to be able to defend from criticisism the guiding theory employed. Hence, in order to justify the kinds of questions asked, even when the objective is to describe, prior consideration of the relevant literature and theory is vital.

In a business context descriptive surveys may be used, for example, to ascertain attitudes to a company's products or the attitudes of a organization's workforce. In their useful book, Reeves and Harper (1981) consider at length most of the issues concerned with managements' use of attitude surveys to ascertain the views and opinions of employees. Such surveys may be undertaken, for example, to assess job satisfaction, motivation, morale and stress; employee grievances and the satisfactoriness of the means of dealing with them; and the reaction to possible changes in working arrangements. This is a field where predominantly descriptive surveys are utilized and these, together with those used to ascertain some of the circumstances of management buyouts, will be used as examples later in this chapter.

It follows that both analytic and descriptive questionnaires are concerned with identifying the 'research population' which will provide all the information necessary for tackling the original research problem. It is from this population that the researcher will attempt to draw a representative (random) sample for research purposes, and it is to this population that any subsequent findings will be generalized or extrapolated. A detailed treatment of random sampling procedures is beyond the scope of this book, but those interested may consult a variety of useful texts (e.g. Kish, 1965; Oppenheim, 1966; Moser and Kalton, 1971; Yeomans, 1973).

At this point it is also necessary to refer to the use of stratified sampling. A prior knowledge of the make up of the population from which a random sample is to be drawn will make the researcher aware that there may be particular population characteristics (e.g. ethnic minorities or age and gender distributions) that make random sampling from within specific sub-groups necessary if the sample is to be representative. A search of the literature will of course aid the task of identifying the stratified characteristics of the research population. Of course, any decisions regarding sample sizes and the sampling parameters for various subsections of the population must also take into account the time and finance at the researcher's disposal.

The objectives of the research will also determine whether or not data is to be collected by only one approach to the sample of the research population or whether information is to be repeatedly collected. In the case of collecting data at successive points in time decisions need to be taken as to whether it is practicable to gain access to the same informants repeatedly and, if not, whether equivalent random sampling will suffice. Moser and Kalton (1971, chapter 6) elaborate this point.

Finally, the size of the sample, together with its geographical dispersion, have a bearing on the researcher's decisions about how respondents are to be contacted and the requisite information to be elicited.

At its most basic this decision involves a choice between sending, probably by post, a questionnaire which the respondent self-administers, or the use of an interviewer to administer the questionnaire. This may either be administered face to face or in some some cases may be economically conducted by telephone (Frey, 1989). Issues other than sample size and location affect this decision: for instance, the complexity of the information required might necessitate the actual presence of an interviewer so that he or she can explain and elaborate the more problematic questions. Further, in considering these issues the researcher needs a prior understanding of the attributes of the target population, for example its degree of literacy and areas of technical competence, so that their ability to cope with questions might be predicted.

Overlaying this decision-making process are the inevitable limits of resources. Postal questionnaires are generally less expensive and time consuming than those administered by an interviewer. However, the use of the latter does raise the problem of interviewer bias (Boyd and Westfall, 1970), while the former can exacerbate 'non response' problems (Scott, 1961). If resources allow, it may be advantageous to undertake interviewing with another co-worker, especially if the investigation is particularly sensitive, as was the case with Braithwaite's investigation into corporate crime in the pharmaceutical industry (Braithwaite, 1985). There may of course be advantages other than corroboration in this approach, for co-workers may provide checks on memory, particularly when note-taking is difficult, and may also bring different perspectives and working hypotheses to the investigation (Bechhofer, Elliott and McCrone, 1984).

So the most appropriate choice of how to gain access to informants and how to collect information is contingent upon the various demands of the research design outlined above. Whatever the eventual decision the result has significant implications for subsequent decisions the researcher must make regarding questionnaire format, which will be addressed in the concluding section of this chapter. At this stage we offer by way of illustration some examples of both analytic and descriptive surveys.

An example of an analytic survey

This study examined the relationship between top managements' entrepreneurial orientation and organizational performance (Covin and Slevin, 1988). It was designed to determine whether organization structure moderated the relationship between entrepreneurial style and organizational performance and, if so, to identify what type of moderating effect structure had on this relationship. A thorough review of the literature seemed to suggest that the use of an entrepreneurial management style and company performance were contingent upon the state of the organization's structure. The following hypotheses were made.

1. In organically structured companies, increases in top managements' entrepreneurial orientation will positively influence performance; in mechanistically structured companies, such increases will negatively influence performance.

    When organization structure was divided into organic and mechanistic, and management style into entrepreneurial and conservative, it enabled a theoretical framework to be constructed of four 'pure' styles:
    (a) effective entrepreneurial companies with entrepreneurial top management styles and organic structures;
    (b) 'pseudo' entrepreneurial companies with entrepreneurial top management styles and mechanistic structures;
    (c) efficient bureaucratic companies having conservative top management styles and mechanistic structures;
    (d) unstructured, unadventurous companies having conservative top management styles and organic structures.
    This classification then gave rise to a second hypothesis:
2. Companies in which the organization structure is congruent with the management style, i.e. cases (a) and (c) above, will perform significantly better than companies in which these variables are incongruent, i.e. cases (b) and (d) above.

Methodologically, data was gathered from business companies throughout the continental United States, randomly selected from a publicly available mailing list. In view of the size of the population, questionnaires were mailed to the most senior executives in 507 firms, roughly equally divided between the manufacturing and service sectors. Eighty usable questionnaires were returned, for a response rate of 15.8 per cent. The low response rate was explicable, it was suggested, as the the mailing list was widely used and the respondents were all senior executives. Examination of response bias revealed no significant difference between the responding and non-responding firms in terms of two key characteristics.

Measures of the variables used in the research, namely, entrepreneurial style, organization structure and organizational performance, were reviewed by a panel of four academicians and pre-tested with a sample of six managers.

A six-item Likert-type scale was used to measure elements of entrepreneurial style characterizing the collective management style of their business unit's top managers. Items such as risk-taking, innovation and proactiveness were derived from the literature and instruments used elsewhere. The ratings on these items were averaged to arrive at a single entrepreneurial style for each business. This seemed warranted when the items were factor analysed to assess their dimensionality or factorial validity. In detail scaling is beyond the scope of this book but the interested reader may consult Kidder and Judd (1986, chapter 9) on scaling generally and the widely employed Likert scales in particular.

Similarly, organization structure was measured by using a five-item Likert-type scale to determine the extent to which organizations were structured in organic or mechanistic ways.

Performance was measured by asking respondents to indicate on a five point, Likert-type scale how their top managers would rate the performance of their businesses over the previous three years on each of the following financial performance criteria: operating profits, profit to sales ratio; cash flow from operations, and return on investment (Table 6.1).

As a check on the validity of these perceptual performance measures secondary performance data, such as sales growth rate, was collected on twenty of the sampled firms. The zero-order correlation coefficient between these figures and the firm's subjective performance scores was very high, indicating evidence of construct validity for the performance measure. It also confirmed that respondents' perceptions of how well their businesses were performing was an acceptable basis for an organizational performance variable.

The first hypothesis was then tested using moderated regression analysis which was considered to be an appropriate technique for testing hypothesized contingency relationships. In moderated regression analysis the statistical significance of interaction effects is tested by regressing the dependent variable on two or more main variables, one being the independent variable and the other the hypothesized moderator variable, and the cross-product of those main variables.

The second hypothesis was tested by dividing the sample into congruent companies, i.e. entrepreneurial style and organic structure; conservative style and mechanistic structure and incongruent companies, i.e. those with entrepreneurial styles and mechanistic structures; conservative styles and organic structures. Then a *t*-test was used to compare the sub-group performance means.

The result of these analyses suggested that organizational performance was jointly determined by the interaction of organizational style and organicity. Since

Table 6.1   Extracts from Covin and Slevin's questionnaire on the relationship between entrepreneurial orientation and organizational performance

---

The following statements are meant to identify the collective management style of your business unit's key decision-makers rather than any one individual's management style or philosophy. Please indicate, by circling the appropriate number, the extent to which the following statements characterize the management style of your business unit's top managers.

THE ENTREPRENEURIAL STYLE SCALE

The operating management philosophy of the top management of my business is . . .

| 1 | 2 | 3 | 4 | 5 | 6 | 7 |

Strong emphasis on the marketing of true and tried products or services and the avoidance of heavy research and development costs

Strong emphasis on research and development technological leadership and innovation

How many new lines of products or services has your business unit marketed in the past five years? Please exclude minor variations.

| 1 | 2 | 3 | 4 | 5 | 6 | 7 |

No new lines of products or services in the past five years

Very many new lines of products or services in the past five years

In dealing with competitors my business unit . . .

| 1 | 2 | 3 | 4 | 5 | 6 | 7 |

Typically responds to actions which competitors initiate

Typically initiates actions which competitors respond to

The operating management philosophy of the top management of my business unit is . . .

| 1 | 2 | 3 | 4 | 5 | 6 | 7 |

Tight formal control of most operations by means of sophisticated control information systems

Loose informal control; heavy dependence on informal relations and norm of co-operation for getting work done

---

the interaction term had a positive regression coefficient it was suggested that an entrepreneurial top management style made a greater contribution to performance in organically structured firms than in those mechanistically structured.

As regards hypothesis two the results of a one-way analysis of variance across the four firm types as well as t-tests between them revealed no significant differences between these firms in terms of numbers of employees. It was therefore concluded that firms in which the structure fitted the management style outperformed those in which the fit was poor.

Despite this the authors note some limitations of the study. The reliability of the entrepreneurial style and organization structure data is based on the perceptions of one organizational member; clearly data collected from multiple respondents would have had more validity.

Further, the data are cross-sectional so causal links among the variables could not be firmly established. Firm performance is a function of prior not contemporary management practices and organizational forms. Accordingly, longitudinal data would be required, rather than data at one point in time, to establish causal relationships and control for time-lag effects such as was suggested in the previous chapter.

Because the principal direction of the causal relationships between firm performance, entrepreneurial style and organization structure is unknown, alternative theoretical frameworks may provide equally plausible explanations of the data: for example, that top management's entrepreneurial orientation moderates the relationship between organization structure and firm performance. This is evident, as in moderated regression analysis the labelling of one of the independent variables as the predictor and the other as the moderator is arbitrary.

Thus, while this study raised the strong possibility that organization structure may exist in a causal relationship with entrepreneurial style and company performance, a potentially fruitful area for research still remained to discover the determinants and consequences of such orientations.

An example of a descriptive survey

There follows an example of research based on evidence from a survey of management buy-outs in the United Kingdom.

Exploratory research was conducted by Wright (1986) to determine some aspects of management buy-outs, a field about which little was known. Management buy-outs were defined as occasions when the management purchase the company for which they work from the previous owners. Buy-outs may occur on the retirement of the previous owners, from an independent or parent company in receivership or from a parent still trading that wishes to dispose of a subsidiary.

An attempt was made to answer issues raised in a preliminary theoretical discussion through a mailed questionnaire survey, and by case studies of a sub-sample of the companies surveyed, both carried out in 1983. The research was designed to find answers to the following questions.

1. What is the extent of management buy-outs involving trading relationships with the former parent?
2. What is the strength of the trading relationship and hence the implied level of dependency of the bought-out company on the former parent?
3. Does continued dependence after the buy-out improve or worsen trading relationships?
4. Are attempts made to reduce dependency on the former parent?

From telephone surveys of the financial institutions and searches of the financial press it had been estimated that up to the time that the sample for the survey was drawn, 580 buy-outs had been completed. Since it had been estimated that the current failure rate was one in ten, the surviving population from which the sample was drawn was approximately 520.

Access was an issue in this research; relatively few buy-outs are reported in the press as the data is often somewhat sensitive, and financing institutions were apparently the only source of the names and addresses of target

Table 6.2   Extracts from Wright's questionnaire on management buy-outs

---

Company details
  1. Location of Head Office and name before buy-out, if changed.
  2. How many companies (subsidiaries, etc.) were bought out?
  3. Have any employees outside the buy-out team contributed any funds for the purchase of the company?
  4. Who provided the finance for the buy-out?

Management
  5. How many were in the buy-out team?
  6. Have there been managerial changes since the buy-out?
  7. Where no changes have taken place, are any planned?

The company
  8. From how many sites does the company operate?
  9. What is/are your principal product(s)/service(s)?
 10. Did you lose any customers as a direct effect of the buy-out?
 11. What changes do you expect in profits before interest and tax in the next financial year?
 12. Have you experienced any cash flow problems since the buy-outs? If so, what were they?

---

companies. All institutions agreed to contact their clients to find out whether they wished to participate, some providing names and addresses, and others preferring to mail questionnaires direct to maintain confidentiality.

In this way, from a distribution of 191 questionnaires, usable replies were received from 111 buy-outs, producing a response rate of 58.1 per cent without a reminder being sent. In assessing the reliability of the results it of course needs to be borne in mind that data was available from only a minority of buy-outs which had taken place. This was because earlier buy-outs were not termed as such, or they had already received much press publicity, or because they were in a precarious position and did not wish attention to be drawn to the fact (Table 6.2).

The second stage of the survey involved writing case studies on twenty companies to discuss issues arising from the buy-out in more detail, to ascertain the kinds of changes and problems that had occurred.

Analysis of the questionnaire survey, which (as can be seen) was concerned throughout with largely factual information, provided evidence that transfers of ownership existed where there were transactional relationships between parent and subsidiary, but that for the most part the level of dependence was likely to be low. The need for independence was also stressed when, in two cases where transactional relationships existed, the parent subsequently went into liquidation after the buy-out. Attempts to reduce dependency apparently began soon after the buy-out but with informal relationships continuing to be maintained.

The choice of questionnaire format

A vital skill in undertaking a survey is the ability to structure, focus, phrase and ask sets of questions in a manner that is intelligible to respondents. Such questions also need to minimize bias, and provide data that can be statistically

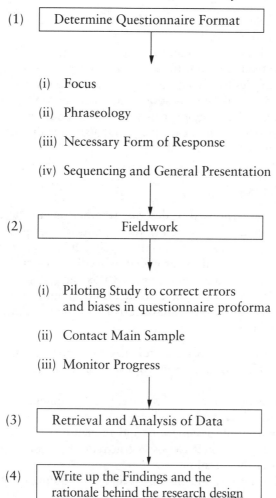

(1)   Determine Questionnaire Format

   (i)   Focus

   (ii)   Phraseology

   (iii)   Necessary Form of Response

   (iv)   Sequencing and General Presentation

(2)   Fieldwork

   (i)   Piloting Study to correct errors and biases in questionnaire proforma

   (ii)   Contact Main Sample

   (iii)   Monitor Progress

(3)   Retrieval and Analysis of Data

(4)   Write up the Findings and the rationale behind the research design

Figure 6.2   The questionnaire format

analysed. To achieve these objectives it is important to consider four inter-related issues in questionnaire design: questionnaire focus, question phraseology, the form of response, and question sequencing and overall presentation (see Figure 6.2).

Questionnaire focus

By focus we mean the extent to which the questions intended to be asked cover the various aspects of the research problem adequately and in sufficient detail. For instance, in analytic survey research it is particularly important that there is provision in the questionnaire for eliciting data on all the important variables. This enables statistical analysis of the relationship between the independent and dependent variables, as well statistical control over extraneous variables, to allow the theory to be tested.

Conversely, it is also important to ascertain whether or not all the questions to be asked are really relevant to the research problem. It is incumbent upon the questionnaire designer continually to assess whether a question is really necessary and to exclude any questions that do not clearly serve the objectives of the investigation. The more incisive a questionnaire the more costs are reduced and, particularly in the case of postal questionnaires, the better will be the response rate.

Questionnaire phraseology

Phraseology is the term used to describe whether or not the ways in which questions are asked are intelligible to respondents, and on these matters generally it will be useful to consult Payne (1951). An important aid in judging these problems will be provided by feedback from the pilot study, a matter which will be considered later. At this early stage in questionnaire design, however, the following considerations should be reviewed by researchers with reference to the characteristics of the population from which the sample is to be drawn.

1. Are the purposes of the research revealed to respondents in a way that will promote the likelihood of their co-operation without biasing subsequent responses?
2. Are any instructions to respondents clear and unambiguous?
3. Can the questions be understood; are they free from jargon, esoteric terminology, inappropriate assumptions and ambiguity?
4. Are the respondents likely to possess the requisite information and knowledge to answer the questions?
5. Is it possible that respondents might find the wording of questions offensive, insensitive or embarrassing?
6. Might the wording of the questions lead to bias through 'leading' the respondent to particular answers or imposing assumptions that may be unwarranted?

The form of response

As we have emphasized, the data provided must be elicited in a form that permits subsequent analysis. This analysis usually entails computer-aided, statistical manipulation. It is therefore vital that measures of the variables important to the research problem are built into the questionnaire by asking questions in an appropriate way and providing an appropriate pro forma for the responses. The key to success is to ensure that the questions will provide data in a form suitable for the statistical techniques the researcher intends to use, bearing in mind the reliability and validity of the measurement scales actually encoded in the questionnaire design.

Scaling

At the outset it is important to be sure to use the type of scale for measuring any variable that is appropriate to the statistical techniques to be used during data analysis. In considering this issue it is helpful to follow Kidder and Judd (1986, pp. 59–62), who differentiate four types of measurement scale: nominal, ordinal, interval, and ratio. For those wishing to pursue more sophisticated aspects of scaling it may be helpful to consult Maranell (1974).

Nominal scales

With this type of scale a variable is measured in terms of two or more qualitatively different categories, e.g. 'male' and 'female'. The scale indicates differences of category but these have no arithmetic value.

Ordinal scales

As with nominal scales, an ordinal scale contains two or more categories that allow differentiation of variables in terms of those categories. As the name implies, however, some degree of ordering is involved as different points on the scale indicate the quantity being measured. For example, Kidder and Judd (1986) illustrate this by the example of how much autonomy workers might have in their jobs: 1 = little autonomy (e.g. assembly line workers), 2 = moderate autonomy (e.g. construction workers) and 3 = much autonomy (e.g. doctors). Different points on the scale indicate greater or lesser amounts of the phenomena being measured relative to other points on the scale. But it does not imply anything other than establishing an order, since an ordinal scale says nothing about the distances between the points on the scale.

Interval scales

These have all the characteristics of an ordinal scale except that the distances between the points on the scale (i.e. the intervals) represent equal quantities of the measure variable (e.g. degrees Fahrenheit on a thermometer). However, interval scales do not have a true zero, rather, zero is arbitrary. So although we can add or subtract the numbers on an interval scale they cannot be multiplied or divided. The lack of a true zero makes the multiplication and division of points on interval scale meaningless. An interval scale is used in Table 6.1.

Ratio scales

These have all the characteristics of an interval scale except that they have a true zero and it therefore becomes possible to say that, for example, a score of ten represents twice as much of the construct as a score of five. So multiplication and division of points on a ratio scale become meaningful.

In the analysis of survey data it is important to use the statistical methods appropriate for the types of measurement scales that have previously been encoded into the questionnaire format. For example, statistical techniques, such as multiple regression, which depend on the distances between quantitative points on a scale being equivalent, cannot be used on, for instance, nominal or ordinal data. So how variables are operationalized and measured, and how this is encoded in the questionnaire design, must fit the statistical techniques the researcher intends to use. This latter choice depends upon the purposes and aims of the research.

The problems surrounding the use of the correct type of measurement scale also raise the issues of validity and reliability. Validity refers to the extent to which a scale encoded into a set of questions actually measures the variable it is supposed to measure. We may assume, for instance, that an examination is a means of measuring the variation in candidates' knowledge of a particular substantive area. However, such an assumption may be invalid in that it may not only measure knowledge of the substantive area, but other variables influencing candidates' performances may be inadvertently measured, such as the ability to cope with stress and the speed of writing.

The only way to assess the validity of such measurement devices is to evaluate the results against some other measures, or criteria, which have already demonstrated its validity. Although this is not without difficulty, a thorough knowledge of previous research literature will aid this calibration process by providing possible criteria (H. W. Smith, 1975; Cronbach and Meehl, 1979). For instance, in our example of analytic research cited above, Covin and Slevin (1988) checked the validity of their measures of managerial perceptions of company performance with secondary performance data such as sales growth rate.

Validity refers to the accuracy of the measurement process while the reliability of measurement refers to its consistency; that is, the extent to which a measuring device will produce the same results when applied more than once to the same person under similar conditions. The most straightforward way of testing reliability is to replicate; either by administering the same questions to the same respondents at different times and assessing the degree of correlation, or by asking the same question in different ways at different points in the questionnaire. More sophisticated versions of these processes are succinctly reviewed by Moser and Kalton (1971, pp. 353–7) and in more detail by Summers (1970). Finally, it is important to note that questionnaire designers need to be aware that, although they may have a highly reliable measure, it may not necessarily be measuring what it is intended to measure: reliability does not necessarily imply validity, whereas if the measure is valid it will be reliable.

By building measurement scales into a questionnaire a researcher necessarily limits subjects' replies to a fixed set of responses which have encoded the requisite measures and thus are readily compared and computed. This form of question is usually called a 'closed' question, and allows comparison and statistical manipulation. It does, however, have the disadvantage of limiting, and perhaps distorting, responses to a fixed schedule, so preventing respondents answering in their own way.

By contrast, 'open-ended' questions do not impose such artificial limitations, and leave respondents free to answer in their own terms. Data might thus be elicited with greater depth and meaning, revealing insights into pertinent issues. The disadvantage is that, due to the lack of structure, information is not readily codable and computable, nor is comparison across respondents easy. Thus, while open-ended questions provide richer data, analysis becomes much more difficult. Again, the nature of the problem being investigated, as well as the aims of the research, has a bearing on all these issues.

Question sequencing and overall presentation

Finally, in designing the format of a questionnaire it is important to consider the sequence of the questions to be asked. This is particularly necessary (as is the overall presentation) where a postal self-completion questionnaire is to be used. With regard to question sequencing it is helpful to both respondents and interviewers if the designer ensures that the questions have a natural and logical order. For instance, it assists both rapport and respondents' understanding of what is required if more general and factual questions precede narrow, detailed questions and questions of opinion.

The quality of the overall presentation of the questionnaire, its conciseness and the attractiveness of the design are also of importance in ensuring a high completion rate, as is a suitable covering letter and a stamped, addressed envelope for its return. Low completion rates are often a feature of surveys by questionnaire, especially if administered by post; the key issue being whether respondents differ in a significant way from non-respondents. Two methods are often used to answer this question: first, to compare the two groups on available characteristics, as was done, for example, in the case of the research reported above by Covin and Slevin (1988); second, to compare the original respondents with those produced by follow-up letters – which, incidentally, can be an effective means of increasing response rates. Factors affecting response rates to mailed questionnaires are covered in detail by Herbelein and Baumgarter (1978).

Fieldwork

Whether it is intended to use a postal questionnaire or an interviwer-administered schedule it is always important to begin fieldwork by conducting a pilot study.

In essence, pilot research is a trial run-through to test the research design with a subsample of respondents who have characteristics similar to those identifiable in the main sample to be surveyed. Piloting is necessary as it is very difficult to predict how respondents will interpret and react to questions. Conducting a pilot before the main survey allows any potential problems in the pro forma of the questionnaire to be identified and corrected. Moreover, where an interviewer-administered questionnaire is to be used piloting provides the opportunity to refine and develop the interviewing and social skills of the researchers and helps to highlight any possible sources of interviewer bias. When the pilot study is completed it is then possible to conclude the design of the questionnaire and finalize any arrangements for its administration.

During the main study it is important to assess its progress by monitoring the postal returns or maintaining contact with the interviewers in the field. In the case of postally administered questionnaires failure to respond by particular sub-groups may be a feature, and in this case it is important to discover any pattern to this.

Data analysis and the presentation of findings

Although this book does not deal in any depth with data analysis and presentation, it is important to remind the reader that a vital aspect of planning a survey is to secure access to any computing facilities necessary for the analysis of data. Similarly, it is important to allow sufficient time for the transfer of data from completed questionnaires and schedules to computer software as well as for the subsequent writing up and critical evaluation of any findings. All these issues are succinctly dealt with by Moser and Kalton (1971, pp. 410–88).

Ethics and survey research

The ethical issues, which will be briefly discussed in the case of the ethnographic approach, also apply when researchers derive data from surveys.

This is particularly the case when data is derived from one organization, and especially so in respect of surveys that are commissioned by one interested party, such as management. This special case is considered at some length by Reeves and Harper (1981, chapter 11), who make the following points:

1. the results may lead to decisions that affect the respondents;
2. as a consequence, interested parties will wish to be consulted about the purpose of the survey and the manner in which it is conducted;
3. choice of questions may need to be governed not only by survey, but also by organizational, considerations;
4. providing opportunities for employees to have their say may be an important consideration in the survey design.

In a discussion of the need for a code of practice governing survey research, such as is contained in the British Sociological Association's 'Statement of Ethical Principles' or the Market Research Society's code of conduct, Reeves and Harper (1981) consider there are four minimum requirements for any code of practice governing survey research within an organization.

1. The researcher should consult with all interested parties before undertaking fieldwork and should proceed only by consent and agreement. This will

probably require free access to employee representatives including representatives of the trade unions.

There may, however, be some difficulties in practice in this regard in the case of analytic surveys designed to test hypotheses where the researcher may not wish to reveal details of the hypotheses to be tested. To state in advance what hypotheses the researcher hopes to falsify or confirm is to invite subjects respond less according to their own feelings but, rather, according to what they believe the researcher wants or does not want to hear. In a full discussion of this dilemma, Barnes (1979) believes that the solution is for the researcher to demonstrate that, as far as possible, anyone interested can find out as much as they wish about the inquiry, its aims and methods, and that the only restrictions are those entailed by the process of data collection itself. He suggests that in this way researchers may hope to gain the confidence of the people they work with.

2. Agreement needs to be reached with all interested parties as early as possible over the dissemination of results before too great an investment of time is made in an inquiry which will lead nowhere.
3. The purposes of an employee survey and most types of survey research should not be concealed, as this prevents any judgement by respondents as to whether their participation may adverseley affect them.
4. Any special circumstance that might affect the interpretation of the results should be clearly reported.

Suggested further reading

There are many basic texts on survey research design, for example, A. N. Oppenheim's *Questionnaire Design and Attitude Measurement*, C. A. Moser and G. Kalton's *Survey Methods and Social Investigation*, and L. H. Kidder and C. M. Judd's *Research Methods in Social Relations*.

Question formulation is succinctly dealt with by S. Payne, in *The Art of Asking Questions*.

A particularly useful book for students of business and management, also available as a student project manual, is T. K. Reeves and D. Harper's *Surveys at Work. A Practitioner's Guide*. It is chiefly concerned with the technology of carrying out employee surveys but in doing so also considers in some detail phases of the research process, such as entry to the organization and drawing conclusions from the data.

Data analysis is covered to some extent in the texts already mentioned above. In addition, a useful guide to basic statistics is A. S. C. Ehrenberg's *A Primer in Data Reduction: An Introductory Statistics Textbook*, which draws many of its examples from market research.

On the computer analysis of survey data, a useful text is the 'SPSS Manual': N. H. Nie, C. H. Hull and others's *Statistical Package for the Social Sciences*.

(Full bibliographical details of these works are given in the References, at the end of this book.)

7
Ethnography: Its Origins and Practice

In this chapter the nature of the ethnographic approach to research is examined with reference to its application to business and management issues. We first discuss the nature of ethnography, then explore its practice through a consideration of business and management cases. In Chapter 8 we consider some matters commonly of most concern to those wishing to utilize an ethnographic approach to research: the nature of the field roles which might be adopted; ethnography as a means of developing theory; the matter of access and the ethical issues that arise.

Ethnography and its development

The ethnographic approach is fundamentally that of anthropology and allows the fieldworker to use the socially acquired and shared knowledge available to the participants to account for the observed patterns of human activity. The key feature of the ethnographic approach is that it is based on what are termed naturalist modes of inquiry, such as participant observation, within a predominantly inductivist framework.

Although the history of ethnography, which is addressed at length in Wax, (1971), probably goes back to the fifth century BC, the first work to be carried out in industry in this tradition was that of Charles Booth in the nineteenth century. He employed a variety of research techniques including statistical data, interviewing and systematic participant observation, the last partly as a lodger with working men's families to study the working people of London in the 1880s. Problems of access and the ethics of solutions were early revealed when Beatrice Potter, one of Booth's co-workers and the daughter of an industrial magnate, wished to study the working class in their homes and workshops. She enlisted the help of her maternal grandmother, who had been the daughter of a powerloom weaver, to arrange an introduction to this working class community but, so that they would not be inhibited by her grand status, a 'pious fraud' was carried out, and she was introduced as a farmer's daughter. Beatrice Potter proceded to carry out participant observation studies in a London sweat shop where she was employed as a seamstress and, with her husband Sydney Webb, later published one of the early texts on research methodology (Webb and Webb, 1932).

Much later, in the USA, there were developments in social anthropology using participant observation techniques in the tradition of ethnographic field-work. In the University of Chicago this came to be known as the Chicago School, and was to be chiefly concerned with the study of ethnic groups in the city. Whyte, (1984), for example, describes these influences upon his first industrial study in the Phillipps Petroleum Company in 1943. During the 1950s and 1960s a few, now classical, ethnographic studies were carried out, for example by Dalton (1959) into managerial practices in four companies in North America, by Sayles, (1964) into the nature of managerial tasks in one division of a large American manufacturing organization and by Gouldner (1954b) into aspects of bureaucracy in a gypsum mine. Sayles (1958) and Gouldner (1954a) also turned their attention to shop-floor matters in eth-nographic studies of industrial work groups and a wildcat strike respectively. A similar focus was also the concern of Lupton (1963), who built upon the participant observation studies of Roy (1960) by studying the work organiza-tion and culture of the shop floor in two manufacturing plants in order to explain the occurrence of restriction of output by employees. These were fore-runners of later business and management studies, some of which we will refer to in more detail later.

In ethnography the focus is on the manner in which people interact and collaborate in observable and regular ways. Typically such work has taken long periods of intensive study and immersion in a well-defined locality involv-ing direct participation with some of the members of the organization in their activities. In understanding primitive societies some anthropologists take the view that the aim is to think and feel like a member of its culture whilst at the same time avoiding 'going native' and being captured by it, and still remaining a trained anthropologist from another culture. So, while a wide portfolio of data collection methods may be used, ethnographers usually place more em-phasis on observation and semi-structured interviewing than on documentary and survey data, although both have frequently been used in ethnographic studies generally as supplementary material.

So while there are a number of divergent trends in the practice of ethno-graphy, practitioners would probably agree that extended participant obser-vation is a central feature of most studies. As participant observers an attempt is made to learn about the culture under study and so interpret it in the way its members do. This approach is based upon the belief that the social world cannot be understood by studying artificial simulations of it in experiments or interviews, for the use of such methods only shows how people behave in those artificial experimental and interview situations.

Ethnographers' commitment to naturalism thus leads them to argue that, in order to explain the actions of people working in organizations, it is necessary to arrive at an understanding of the various cultures and sub-cultures prepotent in particular organizational settings, for it is out of these systems of meanings, beliefs, values and mores that rational action arises. A similar commitment, though for somewhat different reasons, is identifiable in the work of ethnomethodologists, who attempt to uncover and examine the 'taken for granted' meanings and expectations that underpin members' courses of action (Garfinkel, 1967). In this they frequently attempt to 'enter' the daily lives of members, even to the extent of going native in those cultures, with the intention of 'becoming the phenomenon . . . doing reality as its members do' (Mehan and Wood, 1975, pp. 226–8). What may further serve to baffle the uninitiated is the large number of texts referring to work in the 'field', which cover not only ethnographic studies but which may also embrace action research as well as consultancy and may include both quantitative and qualitative methodologies, though the qualitative is usually predominant (e.g. Wax, 1971; Johnson, 1975; Burgess, 1984; Whyte, 1984).

Many of these introductory issues will become clearer as we examine examples of ethnographic research and within it the matters of access, the roles taken by researchers, research design, fieldwork and its analysis, and ethics. Moreover, the wide battery of methods for data collection used by ethnographers will become more apparent, as will their key emphasis upon participant observation.

Ethnography in practice

In the following sections the ethnographic work of a number of investigators who have focused on managerial and shop floor issues is reviewed. While we do not discuss studies of consumer behaviour in this section, it should be noted that a number of articles have recently appeared that describe studies using ethnography as an alternative mode of inquiry to surveys and experiments (see, e.g., McGrath, 1989).

Observational studies of managers

Studies of managers are considered in four subsections. First, a group of studies are reviewed which are concerned with various aspects of managing such as managerial succession and the problems of bureaucracy, the interconnection of informal and formal managerial action, and the managerial way of life in industrial organizations. We then review studies of managers in contexts other than the industrial, such as local government, and in particular in roles such as personnel and marketing. We also explore some issues in researching the roles and activities of managerial élites. Finally, we discuss some ethnographic studies aimed at discovering what managers actually do when engaged in managing.

Studies of managers managing

As mentioned above, Gouldner (1954a, b) studied both shop-floor and managerial matters at a gypsum plant in the USA. In his managerial investigation Gouldner (1954b) wished to clarify some of the social processes that lead to differing degrees of bureaucratization, by studying patterns of factory administration in a case study of one plant. He was careful to make clear that the case would be limited in its generalizability and would not serve as more than a 'potentially fruitful hypothesis' (Gouldner, 1954b, p. 27). It is also made clear at the outset that in the course of the study alternative solutions would become apparent – making policy changes feasible – and these would be reported (Gouldner, 1962). Gouldner headed a team of researchers composed of two teaching fellows from the university and a number of relatively inexperienced undergraduates.

In an appendix fieldwork procedures are described, not to demonstrate how they 'conformed to the canons of scientific method' but simply to state how the data was gathered. The work was to be primarily exploratory and was perceived as developing new concepts that would lend themselves to future 'validation by experimental methods' (Gouldner, 1954b, p. 247).

Entry was through both company management and the trade union. The company was represented by the labour relations director, who was familiar with the social sciences and who wished to gain insights into some of his difficulties while leaving the research team completely free to pursue its own interests. The team was also introduced to managers in the production department, from one of whom final permission had to be secured and who, while supportive of the research, asked to be informed of any foreman who was causing trouble at the plant. Such a request was firmly refused on the grounds that replacing people would not solve problems if the situation causing difficulties remained unchanged.

Two members of the team then attended the local union meeting, which was supportive of the research especially when suspicions that it might be a management attempt to spy were removed after it was made clear that the research team were all ex-GIs. This not only put the researchers in the position of learners but also helped the ex-servicemen in the workforce to feel more comfortable with them.

Despite these careful preparations, however, one influential group had been neglected. It had been assumed that senior management also spoke for local plant management and as a consequence relations throughout the study were less harmonious with this group.

Data sources were interviews, observations and documents; interview techniques being described as 'partially non-directive'. That is to say, interviewers started with some notion of the topics which seemed to be of theoretical importance but after introducing themselves they simply said they were interested in learning about factory life and asked for help. This allowed interviewees to pursue whatever areas they wished while enabling interviewers to probe issues that initial hunches had suggested might be important.

As relationships with interviewees developed the research team found it less necessary to use non-directive methods and began to focus questions. It seemed that, as the team put it, non-directive interviewing suggested a cautious approach and was reciprocated by counter-caution. It was noticeable to the researchers that there were considerable differences between surface workers and miners in their attitudes to being interviewed and this in itself was an important source of data. It also made it necessary to take a flexible interviewing style when the degrees of rapport between researcher and group were qualitatively different. Miners regarded the team as people who were also interviewers whereas surfacemen regarded the team only as interviewers. Although this may suggest over-identification with miners the research team believed this to be much exaggerated, for 'deep rapport has its perils, but to treat the norm of impersonality as sacred, even if it impairs the informant's cooperation, would seem to be an inexcusable form of scientific ritualism' (Gouldner, 1954b, p. 247). Formal interviews lasted between one and a half and two hours and respondents were paid at normal rates while being interviewed.

A second source of data was by observation, in that much time spent walking round the plant, or standing talking casually to a worker, was utilized. The plant's small physical size and the workforce of just over 200 enabled the team to absorb the culture quickly. Observational material was supplemented by one of the research team having been employed full time during a previous summer as a mechanic in the mine, his expertise being useful to the team in their frequent discussions of the data as it emerged.

Finally, the team gained access to a large amount of documentary material such as newspaper reports, memoranda, company reports and union contracts. Much of this material was confidential and the degree of trust established to ensure access was probably assisted by the close proximity of the plant to main company offices, ensuring high frequency of contact.

Dalton's studies in the 1950s had many features in common with those of Gouldner. He too was concerned to immerse himself in the cultures of three manufacturing firms and one department store to investigate problems arising from the gap between unofficial and official ways of doing things. These studies are described in *Men who Manage* (Dalton, 1959) which contains a useful appendix on methods, later expanded with much insight (Dalton, 1964), and which serves as a useful guide to ethnographic practice.

Dalton started with some preconceptions. He believed that natural science methods were inappropriate to the study of social situations. For example, no hypotheses were formulated at the outset as it was considered that what was relevant in forming an hypothesis was unclear until the situation was well known and, further, that a hypothesis could prove restrictive. Rather, Dalton proceded by hunches, some of which were dropped and others followed as knowledge increased. Second, he had a preference for what is described as 'idea over number' (Dalton, 1964, p. 56), by which he meant the avoidance of quantification of data for its own sake; finally, he took a pragmatic view of ethical questions arising from 'insider' research, a matter we consider later.

Dalton was employed as a member of staff at a factory he called Milo when the idea of undertaking an investigation of its managerial culture occurred to him, largely because he was puzzled by many incidents at the plant. He continued his studies when he left the organization and Milo became the focus of his work, which continued for a decade. Unlike Gouldner's study of the gypsum plant, much of Dalton's work was covert in that he did not seek entry to his target organizations through formal channels – believing formal interviews would reveal only official expectations.

Interpretations from Milo were checked at other locations, at some of which he had been employed and at all of which he had 'intimates'. Data was gathered directly by formal interviewing, his own work diaries and participant observation in the course of his normal work as an employee, which he says was uncompromised. This activity was either fitted into his usual duties or more often, interviewing was done after working hours both in the plant and in homes.

Intimates were people who Dalton selected over a period of several years on the basis of mutual trust and the freedom with which they were prepared to speak about their problems and be unlikely to jeopardize his research; they showed acceptance of what Dalton could reveal to them and did not pry into data he was obtaining from others; they also gave him guidance and hints which 'if known would have endangered their careers' (Dalton, 1964, p. 65).

Dalton found female secretaries and clerks particularly helpful in this respect, as acute observers of differences in status and influence as well as having access to records and important events. As he remarks, where 'female secretaries are treated as intellectual menials they are disposed to be communicative with those who show awareness of their insights and knowledge of affairs' (Dalton, 1964, p. 275). In one notable case Dalton tacitly exchanged some counselling help with a female secretary's interest in dating an employee in return for the supply of confidential data on managerial salaries to which she had access. There was clearly danger to the secretary in supplying this information but the bargain was struck and the data flowed while the dating continued. Dalton notes with satisfaction that, despite his crude attempts at counselling the secretary married the employee within a year!

Of the specific techniques used by Dalton to collect data the least significant was formal interviewing, as it was considered inadequate in providing information about unofficial activities. Where formal interviews were used, for example in gathering data on managers' careers from senior officers, questions were prepared but quietly dropped to pursue interesting leads as these emerged. Notes were not taken except at the request of the interviewee, as Dalton considered them to inhibit subjects and to divert him from close observation. Interviews, including notes of non-verbal expressions, were reconstructed as soon after the event as possible.

Dalton used loose-leaf notebooks to record events, gossip, initial hunches and leads which might be followed. His work diaries were increasingly of use as a guide to the research and a source of insight to him through reflection on the data.

The most used method was participant observation. This has its disadvantages; its closeness to unique events, for example, limits attempts to classify and generalize from the data; 'intimates' may be an unrepresentative sample; and the presence of the researcher may distort the data. Friendliness with respondents may provoke leading questions, and unusual events may be mistaken for the typical, particularly if the researcher is new to the situation. In other words, personal observation can have low validity, but Dalton believed that, especially when combined with other methods, these defects are outweighed by its flexibility, particularly in exploratory research. Its advantages are that the researcher is not bound by rigid research plans and interviewing can also be conducted more flexibly and pointless questions avoided. There is time to build greater intimacy, allowing access to covert information and to the motives of informants; and uniquely equipped informants can be treated differently and access to confidential data enabled by a selective and informal process.

Golding's study takes a similar approach to Dalton (Golding, 1979). His data was taken primarily from three industrial organizations in which he had worked as a manager in the previous five years and six additional organizations which he entered primarily as a researcher undertaking a project funded by the Chemical and Allied Products Industry Training Board into managerial approaches to industrial relations. The companies were all given fictitious names to protect the identities of those involved.

Golding, an electrical engineer, had read a master's programme in organization development and had become employed in the personnel department of a medium sized engineering concern, with a brief to take an action research role. He envisaged this post enabling him to complete his master's course by submitting a dissertation on his practice as an internal consultant.

In the event he was blocked from taking such a role, and the aim of his dissertation was consequently changed in order to shed light as to why this was so. This led him to investigate some aspects of power in the organization – an experience that caused him to reflect on similar occurrences in organizations in which he had worked. He thus began to focus on the part played by myth, ritual and ideology in the generation and reinforcement of managers' assumptions about the right to manage. In this way he became interested in the submerged aspects of organizational life using work, for example by Turner, (1971, 1988), as a guide.

He completed his dissertation (Golding, 1977) and when an opportunity occurred to take a full-time (then) Social Science Research Council (SSRC) research studentship leading to work for a Ph.D. he welcomed it even though this entailed a considerable loss of income.

Apart from the data from the six organizations in the chemical industry he had already gathered most of his information in a large number of files over a period of years. The materials were collected in note form written from field notes obtained during a period of observation as a participant living among the managers. He was therefore in a good position, particularly in his last organization by nature of his personnel management role, to have access to most parts of the plant and to most levels of management. He was much helped at this stage by Dan Gowler, one of his supervisors, who advised him to regard the managers under study as a strange tribe about which nothing should be taken for granted.

Observation was the central means of obtaining data and was supplemented with further examples (from memory) of less recent experience; notes were written up as soon as possible after the occurrence. Procedurally an attempt was made to bridge the gap between the phenomenological accounts of organization members and a possible structural significance attached to it by the researcher (Golding, 1986). In order to explore the submerged aspects of power it was clearly necessary to approach methodology as reflexive with content, for to take any other approach to, for example, a ritual by using some research instrument to measure it at a point in time would have simply collapsed the ritual. Observations were supplemented by company documents in the writing of persuasive accounts; the persuasiveness being revealed by the extent to which the reader is prepared to identify with the account of the writer.

Some other studies, which take an ethnographic approach to management research, have explored the role of the marketing and personnel manager (e.g. Watson, 1977; Grafton-Small, 1985); others have been concerned with sectors other than the industrial (e.g. Johnson, 1975; Frame, 1987).

While there is regrettably no full description of method in Watson's (1977) study of personnel managers, made as part of a doctoral programme, it is clear that the methods guiding it are based on participant observation in a personnel department; from documents and the literature; from informal discussions with people working in personnel departments; and from a large number of structured interviews with personnel specialists. Watson worked from an academic base and presented himself as a sociologist who had previously worked in industry and who wished to write not about the nature of the personnel manager's job but about the people doing the job. Throughout the research Watson reports the tensions felt between surrendering to informant experience and returning to reflect on that experience to communicate it to others.

Grafton-Small's (1985) research into the behaviour of marketing managers arose from a specialist academic interest in marketing during study for an MBA. It appeared to him that managing marketing functions bore little relationship to what was taught in the standard texts. As a consequence he undertook to explore their professional behaviour and in doing so was at first attracted to the methodology used in Watson's (1977) study of personnel managers and, like Watson, worked from an academic base but as a (then) SSRC-funded doctoral research student. The first part of his study is thus based upon opportunistic, semi-structured interviewing of marketing managers from forty organizations. Many of the sample were interviewed in off-site locations such as bars, and the background basis of the interviews relied upon academic texts and participant observation as a student when working on placement and in vacation jobs. It emerged from this initial work that an investigation of marketing managers as practising professionals based on oral data alone would be inadequate and the work was expanded to include a methodology which attempted to explicate the complexities of consumption and the everyday importance of industrial artifacts.

There are a number of ethnographic studies in organizations other than the industrial. Johnson's readable account of his field research as an academic into the management of social work activities took place in five offices of two large metropolitan public welfare departments in the USA (Johnson, 1975). His work is particularly helpful on entry issues in bureaucracies and the development of trust in participant observation research, the main method used in the study.

More recently, Frame (1987), a social anthropologist as an undergraduate who had later been equipped at master's level in organizational consultancy, undertook doctoral work sponsored by the (then) SSRC into managerial issues in the social work department of an English metropolitan local authority.

His orientation was to work as an anthropologist but also to do some work of value to the host organization, thus combining both an action research role with that of ethnographer in the way Schein, (1987) discusses in his exploration of the clinical perspective (see Chapter 5). However, in Frame's case the ethnographer role was primary since the maim aim was to carry out doctoral research into the management of financial stringency.

Nevertheless, in his initial approach to the department, although interaction between different organizational subcultures was identified by the researcher as an area of doctoral research interest, he was willing to examine a mutually agreed topic identified by the organization's members – mainly as an inducement to affording access. It transpired that the department was in the throes of externally imposed expenditure reductions and the twin aims were readily combined, as a subcultural analysis was crucial to an understanding of the fundamental organizational dynamics which affected and were affected by cutbacks.

These effects were particularly apparent as cuts began to bite, and so the focus of the research changed to become increasingly concerned with the management of expenditure reductions. Some researchers, including Johnson, (1975), advocate mild deception, such as inventing cover stories to gain access, but Frame found he could be open and indeed was concerned, given his naïvety about the nature of communications in the department, that dissimulation might be detected and his project opportunity lost.

Frame was in the organization on a daily basis for a number of months and was able to observe and participate in its social life; he also found himself assisting in occasional menial tasks which provided some insights into financial stringency. In meetings he acted as an observer in formal events but took part in informal activities as an ordinary member, for example during pre- and post-meeting discussions.

Three methods of data collection were used; semi-structured interviewing, observation and documentary analysis. A rough interview schedule was prepared but this was used flexibly, in the manner described by Dalton (1964), and most managers were interviewed several times, frequently to follow up matters arising from meetings.

Observation took place from an office provided in the central site, where the day-to-day life of the site could be observed and that gave him a base from which he could walk around and where individuals could drop in for a chat. More important, meetings of the organization's three management teams were observed, providing data not only on substantive matters but also material of help in diagnosing team cultures. Further such observation enabled the researcher to compare public contributions with those made to him privately, as a check on the reliability of the former. By observing a large number of meetings the possibility of generalizing from an unrepresentative event was reduced and since meetings generally took place at two hierarchical levels, and sometimes jointly, cultural data could be expanded and strengthened. Further, the criticism that observation without participation can lead to the worst kind of subjectivism, where the observer's surmises are substituted for those of the actor's, is to some degree removed by subsequent informal access to individuals (Schutz, 1967; Blumer, 1971). The degree of observer influence on the group may also be exaggerated, for putting on a show becomes difficult to sustain and members 'enmeshed in social relationships which are important to them' (Becker, 1970, p. 46) are probably a more potent force than researcher influence.

Documents provided the least useful source of data but such records as minutes of meetings were not without significance, even though retrospective, as they could be checked for meaning with their producers and with recipients as to interpretation.

It was therefore in such ways that access was gained to the culture of a small part of an organization in order to understand the management of expenditure reductions. Other methods would probably have been inappropriate in gaining access to subcultures, in the sense of culture as a system of shared meanings or the commonly held fabric of meanings (Smircich, 1983). These could be derived only by gaining access, in the ways described, to the knowledge individuals possessed about their situations, their understanding of others in the organization and their approach to expenditure reductions.

Studies of managerial work

A number of studies have used ethnographic methods to explore various specific aspects of managerial work, in particular the activities of very senior managers or élites. Spencer (1980, 1983) studied the role relationships of non-executive directors as part of her (then) SSRC-sponsored doctoral training, using mainly semi-structured interviewing to understand the non-executive directors' own theories regarding the activity of being a non-executive director. The method used, as we noted in Chapter 3, is termed *verstehen*, or understanding, and is a specialist approach within the broad field of ethnography (Giddens, 1976, pp. 52–3). The work originated from a discussion with her father, himself a non-executive director, who was puzzled by the ambiguities in his role, which although involving him in decision making at the highest organizational levels, at the same time confined him to being an outsider to the organization.

The first issue was the problem of access. Ideally, in order to understand fully the role of the non-executive director as a 'situated activity system' (Goffman, 1971 pp. 84–5) it would have been desirable to observe role performance in the boardroom. Boardrooms are notoriously difficult to access, however, and direct contact was regarded as impractical.

Non-executive directors willing to be interviewed were located with difficulty and even those interviewed, including the researcher's father, were unwilling to introduce her to colleagues. This was probably because they feared accusations of being indiscreet by agreeing to be interviewed or that their competence as a member of an élitist group was being assessed; or, most probably, they did not wish to trouble colleagues on whom they might depend for businesss. Accordingly, all possible contacts available to the researcher were used, the sample eventually comprising a variety of non-executive directors, including a number of academics who sat part time as non-executive directors on company boards as well as those whose entire income was derived from the occupation.

Semi-structured interviewing was conducted in much the same way as has been discussed in other projects save that in these cases tape recorders were effectively used and seemingly caused little concern, in contrast to note taking, presumably because after a few minutes of taping respondents became unaware of the recorder. Finally, it is interesting to note that a young female researcher in a predominantly male preserve had the advantage of being regarded as a naïve student doing a project, in that it enabled her to probe and elicit information which might in a male have been regarded as impertinent or have met with a contemptuous respose.

However, some researchers taking an ethnographic approach have found it possible to enter boardrooms if, unlike Spencer's work, the research has company sponsorship (e.g. Brannen *et. al.*, 1976; Brannen, 1987; Winkler, 1987). Winkler's study was commissioned by the British Institute of Directors, as part of a larger study of the physical and psychological health of members, to find out what directors did. Brannen's work was also part of a larger project to study worker–director participation in the running of the British steel industry and was also sponsored by the main board of the (then) nationalized industry.

Both projects were therefore helped by their client sponsorship in being invited to undertake the work but despite this both researchers, even in these favourable circumstances, speculate on the problematic nature of entering the élitist sanctum of the company boardroom. A variety of techniques was used in both projects: in Winkler's study informal interviews, diary methods and discussion groups were employed but the chief technique used was observation; in Brannen's case the wider project employed a variety of methods including large scale surveys, in-depth interviewing and documentary analysis.

Observation of boardrooms in Brannen's case had not been included in the original design and had to be separately negotiated; first with the corporation chairman, who agreed in principle but left details of access to be negotiated between research workers and managing directors. This became a time-consuming process entailing a variety of elaborate influencing strategies as some divisional boards were reluctant to grant access on the grounds that observation was not 'scientific' and would disrupt normal boardroom behaviour. In a similar fashion Winkler (1987) bemoans the fact that he spent about a third of a three year project negotiating access and experiencing a refusal rate, on the most generous intepretation, of more than 85 per cent. As he mentions, the real issue in observational research, particularly of the powerful, is not the sampling problem but the refusal rate; however, the process was of itself diagnostic – for access to an organization was never negotiated other than through the chairman or managing director, an early indication of the power hierarchy.

Issues that arose in both projects in observing company boards in operation and which both authors significantly describe as 'learning a game', were the defensiveness of directors to strangers observing their work and the projection of anxieties, for example about competencies, on to the researcher as a spy on behalf of the boss.

Brannen particularly explores some of the difficulties of the observer role in determining how far in the context of the boardroom the observer was to be 'one of the lads' or 'a fly on the wall' (Brannen, 1987, p. 171), especially when the focus of the work was on one particular board member, the worker–director. He also felt, in retrospect, that more attention might well have been paid to the informal events which surrounded board meetings, whereas observers regarded their roles rather narrowly to gather data on a simple group process pro forma which nevertheless required a considerable amount of analysis.

He also reflects on stresses on the observer which, in this context, involved 'learning to live with gin and tonic and the problems of eating grouse' (Brannen, 1987, p. 173) as well as acquiring a new language and new patterns of thought. These pressures were not systematically recorded by researchers, an omission regretted with hindsight as providing some insight into the pressures also felt by worker–directors entering the strange world of the company boardroom. Brannen concludes that watching work is a stressful operation: never being able to relax even when others are relaxing; striking a balance between maintaining sufficient distance to be reasonably objective and yet empathizing with the actors; and being self-aware and recording one's self awareness.

Finally, one of the most influential projects designed to discover what senior managers actually do was undertaken by Mintzberg, originally as doctoral work following a master of science programme in management. In common with most training programmes in management nothing had been said about the job of the manager but this strange omission had not occurred to Mintzberg at the time. Later, when he was searching for a thesis topic, the possibility of studying a senior manager's job presented itself but Mintzberg 'hesitated as this seemed to be a risky project in a science based business school' (Mintzberg, 1973, p. ix). His book (Mintzberg, 1973) published five years after his Ph.D. thesis was completed, was an edited version of his doctoral work, based on a study of five anonymous senior managers and additional empirical work. Significantly in the context of this book, and less common in British ethnographic studies, it also contains particularly readable appendices on his research methods, including a comprehensive justification of his choice of structured observation. We consider this in more detail in Chapter 10 (see Table 10.1) as an excellent example of the justification of methodology.

Mintzberg decided that a combination of the advantages of unstructured observation, with its reliance on living in the system and working inductively,

would be an appropriate method if combined with the development of categories to make some sense of complex, voluminous data. Categories would,
however, be developed only during and after observation, that is to say, they
would be 'grounded' in the data (Glaser and Strauss, 1967). He was thus
especially influenced by Dalton's (1959) and Sayles's (1964) ethnographic
studies of managerial work together with the systematic diary methods of, for
example, Carlson (1951) and Stewart, (1967).

Little is mentioned on the difficulties or otherwise of access to the five chief
executives studied, but the sample size was necessarily limited by the time-
consuming nature of the method and the restrictions placed on the study by the
resources available to one research student, which included confining observation to spending one week with each manager. The field study proceeded
through three stages: preliminary data collection, recording of observations
and coding of observations. In preparation for each week's observation preliminary information was collected by interview and from documents about
the manager and the context in which he worked. Two types of data were
collected by observation: 'anecdotal' data on interesting and critical incidents
and 'structured' data gathered on the pattern of activity throughout every
minute of the day. Raw field data was thus gathered with no special concern
for consistency at that stage and was tidied up through an inductive process of
recording, tabulating, coding, recoding and analysing until meaningful ideas
emerged. This clearly demanded patience, hard work and above all a suspen-
sion of anxiety about progress and an ability to cope with ambiguity.

In discussing the results of using his method Mintzberg (1973) reflects on the
validity of such a small sample, and more generally on issues arising from the use
of structured observation as a means of discovering what managers do. Evidence
from other work suggested that the one week observation periods were for the
most part representative and that the work of the five men was typical of chief
executives in large organizations. Some support for the choice of only five chief
executives was provided in the surprisingly high consistency of the data from all
five cases. Other empirical data, including data from diary studies, suggested that
basically the work of these men was similar to those in similar jobs.

Five matters are mentioned on the use of structured observation: the difficulties of collecting data on the rare occasions of missed meetings when, for
example, the researcher was excluded; the problems of access to evening work
and telephone calls; difficulties due to the pace of work and the wear and tear
on the researcher who is also trying to record it; problems of coding and,
finally, the effects of the presence of the researcher on the data. The first three
matters were fairly readily overcome. In Mintzberg's view his presence had
very little effect on the data, primarily as work activity rather than style (potentially more sensitive) was under investigation. During meetings questions generally reflected an interest in the research rather than concerns about it and the
presence of the researcher seemed to be quickly forgotten.

Others, such as Kotter (1982), have built on this work which will be considered later in Chapter 10 on choosing and justifying methods. We now turn
to ethnographic studies of industrial relations and the shop floor.

Studies of shop-floor relations

Ethnographic studies of shop-floor relations have become more common since the pioneering work of, for example, Gouldner, (1954a), Walker and Guest (1957), Sayles (1958), Roy (1960), Lupton (1963) and Cunnison (1966).

More recently, shop-floor research, primarily using participant observation methods, has been conducted, for example, into a strike at Pilkington (Lane and Roberts, 1971), into shop-floor politics in a large chemical plant (Nichols and Armstrong, 1976) and into management and shop-floor notions of legitimacy in workplace rule-making in manufacturing plants (Armstrong, Goodman and Hyman, 1981). The importance of humour in the maintenance of culture and the incidence and role of sabotage in a very large confectionery-making plant were investigated by Linstead, (1984); women's work in factories by Westwood, (1985); what it feels like to work at Ford by Beynon (1973, 1988); and an exploration of two shop steward organizations in the same motor car assembly plant, by Batstone, Boraston and Frenkel (1977). Since the methods used in the study of Pilkington and the chemical plant are unfortunately not discussed except inferentially, the research by Armstrong, Goodman and Hyman (1981), Beynon (1973), and Batstone, Boraston and Frenkel (1977) are chosen for consideration in more detail below.

Armstrong, Goodman and Hyman (1981) explored the day-to-day conflicts and compromises that occur on the shop floor in the process of rule generation and change. They were supported by a grant from the (then) SSRC and the research took place in three anonymous manufacturing plants on the periphery of the Manchester conurbation.

The principal method used in the research was participant observation supplemented by access to documents and some semi-structured interviewing, particularly with managers, in the early stages of the work. Observation was conducted continuously for four months in each factory, with investigators working the same hours as the workforce, partly to achieve close identification with it and more accurately to absorb the context in which the data was gathered. The researchers were aware of the limitations of generalizing from a few cases and the potential methodological deficiencies of observation in being 'impressionistic', though in most cases they sought to validate accounts by discussing the same material with others. They were open about their purposes and made no secret of their intention to write a book on industrial relations. They discovered that, as a consequence, they were often spontaneously helped with information for the book; on the other hand, they found themselves fending off those eager to pick up information about others in the organization and occasionally those seeking advice on problems. They believed this reticence heightened trust and enabled informants to take greater risks with the researchers.

Working for Ford is Beynon's (1973) very readable analysis of events and problems at the Ford Halewood plant in a five-year period from 1967 to 1972. Beynon uses a combination of survey techniques, participant observation,

observation, informal interviews and documentary sources in endeavouring to interpret the behaviour of Ford workers in terms of their own culture.

In reviewing his research Beynon (1988, p. 26) mentions the difficulty of gaining access to 'tell it like it is'. In the case of the Halewood plant he was invited in by the personnel manager following a talk the latter had given on the subject of local industry. At the talk Beynon's supervisor had asked some questions about the high rate of labour turnover on Merseyside, suggesting that the type of work might be a factor. An invitation followed from the company to see for themselves.

Nevertheless, despite this favourable start towards mutual understanding between researcher and company a number of factors worked against it. Agreement had of course also been reached with both lay and full-time officials of the Transport and General Workers' Union, but the work was done at a time of great industrial relations change resulting in a period of severe conflict and strikes. This occasionally left Beynon under pressure from both management and union to reveal information given in confidence by the other party. Beynon coped with these difficulties by leaving the plant until the crisis blew over but at the risk of jeopardizing his project. However, much the fullest report of the methodological issues entailed in undertaking industrial relations fieldwork using an ethnographic approach is reported by Batstone, Boraston and Frenkel (1977), to which we now turn.

The aim of Batstone's project was to describe and analyse how shop stewards and their members act within the workplace as trade unionists, the project being supported by the SSRC. The study focused on what the researchers term 'domestic organization', that is to say, not only the shop stewards but the members they represent; emphasis being on the organizational aspects of their behaviour.

It was expected that such objectives would be most readily achieved by using observation as the primary research method as the research team were not trying to test specific hypotheses. Rather, they were focusing on particular areas of interest which required a high degree of flexibility and the maximum collection of data of the social life of the plants. It was appreciated that observation would be very time consuming, which limited the situations that might be economically covered to two shop steward organizations in the same large multinational company engaged in vehicle manufacture. Access was gained by agreement with full-time union officials, conveners and management. Access was, however, conditional on the preservation of anonymity and confidentiality.

Batstone had previously been engaged in the study of worker–directors discussed above, and had been convinced that observation was a reliable method provided that data was recorded as widely as possible in all situations, formal and informal. It was also felt possible to record contacts and statements fully through observation even in complex, confusing situations. Data was recorded by note-taking at the time events occurred; tape recorders being found to be unserviceable given the noise of factory work. Rules for note-taking were synchronized between researchers and, in addition, two or more of the researchers would occasionally be involved in the same event comparison of which suggested 80 to 90 per cent agreement between observers. The period of observation spanned four months and the three researchers were in the plant for the whole of each working day apart from night shifts. However, in view of the difficulty of covering over 5,000 people spread over a site of many acres, and following a principle of choosing intensity of investigation rather than broad coverage, it was decided to concentrate on particular stewards; using these as focal points to develop networks of stewards and managers. In these exchanges there was an avoidance of active participation with either managers or stewards in their activities.

Throughout the research team met at least weekly to discuss research strategy and to exchange summaries of field notes, facilitating comparability and insight. The result of this activity ran into many thousands of words of field notes, which were indexed to outline who was observed, their contacts and the issues concerned. In addition, informal interviews were similarly analysed as were steward and mass meetings. Finally, one of the research team did the bulk of the analysis, which took many months. A high level of agreement was found between each researcher, and in cases of disagreement the matter was discussed until resolved.

Other sources of data were structured interviews, self-administered questionnaires and documentary sources, all of which were administered after observation was completed. Documents were obtained from both trade union sources and, particularly, management which, for example, was the only source of information on stewards over a period of time. Wherever possible data from different sources was compared.

In the following chapter we turn to some issues in undertaking ethnographic research raised by the cases outlined above: the variety of roles in ethnography and their implications for fieldwork, the development of theory from case material and the issues raised by problems of access and ethical matters.

Suggested further reading

The history and early development of ethnography are comprehensively covered in R. H. Wax's *Doing Fieldwork: Warnings and Advice*. A useful collection of readings largely concerned with the practice of ethnographic fieldwork in work organizations such as car assembly plants, banks, local authorities and insurance companies is contained in A. Bryman's *Doing Research in Organizations*.

Reportage of some ethnographic research in business and management has also been outlined above; as we have noted, among the most useful – providing descriptions of the methods employed – are M. Dalton's, 'Preconceptions and methods in *Men who Manage*'; E. Batstone, I. Boraston, and S. Frenkel's *Shop Stewards in Action: The Organization of Workplace Conflict and Accommodation* see especially 'Research strategy', pp. 13–17, and Appendix A, 'Research methods'; H. Mintzberg's, *The Nature of Managerial Work* see especially Appendices B and C on methodology); and T. Lupton's, *On the Shop Floor*, for an account of research conducted as an overt participant-as-observer.

(Full bibliographical details of these works appear in the References, at the end of this book.)

8
Issues in Ethnographic Research

We now turn our attention to some recurring themes in ethnography which seem to emerge from an examination of the cases, discussed in the previous chapter, of ethnography in practice.

It is not possible to define ethnography as a single mode of collecting information since it usually entails the varying application of a battery of techniques so as to elucidate the subjective basis of the behaviour of people. Nevertheless, it is still possible to review the practice and design of ethnographic research in terms of the various choices available to an ethnographer in undertaking a piece of research. Many of these decisions appertain to the way the ethnographer is to observe the phenomena of interest in a systematic fashion and are contingent upon various factors, including the purposes of the research, the setting in which the research will take place, the resources available to the researcher and the nature of the study. As we have indicated, these various choices are usually taken in the context of an ethnographer's philosophical commitment to comprehending the behaviour of subjects in their natural and everyday settings through an inductive development of an empathetic understanding of those actors' rationality.

Smircich (1983) considers there to be three main available approaches: observation, participation in the setting and gathering reports from informants that use

> the capacity that any social actor possesses for learning new cultures and the objectivity to which this process gives rise. Even where he or she is researching a familiar group or setting, the participant observer is required to treat it as anthropologically 'strange' in an effort to make explicit the assumptions he or she takes for granted as a culture member. In this way the culture is turned into an object for study.
>
> (Hammersley and Atkinson, 1983, p. 8)

However, which of these techniques are available to the researcher, and how they are to be used to collect information, are largely governed by decisions about the type of 'field' or 'social' role to be adopted (Junker 1960; Adler and Adler, 1987). It is to these issues that we now turn.

Field roles in ethnography

As we have seen, there are numerous aspects to the field role which an ethnographer may adopt, and perhaps the most important relate to the extent to which the researcher decides to 'participate' in the natural setting of subjects' behaviour, and the extent to which the identity and purposes of the ethnographer are revealed to those subjects.

Participant and non-participant observation

In essence these choices may be conceptualized as varying from the observer's complete immersion in a social setting, by adopting a role of full participant in the everyday lives of subjects, to that of spectator in which the ethnographer only observes events and processes and thereby avoids becoming involved in interactions with subjects.

In the former the researcher attempts to participate fully in the lives and activities of subjects and thus becomes a member of their group, organization or community. This enables the researcher to share their experiences by not merely observing what is happening but also feeling it. Although this form of observation was first developed by anthropologists investigating 'exotic' tribal cultures, as we have previously shown it has been successfully applied to the study of people in organizations, including managers. This field role usually enables a great deal of depth in research since it allows the researcher to get very close to the phenomena of interest 'catching reality in flight' by experiencing the often hidden experience (Madge, 1953) of members. For Douglas (1976), participant observation can enable the researcher to penetrate the various complex forms of 'misinformation, fronts, evasions and lies' that are considered endemic in most social settings, including business. So in management research, as in our example in Chapter 7, Mintzberg (1973) discovered it can enable access to what people actually do (the informal organization), as opposed to what they might claim they do and which official sanctions impel them to do (the formal organization). Particularly where the phenomenon of interest is rather controversial or surrounded in secrecy (e.g. Roy, 1960; Lupton, 1963; Golding, 1979), participant observation may be the only viable means of discovering what is actually happening. This dual purpose of empathetically experiencing hidden data and thereby penetrating secrecy is illustrated in Douglas's articulation of 'depth-probe' research. In this

> the researcher surrenders to the everyday experience while in the natural setting but, instead of going native, remains latently committed to being a researcher, and comes back to reflect and report upon the experience as a

member. Depth-probes are vital in getting at deeper, more secret aspects of social life, those about which members would not talk or possibly even think. In these forms the researcher's knowledge of his own feelings becomes a vital source of data.

(Douglas, 1976 p.16)

Thus, for Douglas, depth-probes involve 'de-focusing', that is, immersion in and saturation by the setting through allowing oneself to experience that setting as much as is possible, in the same way as any other organizational member. At the same time the researcher retains a commitment to being a researcher and later moving to more systematic observations and analyses of that setting. However, without such direct or 'lived' experience of the setting the researcher might be forced to 'rely upon the members to communicate it to him, which makes him dependent upon their honesty and their abilities to symbolise their experience' (Douglas, 1976, p. 111). Douglas would find the truthfulness of such accounts exceedingly problematic for they would remain uncheckable, and as such the researcher might be unable to avoid 'being taken in, duped, deceived, used, put on, fooled, suckered, made the patsy, left holding the bag, fronted out and so on' (Douglas, 1976, p. 57).

While participant observation does allow for these significant strengths in research, however, there is also the imminent danger that, by becoming embroiled in the everyday lives of subjects, the researcher internalizes subjects' culture and becomes unable to take a dispassionate view of events and unintentionally discards the researcher elements of the field role. That is, they actually become a member of the organization, or 'go native'.

Where the field role is limited to that of a spectator the consequent lack of interaction with subjects can raise the opposite problem of ethnocentricity: that is, the observer fails to gain access to and to understand the cultural underpinnings of subjects' overt behaviours and actions. Indeed, the observer may inadvertently analyse and evaluate those events and processes from the perspectives and rationality of his or her own culture. Such distortions may be compounded by an inability to penetrate the 'fronts and evasions' alluded to by Douglas (1976). It might, however, be claimed that since the role of the spectator entails no interaction with subjects it is less likely that the observer's presence will affect the situation and cause some change in their usual behaviour; particularly where such observation is being undertaken secretly, for example by means of a two-way mirror. This last point involves consideration of the next important aspect of field role choices, namely, overt or covert observation.

Overt and covert observation

This refers to whether the subject(s) know about, or are aware of, the presence of a researcher, or where the actual purpose of the observer is hidden. There are usually two main rationales behind the use of covert observation.

First, it is often argued that people may behave quite differently when aware that they are under observation. Indeed, this is frequently a managerial view – exemplified by Batstone, Boraston and Frenkel's (1977) research considered in Chapter 7, when access was at first refused on the grounds that participative methods were 'unscientific'. Thus the degree of naturalism or ecological validity is reduced if observation is not employed covertly. So in many versions of ethnography there is an obsession, similar to that in nomothetic methodologies, to eliminate the effects of the researcher upon the data (although a very different set of strategies is adopted in attempting to achieve this goal). This objective has two important dimensions: first to eliminate reactivity by subjects to the researcher's personal qualities and research techniques; and, second to eschew the idiosyncratic imposition of the researcher's own frame of reference upon the data. Here we shall concern ourselves only with the former since the latter is reviewed in Chapter 9 when we consider the issues surrounding the contentious possibility of a theory-neutral observation language for social science in general.

Often the most vaunted advantage claimed for ethnography over other research procedures is its greater ecological validity because it entails studying social phenomena in their natural contexts. This, it is argued, reduces subjects' reactivity to the researcher and his or her data collection procedures. However, where participant observation is being used, even where the ethnographer's presence is covert, he or she is present and involved as a member and inevitably must affect the phenomena under investigation in some way. It seems certain that members must react to the various qualities and attributes 'given off' by the covert researcher and, as such, their everyday lives are being disturbed to some degree. This problem has important implications for the practice of ethnography, in that 'instead of treating reactivity merely as a source of bias, we can exploit it. How people react to the presence of the researcher may be as informative as how they react to other situations' (Hammersley and Atkinson, 1983, p. 15). As we saw in Chapter 7, with hindsight Brannen (1987) realized this possibility of considerably enhancing his study of worker directors.

Hence there is a need for the researcher to be 'reflexive'. Rather than to attempt to eliminate the effects of the researcher on the phenomenon under investigation, the researcher should attempt to understand his or her effect upon, and role in, the research setting and utilize this knowledge to elicit data. Therefore the social and interactive nature of ethnographic research becomes clear:

Once we abandon the idea that the social character of research can be standardised out, or avoided by becoming a 'fly on the wall' or a 'full participant', the role of the researcher as an active participant in the research process becomes clear. He or she is the research instrument *par excellence*. The fact that behaviour and attitudes are often not stable across contexts, and that the researcher may play an important part in shaping the context becomes central to the analysis. Indeed it is exploited for all it is worth.'

(Hammersley and Atkinson, 1983, p. 18)

Thus, 'rather than seeking by one means or another to eliminate reactivity, its effects should be monitored, and as far as possible brought under control. By systematically modifying one's role in the field, different kinds of data may be collected whose comparisons may greatly enhance interpretations of the social processes under study' (Hammersley and Atkinson, 1983, p. 104). It follows that these prescriptions revolve around the need for the ethnographer to be 'reflexive'; that is, the researcher should attempt to understand the effects of the field role upon subjects in the research setting. The 'problem' of reactivity is thus converted into a research tool: the researcher attempts to shape aspects of the social context in which interaction takes place by manipulating dimensions of the role to promote controlled types of reactivity.

It would appear then that one of the notional advantages of covert over overt participation might be chimerical in many circumstances. Indeed, the latter may enable the researcher to manipulate dimensions of the field role more effectively since the overt researcher may be allowed by members to behave strangely or variably; behaviours which if entered into by a presumed member would result in sanctions being applied if group norms were broken.

A second reason for using covert research is often because it would be impossible to obtain access to do the research if the subjects knew one was a researcher , or knew the true nature of the research. Certainly in such circumstances some degree of deception may be ethically defensible. In covert participant observation, however, since the researcher is publicly perceived as an 'ordinary' member, inevitably his or her freedom of action may be curtailed.

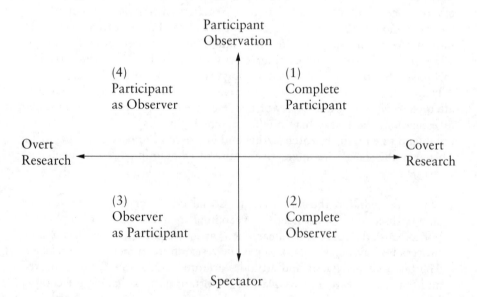

Figure 8.1   A taxonomy of field roles

Such limitations may not only restrict the ability to shape aspects of the social context reflexively but also affect the freedom to sample different social settings by moving around the organization unhindered. Hence covert research might allow some access to the phenomena of interest but it might be severely limited, particularly by the norms that govern members' interactions and freedom of movement. Clearly, many of these advantages and limitations of covert and overt participant observation apply equally to circumstances in which the field role is limited to that of spectator.

Two of the most significant choices the researcher must make on starting fieldwork are the extent to which the work is covert and the extent to which the researcher interacts with members by performing an existing role within the organization. A useful conceptualization of these choices is provided by Gold (1958), later modified by Junker (1960), whose taxonomy of four field roles might be represented by Figure 8.1.

While Gold usefully summarizes the various advantages and disadvantages attached to each role, we wish to emphasize that these choices are largely contingent upon the aims of the research, the skills and experience of the researcher and the nature of the social setting to be investigated. In many respects the difficulties surrounding access are highly influenced by the researcher's choice of role, which we next consider.

Access

The problem of access, frequently addressed in our earlier examples, stems from the very nature of ethnography, for in most cases the researcher initiates a process of inquiry which at the outset is necessarily vague in its aims. Its methods too are difficult to describe, particularly to gatekeepers brought up in a different research tradition.

Access is also affected by the approach to the study. The typology in Figure 8.1 of four possible modes of observational research is useful in clarifying some aspects of the access issue.

In the complete participant role the researcher's activities are concealed and the investigator joins the organization as a normal member but to carry out research covertly. There are a number of examples of ethnographers undertaking covert work of this nature in the wider literature but few in business and management; by definition, in this role access clearly presents little problem for a researcher. Alternatively, as in the cases of Dalton (1959) and Golding (1979) referred to in Chapter 7, both were already members of the organization when they decided to study it. At the other extreme is the complete observer, who has no contact at all with those being observed and is also in a relatively unusual role in ethnographic studies in business, but access again of course presents little problem.

Mostly the researcher roles described earlier fall into the categories of participant-as-observer and observer-as-participant. In the former the primary role is that of participant but both fieldworker and informant are aware that theirs is a field relationship. This again is not a common role in the cases previously mentioned but is probably best exemplified by Lupton (1963) who overtly played the part of industrial worker for several months in two shop floor pieceworking groups, which he termed 'open participant observation'. It is, however, likely to be the role played by part-time management students engaged in dissertations and project work who, if working in their own organizations, will take various positions within the broad participant-as-observer role. In most of the studies previously discussed researchers have primarily been observers who have not been members of the organization although some have at times taken part in its activities as a member (e.g. see Frame, 1987 in Chapter 7). On the other hand, others have carefully avoided involvement with organizational issues (e.g. Batstone, Boraston and Frenkel, 1977). For this group access has generally been difficult and since the activity has been completely open has had to be negotiated with the organization.

Issues that generally arise when access is negotiated include the benefit which might be afforded to the organization such as feedback on some aspects of the study; the amount of organizational time likely to be taken up; and particularly the extent the work is to become public through publication. In most of the cases we have instanced eventual publications have been agreed provided the identity of the organization was disguised and the anonymity of individuals preserved. Some form of feedback has generally been negotiated and in some cases specific organizational help offered.

While negotiations may be protracted, initial reactions at this stage generally provide crucially important insights into the organization's culture (Alderfer, 1968). Clearly, particular care needs to be taken if, as in a number of our examples, the issues to be investigated are matters of conflict and involve more than one party, such as trade unions and middle or senior managements, otherwise, at the very least problems may emerge later.

Access, then, is time consuming and often difficult, especially when the researcher lacks powerful support or a prestigious academic base. The use of all possible sources of help, such as friends and business contacts, has frequently been found to be useful in successful entry strategies (Glidewell, 1959).

Direct and indirect observation

So far we have focused upon the use of direct observation in ethnography, where the researcher observes by directly watching and listening to the behaviour of subjects. The ethnographer may, however, choose to gain access to data through indirect observation of an event not personally witnessed but which may be reported by an informant either orally or in writing. Other ingenious way of gaining access to such data are covered by Webb *et al.* (1969).

Although all four of the field roles shown in Figure 8.1 involve some degree of indirect observation, the observer-as-participant role may rely particularly upon interviewing informants about events the researcher has been unable to observe. Similarly, the complete observer may rely particularly on the use of various organizational documents, or 'secondary data', to supplement the primary data gathered through observation. In the case of the former, as with any interview, whether it is directive and structured or non-directive and unstructured, there is the problem of interpreting and verifying the informant's statements. Nevertheless, it has the advantage of allowing some access to events to which, for whatever reason, the researcher was unable to gain access. However, it needs to be borne in mind that interviews are an outcome of the social interaction of the participants. Similarly, the secondary data provided by various types of organizational documents such as correspondence, memos and personal files can provide useful insights into organizational events and processes, though of course great care needs to be taken in interpreting their meaning and significance. It is particularly important to avoid taking such documents at face value and to make some allowance for the audience for whom they were originally intended and the possible motives the author(s) might have in saying what they said. Although such data might be gathered in an unobtrusive manner the dangers of misinterpretation and ethnocentricity must be checked out against other ethnographic procedures. Clarification of some of the key issues in ethnographic fieldwork, and particularly those concerned with fieldworker roles, may be assisted by Exercise. 8.1.

Exercise 8.1

Tasks:
1. To observe and describe the social norms that regulate employees' (e.g. cleaners, library staff, secretaries) behaviour during breaks.
2. To observe and describe the social norms that regulate fellow students' behaviour during breaks.

Discussion:
(a) Compare and evaluate the different types of field role and their particular difficulties used for each of the above tasks.
(b) Reflexively consider the different sources of bias that may have influenced what you observed.
(c) From (a) and (b) devise a checklist of the issues ethnographers need to be aware of before, during and after ethnographic fieldwork.

The development of theory: theory building from cases

Much ethnographic work may not be explicitly concerned with the collection of data so as to enable the inductive development of theory. Rather, it may often be concerned primarily with the description of subjects' cultures so as to gain 'access to the conceptual world in which our subjects live so that we can, in some extended sense of the term, converse with them' (Geertz, 1973, p. 24).

Although rigour regarding sampling both within and among settings is evident in much descriptive ethnography, in such research theory largely remains implicit and undeveloped. However, where ethnographers adopt a more 'behaviouristic' ethnography (Sanday, 1979) they are overtly concerned with the development of 'grounded theory' (Glaser and Strauss, 1967) so as to explain variations in phenomena observed in the field. Through induction, theory building and data collection are closely interlinked (Wiseman, 1978). This interplay between data and analysis is to some extent illustrated by a model for induction that tries to enable the development and testing of theory and which is called analytic induction.

Znaniecki (1934) in his original formulation of analytic induction, implies that, if well done, the study of one instance of the phenomenon of interest will suffice and no subsequent investigations are necessary into the same phenomenon. In practice, however, 'any one set of data is likely to manifest *only some* of the elements whose explication would contribute to a cogent theoretical interpretation of the processes involved. An indeterminant number of *strategically selected* sets of events would need to be examined' (Mitchell, 1983, p. 202, our emphases).

In his attempt to make qualitative research more rigorous, Denzin (1970) elaborates upon the approach used by Cressey (1950) in his study of the criminal violation of financial trust. This approach manifests Mitchell's prescription for the 'strategic selection' of cases through the articulation of a 'formal' model for a research strategy that forces the researcher 'to formulate and state his theories in such a way as to indicate crucial tests of the theory and permit the explicit search for negative cases' (Mitchell, 1983, p. 197).

In this version of analytic induction, Denzin (1970) suggests six stages allowing 'fact', observation, concept, preposition and theory to become closely articulated, which enables the researcher to develop theory. Denzin's six stages are as follows:

1. A rough definition of the the phenomenon to be explained is formulated.
2. A hypothetical explanation of the phenomenon is formulated.
3. One case is studied in the light of the hypothesis, with the object of determining whether or not the hypothesis fits the facts in that case.
4. If the hypothesis does not fit the facts, either the hypothesis is reformulated or the phenomenon to be explained is redefined so that the case is excluded.
5. Practical certainty may be obtained after a small number of cases have been examined, but the discovery of negative cases disproves the explanation and requires a reformulation.
6. The procedure of examining cases, redefining the phenomenon and reformulating the hypothesis is continued until a universal relationship is established, each negative case calling for a redefinition or reformulation.

By following this model, theory might be developed and elaborated through an exhaustive examinaton of strategically selected cases to develop grounded theory. Such cases must provide comparative observations that involve the search for a 'decisive negative case' (Lindesmith, 1952, p. 492; Becker, 1966, p. xi) and thereby subject the theory to test (Hammersley and Atkinson, 1983, p. 201–4). This enables modification to occur in two ways. As Robinson (1951) demonstrates, either the hypothesis itself is modified so that new observations may be embraced by it, or the range of application of the hypothesis is limited to exclude observations that defy explanation, thereby 'limiting the universal' (Dubs, 1930). In this fashion a statement is slowly built up which is applicable to a number of cases and which constitutes a generalization. How these cases are chosen is, however, dependent on 'theoretical sampling', which is based upon the relevant theoretical criteria that have evolved out of antecedent analyses. Although discussing a related but somewhat different qualitative methodology, Glaser and Strauss (1967, p. 184) emphasize how, in order to achieve theoretical integration, the researcher must sample theoretically for case histories: 'This means that if he has a case history, and a theory to explain and interpret it, then he can decide on theoretical grounds about other possible case histories: which would provide good contrasts and comparisons.' Thus the basic logic followed in this type of research involves the scrutiny of one case in detail and then the pursuit of further cases that enable modification of the emergent theory. Cases are selected strategically in terms of the theoretical criteria that have been developed out of prior investigation, and thus are selected because they are believed to exhibit some general principle(s), and thereby confront the theory with the patterning of social events under different circumstances. Glaser and Strauss (1967) term such cases 'case studies' as opposed to 'case histories' as the latter's emphasis on description is subordinated to the abstract purpose of theory verification and generation.

The whole scheme has, however, been heavily criticized by Robinson (1951). In his critique of Znaniecki (1934), Cressey (1950) and Lindesmith (1952), and by implication Denzin (1970), Robinson (1951, p. 200) argues that in their version of analytic induction the procedures used remain inadequate because they result in 'only the necessary and not the sufficient conditions for the phenomena to be explained'. This is because it fails to analyse situations in which the phenomena do not occur. Therefore, Robinson argues, if analytic induction is to provide 'adequacy' it must inevitably rely on statistical inference.

However, M. Bloor (1976, 1978) appears effectively to refute Robinson's argument. He develops an analytical framework which demonstrates how sufficient and necessary conditions may be differentiated in analytic induction without resort to enumerative induction. In regard to Lindesmith's and Cressey's work Bloor points out that the 'main difficulty with both studies was that the researchers were unable to distinguish between the necessary and sufficient causes of addiction or embezzlement' (Bloor, 1978, p. 547). This was not because they had not used enumerative induction, but because 'they lacked control groups in which necessary but not sufficient cases could be located. I was free of this difficulty because the cases in other categories could stand as a control group for those cases in the category I was analysing' (ibid.).

Bloor's approach has significant design implications for analytic induction, which are summarized as follows.

1. Define the phenomenon whose variance is to be explained. Identify variations of that phenomenon and categorize or classify these variations in terms of their shared characteristics and differences.

2. Create a provisional list of 'case features' common to each identified category of the phenomenon. It is in terms of these features that explanations of the observed variation in the phenomenon will be postulated.

3. Identify any 'deviant' cases of the phenomenon that lack the case features common to other cases initially put into the same category. These deviant cases of the phenomenon are examined so as to:
   (a) modify the list of common case features so as to accommodate the otherwise deviant case;
   (b) modify the scheme of classifying variation in the phenomenon so as to allow the inclusion of deviant cases within a new or modified category thereby creating a new list of categories of the phenomenon.
   So, (a) and (b) allow an analytic framework to be developed in order to incorporate all the cases of the phenomenon observed during fieldwork.

4. Compare across all the categories of the phenomenon by looking for those case features which are shared by more than one category and for those unique to a particular category. Bloor judges case features as necessary rather than sufficient for the occurrence of a particular category of the phenomenon; whereas unique features are sufficient to generate the category. It is on the basis of these necessary and sufficient conditions associated with each category of the phenomenon that it is possible to postulate theoretical explanations (i.e. causes) of variance in the phenomenon that in essence have already been tested through observation.

Eisenhardt (1989) similarly suggests a 'road map' for building theories from case study research by synthesizing previous work (Glaser and Strauss, 1967; Yin, 1981, 1984; Miles and Huberman, 1984) and suggests a processual framework leading to theory building from case study research essentially similar to that mentioned above, though in considerably more detail. Her procedure is directed towards a positivist approach to research, with the aim of developing testable hypotheses and theory generalized across settings.

In reviewing the strengths, weaknesses and applicability of theory building from cases, Eisenhardt (1989) argues that the process of reconciling differences across cases, or among different investigators as, for example, we saw in Batstone, Boraston and Frenkel's (1977) work mentioned in Chapter 7, increases the likelihood of generating new theory. So in the same way does comparing case material with the literature. Testable theory is also likely to be produced with constructs which can be easily measured as they have already undergone repeated verification during the theory-building process. It is also suggested that emergent theory is likely to be empirically valid as it has been built up through intimate interaction with reality.

There are, however, some potential weaknesses of theory building from cases. Both Mintzberg (1973) and Batstone, Boraston and Frenkel (1977), for example, mention the large amount of information that is generated in the course of quite brief periods of ethnographic fieldwork. This may lead to the researcher being swamped by data and being unable to distinguish the most significant variables from those peculiar to a particular case. Eisenhardt (1989) also argues that there is a possibility that theory generated inductively is likely to be testable, novel and empirically valid but lack the sweep of 'grand theory' and remain at a modest, idiosyncratic level. The major solution to the generalization problem may be that research findings generated by single case designs need to be replicated and tested under a variety of conditions to allow generalization from one setting to another with a reasonable degree of confidence (Hersen and Barlow, 1976).

Theory-building, case study research may perhaps be most appropriate when little is known about a topic and where in consequence there can be little reliance on the literature or previous empirical evidence. Such approaches may also be most useful in the early stages of research or to provide a new perspective in a well-researched area.

Readers will note that the logic underpinning this form of analytic induction entails the search for 'differences' so central to those discussed earlier in Chapter 4 on experimental approaches. As such it is hardly surprising that some commentators have accorded it the status of a 'plausible reconstruction of the logic of science, not just ethnography' (Hammersley and Atkinson, 1983, p. 204).

Ethics and ethnography

Ethical issues in ethnography arise from the nature of the relationship between researcher and host organization and between the researcher and the subjects he or she studies, both of which may block other researchers if hostility is aroused.

The findings of ethnographic investigations are often eventually published and this may bring with it a number of ethical problems. These are mentioned, for example, by Morgan (1972), who discusses a case in which he gave a paper on a piece of research in a factory which was distorted by some sections of the press, who also discovered the identity of the company; this caused him embarrassment, particularly with his informants on the shop floor. Nevertheless, in apologizing for the affair Morgan was incidentally enabled to add considerably to his understanding of the plant.

More commonly, researchers who have agreed to have work checked for accuracy by host organizations are sometimes requested to delete passages found to be offensive, perhaps because they are perceived to suggest a negative public image. Whyte (1984), for example, presents several amusing cases of this sort one of which explains why his classic study, *Human Relations in the Restaurant Industry* (1948), has two appendices, one of which – on 'job attitudes' – is seemingly superfluous. This evidently occurred as the outcome of a negotiation to allow the publication of his work.

Clearly, it is crucially important to contract unambiguously with organizations in such matters and to fulfil the researcher's side of the bargain, including offers to make presentations and provide reports to the host organization.

Another key matter that arises is whether or not to use deception in research, and the answer should perhaps be clear cut: that producing a more comprehensive study is never justified by putting the job of an informant at risk. While the risks were probably very small, and particularly so in the case of Golding's (1979) work, both he and Dalton (1959) might have put employees' jobs in danger. In the final analysis, 'ethical fieldwork turns on the moral sense and integrity of the researcher negotiating the social contract which leads his subjects to expose their lives' (Dingwall, 1980, p. 885) and at the heart of the contract lies the matter of trust between the parties. In the case of student research work the need for confidentiality frequently arises, particularly when the work is being undertaken in the student's own organization. Although often an inadequate solution to the problem, most institutions recognize these difficuties by offering protection of dissertations and theses by restricting their publication for a period. It is, of course, also possible to protect the identity of individuals and context, as Golding (1979) achieved through the use of fictitious names, although this may frequently prove to be difficult.

Suggested further reading

M. Hammersley and P. Atkinson's *Ethnography, Principles in Practice*, is a useful brief text written for the beginner and covering most aspects of ethnography including its philosophical basis. It is not written with the business and management reader particularly in mind but is nevertheless an adequate introductory text to ethnography.

Also helpful are D. M. Fetterman's *Ethnography: Step by Step*, a readable, practical guide to ethnography by an anthropologist, and E. H. Schein's *The Clinical Perspective in Fieldwork*, which clarifies ethnography by comparing it with the clinical perspective.

On the politics and ethics of fieldwork, see M. Punch's *The Politics and Ethics of Fieldwork*, and J. F. Gubrium and D. Silverman's *The Politics of Field Research*.

For two useful short texts on the in depth interview see W. H. Banaka's *Training in Depth Interviewing* and G. McCracken's *The Long Interview*.

(Full bibliographical details of these works are given in the References, at the end of this book.)

9

Making Methodological Choices: The Philosophical Basis

In the earlier chapters of this book we have tried to provide the aspiring researcher with an overview of several research approaches or strategies. In undertaking a piece of research, inevitably the researcher must choose between these different approaches in making an area of interest researchable. The nature and content of the 'problem', as well as the extent of the available resources, clearly influence this choice. It is also important to be aware that the different methods available have differing inherent strengths and weaknesses, which need to be taken into account in relation to the goals of the research when an approach is selected.

In an attempt to illuminate these various strengths and weaknesses we briefly review the strategies we have presented in earlier chapters by comparing and contrasting them in terms of several criteria which derive from the validity and reliability of findings.

Evaluation criteria

With regard to the validity of any research findings, it is possible to distil four criteria that might be used in evaluation.

1. *Internal validity* This criterion refers to whether or not what is identified as the 'cause(s)' or 'stimuli' actually produce what have been interpreted as the 'effects' or 'responses'.
2. *External validity* Generally, this criterion refers to the extent to which any research findings can be generalized or extrapolated beyond the immediate research sample or setting in which the research took place. The matter of external validity is often subdivided into:
   (a) *Population validity* This criterion concerns the extent to which it is possible to generalize from the sample of people involved in the research, to a wider population.

(b) *Ecological validity*   This criterion is concerned with the extent to which it is possible to generalize from the actual social context in which the research has taken place and data thereby gathered, to other contexts and settings. This is also related to the issue of how artificial or atypical the research setting is relative to 'natural' contexts typical of normal, everyday life.

3. *Reliability*   This criterion basically refers to the consistency of results obtained in research. To satisfy this criterion it should be possible for another researcher to replicate the original research using the same subjects and the same research design under the same conditions.

Armed with these criteria, it is now possible to use them to evaluate each of the research strategies or approaches we have considered previously, and thereby elucidate their potential strengths and weaknesses.

Application of the criteria to research methods

Ideal or laboratory experiments

The highly structured nature of experimental research designs, with their identification and manipulation of independent and dependent variables and assignation of subjects to control and experimental groups, endows this approach with significant strengths of internal validity and reliability. Being highly structured, it is comparatively easy to replicate many aspects of an experimental research design. Moreover, its utilization of matched control and experimental groups enables observation of the effects of manipulating an independent variable while providing a high degree of confidence that the effects of any potential extraneous variables have been ruled out, or controlled, thus allowing the establishment of causal connections.

However, the ideal experiment, in gaining these strengths through its high degree of structure, loses or 'trades off' naturalism: experiments are low in ecological validity because of the artificial nature of the research process and context created by their very structure. Such weaknesses raise the issue of the extent to which any conclusions from ideal experiments are mere artifacts of the research process and context and thus inapplicable to social contexts outside those in which data has been collected.

A further significant weakness in much experimental research is that it is often low in population validity since it may involve small numbers of subjects, who may often be volunteers. Researchers using experiments can, however, increase population validity by giving greater attention to the random sampling of subjects.

Quasi-experiments and action research

Both quasi-experiments and action research attempt to take the research design of the ideal experiment out of the laboratory and into the field. By attempting to undertake research in relatively natural, non-artificial settings both are seen to gain naturalism and therefore are relatively higher in ecological validity.

But here we confront the paradoxical relationship which exists between control and naturalism in research design. Through venturing into the field naturalism may be gained, but only at the expense of losing the ability to manipulate the incidence of independent variables and control the incidence of extraneous variables. Except on rare occasions, in action research it is usually much more difficult for a researcher to manipulate the independent variable and assign subjects to matched and experimental groups. Indeed, to attempt to create such groups often disturbs the normal lives of subjects and so reduces naturalism. So, by increasing ecological validity quasi-experiments and action research trade off internal validity when compared with the ideal experiment. Similarly, in order to preserve the context in which research is undertaken, this reduction in structure will frequently result in a relative decline in reliability as it becomes more difficult to replicate.

As with the ideal experiment, it is often the case that researchers using either a quasi-experimental design or action research fail to give sufficient attention to sampling. This causes problems regarding population validity. While this may be understandable given the difficulties of gaining access in the field, it is not necessarily an intrinsic weakness of these research approaches.

Surveys

It should now be apparent that the qualities displayed in survey research give it much strength in population validity and reliability. Surveys usually entail the careful random selection of samples that enable results to be generalized to wider populations with a high degree of confidence. Concurrently, by using highly structured questionnaires to gather data in a form that is quantitatively analysable survey based research is usually regarded as easily replicable and hence reliable. However this high degree of structure, although conferring strengths, appears to create a relative lack of naturalism. The context in which data collection takes place will not usually be as artificial as the context of the ideal experiment. Nevertheless respondents might often be constrained or impelled by the prompts of an interviewer or the rubric of a self-completion questionnaire. This may lead them to make statements which, although fitting into the conceptual and theoretical proforma of the research, give little opportunity for the respondent to articulate the ways in which he or she personally conceptualizes and understands the matters of interest. It is usually for these reasons that survey research is often considered to be relatively low in ecological validity.

Surveys are also considered to be relatively weak in internal validity as compared with experiments; that is, they have difficulties in their control of rival hypotheses. For instance, analytic surveys rely on the use of the statistical controls of multivariate analysis to control extraneous variables, and this potentially weakens any causal conclusions arrived at. This is because correlation does not prove causation; the presence of a correlation is a necessary but not sufficient proof of a causal relationship. Moreover, the presence of a correlation gives little indication of the direction of causation between independent and dependent variables unless some temporal ordering is evident.

Ethnography

As we have attempted to make clear in earlier chapters, the more research is structured the more easily it can be replicated. Ethnography, with its commitment to induction and unstructured methods of data collection, creates severe problems regarding replicability, and consequently reliability also appears problematic. Moreover, as we have seen in the last two chapters, since ethnography usually entails the intensive study of a small number of cases its claims to population validity are usually considered to be limited to the actual phenomena under investigation during fieldwork. Although this apparent limitation regarding population validity has been thoroughly disputed by Mitchell (1983) and others in their discussion of the use of analytic induction, the main strength of ethnography is generally considered to be ecological validity.

It is often considered that ethnography has inherent advantages over positivistic research methodologies (e.g. laboratory experiments and surveys) that suffer from deficiencies in ecological validity (Brunswick, 1956; Bracht and Glass, 1968). That is, ethnographic research (unlike other research strategies) takes place in the natural setting of the everyday activities of the subjects under investigation. This, and the research procedures used, reduce contamination of the subject's behaviour by the researchers themselves and the methods they use for collecting data.

However, few ethnographers would claim that it is possible completely to eliminate subjects' reactivity to the researchers' personal qualities or techniques. As we have already discussed in the previous two chapters, the ethnographer rather attempts to be reflexive; that is to say, an attempt is made by the researcher to understand his or her own effect upon, and role in, the research setting and to utilize this knowledge to elicit data.

Where ethnographers are concerned with inductively generating grounded theory, their commitment to naturalism may often obstruct their establishment of control and experimental groups and hinder their ability to manipulate independent variables. As such, ethnography is often considered to have difficulties regarding the clear establishment of cause and effect relationships and consequently is taken to be low in internal validity. This situation is, however, problematic for several reasons.

Because ethnographers produce large amounts of qualitative data in an inductive fashion it is perhaps the most likely of all strategies to identify and include all the relevant variables in any subsequent theoretical analysis. In contrast, the experimental and survey approaches entail the formulation of theory prior to data collection through operationalization and instrumentation. At each stage of this process the deductive researcher is, in effect, excluding variables from consideration and limiting the extent and form that data takes in an a priori fashion. To put it crudely, the researcher is throwing information away!

Despite the ethnographer's inevitable selection of relevant aspects to study, he or she is more likely than deductive researchers to become aware of important factors that did not form part of his or her preconceived notion of the situation. This is particularly so when this process is combined with forms of analytic induction (M. Bloor, 1976, 1978), which enable the establishment of what are in effect control and experimental groups. In this way the criticism that ethnography is inevitably low in internal validity is increasingly open to question. Moreover since ethnographers have a varying commitment to naturalism, they have the scope to rule out some of the threats to internal validity that stem from the artificiality of the research context and procedures; something to which the more structured research styles are evidently victims.

In conclusion, it seems that the internal validity of ethnography is problematic as it depends largely upon rigorousness and the specific concerns of the ethnographer. When that entails analytic induction and reflexivity the internal validity of the ethnographer's theoretical conclusions may well be very high in comparison to many of the deductive approaches.

So far in this chapter we have shown how the making of methodological choices involves a consideration of the inevitable trade-offs that occur when issues such as internal validity, ecological validity, population validity and reliability are considered. As we have seen, such trade-offs occur because of the various strengths and weaknesses the different approaches have built into them. Moreover, researchers' evaluations of these trade-offs, and their consequent methodological choices, need to take into account the nature and organizational context of the substantive 'problem' to be investigated; as well as a consideration of the resources they have at their disposal and any potential ethical dilemmas.

Such decisions on methodological matters are also determined by the philosophical assumptions researchers implicitly and explicitly make by adopting what Morgan (1983, p. 19) terms a 'mode of engagement'. We have deliberately used Morgan's terminology at this point since his use of this term is intended to indicate how empirical research is not simply a choice of method; rather, as he points out, research as a mode of engagement is part of a wider process 'that constitutes and renders a subject amenable to study in a distinctive way. The selection of method implies some view of the situation being studied, for any decision on how to study a phenomenon carries with it certain assumptions, or explicit answers to the question "what is being studied?" ' (Morgan, 1983 p. 19).

It is to these wider, essentially philosophical questions and choices that we now turn. This will be facilitated by a discussion of some of the problems associated with positivism, to which we first alluded in chapter 1.

Ontology, epistemology and methodology

We argued, particularly in chapter 1, that interpretative approaches to research, such as ethnography, arise out of a critique of positivism's tendency to reduce human action to the status of automatic responses excited by external stimuli. Essentially we argued that this reduction was achieved by positivism through ignoring the subjective dimensions of human action, that is, the internal logic and interpretative processes by which action is created. Many positivists (e.g. Neurath, 1959, p. 295) justify such an approach by being concerned to prevent a divorce of the social sciences from the natural sciences; attempts at such a severance being perceived as a result of the 'residues of theology' (Neurath, 1959, p. 295). Other positivists, as Smart (1975) indicates, have justified their concern to follow what is assumed to be the approach of the natural sciences by expressing a desire to achieve in the social sciences the evident operational successes of the former. The result of the positivist's concern to emulate natural science methodology thus necessitates a denial of the importance of human subjectivity, a denial usually supported by further methodological criteria. As Giddens (1976) points out,

> the specific unreliability of the interpretation of consciousness, indeed whether by self or by an observer, has always been the principal rationale for the rejection of verstehen by such schools. The intuitive or empathetic grasp of consciousness is regarded by them merely as a possible source of hypotheses of human conduct.
>
> (Giddens, 1976, p. 19)

On the other hand, interpretative approaches such as ethnography reject what they perceive as the positivist's over-deterministic orientation towards an understanding of human action and behaviour. Instead they argue that, unlike animals or physical objects, human beings are able to attach meaning to the events and phenomena that surround them, and from these interpretations and perceptions select courses of meaningful action which they are able to reflect upon and monitor. It is these subjective processes that provide the sources of explanation of human action and thereby constitute the rightful focus for social science research. Thus the aim of such interpretative approaches is to understand (*verstehen*) how people make sense of their worlds, with human action being conceived as purposive and meaningful rather than externally determined by social structures, drives, the environment or economic stimuli.

We are therefore confronted with a philosophical choice regarding the nature of human action and its explanation which has direct methodological implications. Which set of philosophical assumptions we implicitly or explicitly adopt regarding what Burrell and Morgan (1979, p. 6) have termed 'human nature' influences our subsequent choice of particular 'modes of engagement' and what we see as warranted in research. If we accept the philosophical assumptions of positivism and its consequent epistemological prescriptions, we are invariably drawn towards the exclusive utilization of nomothetic methodology. Conversely, if our philosophical orientation is interpretative the ensuing epistemological mandate impels us towards a more ideographic methodology such as ethnography as it enables *verstehen* (Burrell and Morgan, 1979, pp. 1–37).

Methodological pluralism

The choices we may make in these matters may not necessarily entail a simple decision between what appear as the incommensurable alternatives of an ideographic or nomothetic methodology. Indeed, it would appear that such a view of methodology, purely in terms of a dichotomy, is fundamentally flawed. What it ignores is the adoption of what may be termed a 'methodologically pluralist' position. Such a position is articulated, for instance, by Trow (1957) when he proposes that

> different kinds of information about man and society are gathered most fully and economically in different ways, and the problem under investigation properly dictates the methods of investigation . . . This view seems to be implied in the commonly used metaphor of the social scientists's 'kit of tools' to which he turns to find the methods and techniques most useful to the problems at hand.
>
> (Trow, 1957, p. 33)

The position above implies the possibility of *rapprochement* between ideographic and nomothetic research methodologies, as articulated, for example, by McCall and Simmons (1969). From this stance the difference between the methods of the social scientist are perceived as being ones of trade-off around reliability, internal and external validity, and their appropriateness to the research topic. In this context Zelditch (1962) discusses information adequacy and efficiency as a criterion by which to judge the appropriateness of the researcher's choice of method. Alternatively, what has also been termed methodological pluralism may be based on the conception, demonstrated by H. W. Smith (1975), that different kinds of complementary data about a 'problem' may be acquired by using different research techniques in the same empirical study. This 'methodological triangulation' is thought to overcome the bias inherent in a single-method approach (Campbell and Fiske, 1959; Denzin, 1970, p. 313; Jick, 1979a), and we will return to this matter in the final chapter. According to Smith it illuminates different aspects of a problem. Therefore,

> We are really like blind men led into an arena and asked to identify an entity (say an elephant) by touching one part of that entity (say a leg). Certainly we might make better guesses if we could pool the information of all the blind men, each of whom has touched a different part of the elephant.
>
> (H. W. Smith, 1975, p. 273)

It would appear implicitly that many of the researchers working within this approach would argue that the nomothetic/ideographic debate does not necessarily reflect a fundamental conflict, rather, it reflcts different interests, which are reconcilable. However, it seems that this *rapprochement* is tenable only within certain webs of ontological assumptions. In particular it appears that such 'pluralism' is founded upon what Burrell and Morgan (1979) term 'realist' assumptions about the ontological status of social reality, which postulate that the world is a real world made up of hard, tangible and relatively immutable structures. Whether or not we label and perceive these structures the realists maintain, they still exist as empirical entities. We may not even be aware of the existence of certain crucial structures and therefore have no 'names' or concepts to articulate them. For the realist the social world exists independently of an individual's appreciation of it. The individual is seen as being born into and living within a social world which has a reality of its own. It is not something which the individual creates – it exists 'out there', ontologically it is prior to the existence and consciousness of any single human being. For the realist, the social world has an existence which is as hard and concrete as the natural world.

(Burrell and Morgan, 1979, p. 4)

Thus social reality has a concrete existence independent of human consciousness and cognition, which is in many respects empirically indefinable and presumably measurable in some way. Therefore experimental or analytical survey researchers may legitimately impose their operationalizations of social reality upon their subjects, which become measured stimuli to which subjects' responses are also measured in some fashion. Indeed, operationalization and measurement of social reality (stimuli) and action (responses) become the key activity in scientific inquiry and are clearly underpinned by the assumption that we all live in the same independent and external social world (Gouldner, 1970). Such methodological pluralists would follow Laing (1967) in attacking the positivist contention that social phenomena are analogous to the 'it-beings' or 'things' of nature and are thereby amenable to a similar type of causal analysis in which human beings are reduced to entities that automatically react to external stimuli in the same fashion as inanimate phenomena behave.

In the methodological pluralist position outlined here, human action has an internal logic, for human beings have been freed from the 'reflexive arc' (Mead, 1934). It therefore creates a perceived necessity to explore the meanings people attach to that all-embracing, identifiable, concrete social reality – meanings integral to the construction of responses, i.e. action.

Ideographic methods that enable *verstehen*, such as ethnography, are for the pluralist the methods appropriate for fulfilling their commitment to exploration of actors' phenomenological worlds. Therefore in the methodological pluralist's web of what are essentially philosophical choices, ethnography takes its place within a version of 'variable analysis' (Blumer, 1967). This position is often promulgated through attempts at providing what Fay (1975, p. 84) has termed 'quasi-causal' accounts. In clarifying what he means by this term, Fay states that, 'in these sorts of conditionship relations, consciousness functions as a mediator between the determining antecedent factors and the subsequent actions, in other words, men act in terms of their external conditions, rather than being governed directly by them' (Fay, 1975, pp. 84–5). In this, stimuli (social reality as measured and defined by the social scientist) and responses (human actions as measured and defined by the social scientist) are mediated by the actors' subjective processes of attaching meaning to and interpreting stimuli. For example, within this epistemological stance, the experimental and survey researchers can legitimately follow their 'crafts' by imposing operationalizations of their versions of social reality upon subjects and subsequent data, through highly structured research strategies. The relationship between stimuli and responses may often be investigated while taking into account (or controlling for) the creative processes of interpretation and meaning construction by subjects with some kind of ideographic analysis aimed at ruling out competing hypotheses. In other words, pluralists would attempt to increases the internal and ecological validity of their findings by attempting to 'control' for the indexicality of their experiment or survey by using the research methods most suitable for that purpose.

Within this pluralist position, however, ideographic methodology is not used purely within a hypothetico-deductive framework to control extraneous variables deriving from indexicality. Alternatively, methodological pluralism may arise from a commitment to linking micro analyses of individual or group action(s) with a macro-structural analysis of society. So in summary , the methodological pluralist position suggests that not only are different ideographic and nomothetic methodologies suitable for different kinds of problem (e.g. Trow, 1957), they also complement one another in a variety of ways that add to the credibility of a study by providing an internal cross-checking or monitoring device during the research process (e.g. McCall and Simmons, 1969; H. W. Smith, 1975; Denzin, 1970), as well as constituting aids for spanning the micro–macro divide (Godsland and Fielding, 1985; Fielding, 1988). We shall return to this discussion of methodological pluralism or multi-methods briefly in Chapter 10.

It should be remembered that within a realist ensemble of philosophical assumptions, once the role of human relationships (for whatever reason) is understood as irrelevant to the explanation of social phenomena, an increasingly positivist methodology is likely to be adopted. This implicitly or explicitly re-establishes a dichotomy between the nomothetic and the ideographic by dismissing the latter as irrelevant to social science research. However, an alternative form of methodological parochialism to that proposed by the philosophical choices of the positivist also arises when the importance of human subjectivity is not denied as irrelevant to social science but rather a realist ontology is questioned and the possibility of a nominalist conception of the ontological status of social reality embraced. Nominalism

> sees the social world as an emergent social process which is created by the individuals concerned. Social reality, in so far it is recognised to have any existence outside the consciousness of any single individual, is regarded as being little more than a network of assumptions and inter-subjectively shared meanings. The ontological status of the social world is viewed as extremely questionable and problematic.
>
> (Burrell and Morgan, 1979, pp. 30–31)

The position of methodological pluralism again becomes increasingly problematic, as the implicit acceptance of a realist position is necessary in all versions of experimental and survey methodologies. The operationalization of theoretical concepts, the measurement of those concepts and the assignment of explanatory or independent variables imply 'this is concrete social reality' – either the stimuli which people interpret in their construction of action or, alternatively, the stimuli which cause action. This is apparent in positivist surveys and experiments and the methodologically pluralist surveys and experiments which accept the importance of human subjectivity. The latter posit that subjectivity within a stimulus response relationship, or macro–micro duality, is inevitably based upon realist, ontological assumptions. Once nominalism is accepted, methodological pluralism, and the methodology of the positivist become inappropriate.

In regard to experimental and survey forms of social inquiry, what happens in nominalist terms is that 'scientists' are imposing their shared versions of social reality upon subjects before data collection begins, therefore giving their version of social reality an unwarranted superior status (i.e. privileged to that of subjects). However, ideographic methodology, such as ethnography, with its usual commitment to induction as well as explanation by understanding actors' cultures, can avoid this problem and therefore becomes the only appropriate form of social inquiry to the nominalist. Thus another version of methodological parochialism emerges which emphasizes the use of ethnographic methods to describe actors' commonsense thinking (Schutz, 1966, pp.62–3) through an inductive compilation of empirical 'facts' that are 'understandable for the actor himself as well as for his fellow men in terms of common sense interpretations of everyday life' (Schutz, 1967, p. 44).

So the researcher's constructs must be consistent with the constructs of commonsense experience of social reality employed by actors. Therefore the researcher's constructs and accounts must appear plausible and understandable to subjects; this implies that the veracity of a piece of research is determinable only through that consensus.

Thus, due to his nominalism, Schutz (1967) argues that the observer must discard any claim to a privileged position *vis-à-vis* conditions of action unacknowledged by the actor(s), for social science must not, and cannot, go beyond commonsense experience. Thus, research methods that rely upon the imposition of an external and alien logic through, for instance, the deductive classification of phenomena as independent, dependent and extraneous variables, are perceived from this particular philosophical standpoint as inappropriate to social science.

So one's 'modes of engagement' (Morgan, 1983, p. 19) not only make one's area of interest amenable to investigation in a distinctive way but also entail entering into a particular 'methodological subculture'. For Diesing (1972, p. 18), each subculture is 'justified and explained by an ideology or philosophy which specifies the goals of science, the available and permissible means, the impermissible errors, the proper subject matters, the heroic exemplars, the unfortunate failures or pseudoscientific villains'.

We have discussed some of these choices and consequent subcultures and these are represented by the matrix in Figure 9.1.

Philosophical choices	Non-recognition of the relevance of human subjectivity	Recognition of the relevance of human subjectivity
Ontological realism	Positivist methodological parochialism (e.g. Neurath, 1959)	Methodological pluralism (e.g. Trow, 1957; Denzin, 1970; H. W. Smith, 1975)
Ontological nominalism		Interpretative methodological parochialism (e.g. Schutz, 1964b, 1966, 1967; Garfinkel, 1967)

Figure 9.1   Philosophical choices and research subcultures

Choices and the problem of justification

It is now necessary to consider the issues that surround the evaluation of the status of our empirical findings on completing a piece of research. That is, what claims can be made for these results? In particular, these issues must lead us to consider the extent to which it is possible to claim that any empirical findings are justified and warranted in the sense that they correspond to the facts of the independent reality. Moreover, if the possibility of such a claim is found to be dubious, or indeed impossible, where does this leave us? What alternative criteria are then left for evaluating and justifying any claim to warranted knowledge?

Here we are raising very difficult philosophical issues that inevitably pervade our assessment of the veracity of any research findings. That is, what do we mean by the concept 'truth' and how do we know whether or not it is present? In other words, what is our theory of truth? These are major epistemological issues and we can only introduce the reader to some of these debates and thereafter direct those interested to further reading.

Perhaps it is again useful to begin this review from the epistemological standpoint advanced by positivism. According to many commentators (e.g. Keat and Urry, 1975; Giddens, 1979) two of the most significant characteristics of positivist epistemology contain the claims that warranted science is concerned with:

1. only directly observable phenomena, with any reference to the intangible or subjective being excluded as being meaningless; and
2. the testing of theories, in a hypothetico-deductive fashion, by their confrontation with the facts of a readily observable external world.

Thus, positivist epistemology limits its conception of valid or warranted knowledge (i.e. science) to what is taken to be unproblematically observable 'sense-data'. If a theory corresponds with a researcher's observations of these facts its truthfulness is taken to be established. If it fails to correspond, it is discarded as fallacious. Thus the theory of truth that is proposed, implicitly and explicitly, is a correspondence theory of truth. Such a view of truth is made viable only through the prior assumption that it is possible to observe the facts of the external world neutrally and objectively by the application of rigorous procedures and protocols. This latter assumption is often called the assumption of a theory-neutral observational language. As Hindess (1977, p. 18) points out, 'it makes possible a very precise conception of the testing of theory against observation. The testing of theory against irreducible statements of observation is equivalent to a direct comparison between theory and the real world. If they fail to correspond then the theory is false and therefore may be rejected.'

In this way *doxa* (what we believe to be true) becomes transformed into *episteme* (that which we know to be true), hence epistemology. At first sight, particularly from a standpoint imbued with Western cultural norms, this positivistic epistemology appears as eminently rational – indeed commonsensical. However, there seem to be major problems with this view of scientific endeavour: first, it seems self-contradictory; and, second, the possibility of directly and objectively observing phenomena, and thereby accumulating the 'facts' of the world so as to test the veracity of a theory, seems dubious.

We shall now proceed to discuss each of these problems in turn.

Self-contradiction

In order to observe directly, and objectively, the phenomenon in which they are interested, positivists must assume what is called a dualism between 'subject' and 'object'; that it is possible to separate the 'subject' (the knower, the observer, the researcher) from the 'object' (the known, the observed, what are taken to be the 'facts' of the world) by the application of scientific method. Therefore, by using rigorous methodology it is possible to have knowledge that is independent of the observer and uncontaminated by the very act of observation. Thus, it is only through the prior assumption that such a dualism is possible, and consequently that a theory neutral observational language is available, that the correspondence criteria of the positivist (i.e. his or her epistemology) become viable. This is illustrated by Figure 9.2.

According to both Hindess (1977) and Gorman (1977), however, the contention above about the nature of subject/object relations (i.e. a dualism) demonstrates the contradictory nature of positivism. As we have tried to show,

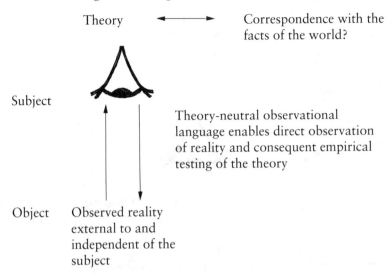

Theory ←——→ Correspondence with the facts of the world?

Subject

Theory-neutral observational language enables direct observation of reality and consequent empirical testing of the theory

Object   Observed reality external to and independent of the subject

Figure 9.2   Positivist Dualism

positivism ostensibly excludes from what is taken to be warranted knowledge, the metaphysical that is to say the intangible, and the subjective or abstract.

But in rejecting the metaphysical it rejects as meaningless the very knowledge of subject/object relationships on which any epistemology, including its own, is ultimately grounded. There is therefore a contradiction since it excludes from its conceptualization of warranted knowledge its own grounds for warranted knowledge (Hindess, 1977, p. 135).

Thus it would appear that since positivism cannot account for itself on its own terms, it becomes indefensible in its own terms, and is thereby incoherent.

Is a theory-neutral observational language possible?

As we have shown, positivism, with its articulation of a subject–object dualism, assumes that there is some neutral point from which the observer can stand back and observe the world objectively. That is, the observations that are registered are independent of the very process of the observer observing and thus 'truth' is to be found in the observer's passive registration of the 'sensory givens' (Mattick, 1986), or facts, that constitute reality. This is illustrated by Figure 9.3.

Figure 9.3 illustrates the empiricist maxim that science should be, and can be, a neutral, value-free and disinterested endeavour. So as Rorty (1979, p. 46) argues, a correspondence theory of truth relies upon the received wisdom that the veracity of competing theories may be adjudicated through an appeal to their correspondence with the facts of an external objective reality that is 'mirrored' in the 'Glassy Essence' of the observer. However, in assuming the possibility for an observer to register passively the facts of reality, positivism ignores the possibility that the observer's perceptual apparatus does not

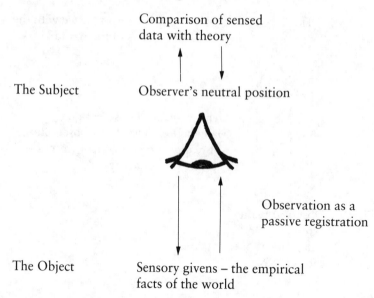

Figure 9.3   Science as a Neutral Endeavour

provide mere reflections of what is out there, but is proactive and creative in influencing what we apprehend. As Habermas (1974b, p. 199) contends, 'even the simplest perception is not only performed pre-categorically by physiological apparatus – it is just as determined by previous experience through what has been handed down and through what has been learned as by what is anticipated through the horizons of expectations.'

Factors that might influence observation

It is now important to turn to considering how various factors might influence observation/sensory experience and thereby consider their implications for the possibility of a theory-neutral observational language. In this we shall review the process of perception and the theory-laden nature of observation.

The process of perception

For many scientists, warranted knowledge about the world emanates from that reality, that is an external world directly and objectively accessible through human sensory experience. As such, warranted knowledge has a correspondence with the world that has been established through our neutral and passive registration of various sensory imputs.

Unfortunately, such a claim for perception seems questionable. Often the same event or identical set of sensations is perceived and experienced by people in different ways. For instance, consider the two objects in Figures 9.4 and 9.5. How many women do you see in Figure 9.4?

Figure 9.4   Old woman or young woman?

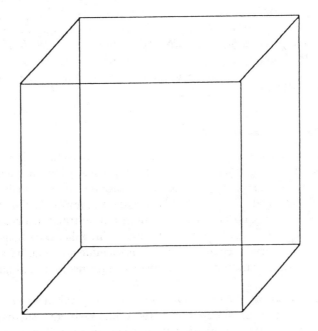

Figure 9.5   Necker's cube

Do you see the object in Figure 9.5 in three dimensions? If so, how many cubes do you see? Can you also see it as one dimensional and composed of squares, triangles and parallelograms? People outside Western cultures may perceive this figure in only one dimension.

If the sensory process of perceiving even relatively simple objects was indeed merely a matter of the passive reception and registration of their evident characteristics, how is it that the same object can be apprehended so differently? This must surely imply that we are not passive receivers of external stimuli and data but rather that we apply various inferences and assumptions which mediate what we 'see'. Indeed, it suggests that we are important participants in the process of perception as we experience an interpreted world and not one that is directly accessible through our sensory capacities (Spinelli, 1989, pp. 32–59). So what we perceive as being external to and separate from us is just as much an expression of our subjective processes as what is actually going on 'out there'.

We are continually bombarded by sensations and stimuli and we project on to those inputs a form and substance that derives from within, from our 'cognitive processing mechanisms' (Unwin, 1986, p. 300). Such projection entails selection, as we choose what we sense by giving attention to particular stimuli while de-emphasizing, filtering out or ignoring others. The selected sensory stimulations are simultaneously organized and interpreted by being put into a coherent and meaningful whole. This organization, interpretation and consequent imposition of order may be highly influenced by the schemas built up from our previous experience, or received as stocks of knowledge through our interaction in various cultural milieux. We usually do these things rapidly and automatically and often unconsciously. Although the result may appear objective and separate from ourselves, – as 'out there', – in many respects we are creating what we apprehend. So 'perception allows us to impose a logic and order on the chaos of the thousands of sensations that bombard our senses . . . perception allows us to make sense out of all these sensations' (Spinelli, 1989, p. 38).

The theory-laden nature of observation

The ways in which we make sense of the various sensations that bombard our senses also direct attention to the issue that has usually been termed the 'theory-laden' nature of observation. This term refers to the way in which prior theories influence what we take to be factual observations. Hanson (1958) contends that, rather than a theory and the data accumulated to test that theory being separate elements, they are actually intimately linked. In other words, he claims that observation is theory-laden in that our theories influence what we see, and hence there is no actual separation between theory, interpretation and data.

Our brief discussion of the various processes involved in perception and the theory-laden nature of observation casts doubt upon the possibility of there being a theory neutral observational language that would enable theory to be tested directly against empirical reality. Thus, the assumption of a subject –

object dualism, so necessary for epistemology based on a correspondence theory of truth, appears implausible. Advocates of such coresspondence criteria fail to acknowledge what is known as the 'hermeneutic circle', that no 'pure' description of data free from interpretation based upon presuppositions is possible. As Spinelli (1989, p. 58) comments, 'the assumed separation between the data being analysed and the person who analyses them . . . becomes questionable'.

Inevitably the observer, explicitly or implicitly, projects prior beliefs and sentiments upon sense-data and thereby moulds them through this imposition of common sense (Hooker, 1973), or theoretical (Hanson, 1958; Quine, 1960; Habermas, 1974a) or paradigmatic (Kuhn, 1970) or unconscious (Hunt, 1979) assumptions and background expectancies (Giddens, 1976). It may of course also be moulded by cognitive phenomena to which researchers may be emotionally committed (Mitroff, 1974) and whose nature is highly influenced by social factors (Barnes, 1974, 1977; D. Bloor, 1976; Law and Lodge, 1984). Indeed, as Gadamer (1975) in his critique of Dilthey argues, the notion of a neutral, detached observer is a myth. Interpretations cannot escape background preconceptions embedded in the language and life of their authors. So it follows that the processes described in the previous sections are not merely interesting curiosities that we should try to subliminate or ignore in considering the status of our research findings. Rather, their implications demand that we should attempt to develop epistemologies capable of coping with their burgeoning critique. It is now therefore imperative to consider some of these attempted escape routes, albeit briefly.

The debate between two alternatives: conventionalism versus pragmatism

It seems that the possession of a theory-neutral observational language is impossible. Further, it implies that what we take to be warranted knowledge is not objective and independent but is imbued with the partiality and theoretical dispositions of the observer, through the action of our 'cognitive processing mechanisms' (Unwin, 1986, p. 300). This has led to the creation of several escape strategies.

One choice or strategy appears to involve a suppression of philosophical issues in undertaking research through the maintenance of a naïve and unreflective empiricism that makes various research methods used appear as philosophically expurgated techniques and protocols, especially in regard to 'questions of epistemology, of truth' (Douglas, 1976, p. 3). Obviously, this is a strategy with which we have little sympathy. We would particularly concur with Giddens's (1984, p. xviii) warning that 'the social sciences are lost if they are not directly related to philosophical problems by those who practise them'. An alternative strategy entails adopting a 'conventionalist' or 'consensus' approach to truth. For Keat and Urry (1975, pp. 60–1) this has the following characteristics. First, that scientific statements are not seen to be true or false descriptions of some external reality but are creations of the scientist. Second, the acceptability of a statement is not the product of the existence of universally valid criteria and standards of evaluation but, rather, the product of the value-laden subjectivity of an individual scientist or a community of scientists. Finally, the truth or falsity of statements is 'under-determined' by empirical data in that observation cannot provide objective control over scientific statements.

So the only way to establish the veracity or truthfulness of our research findings is through agreement between the concerned parties. Such a consensus might be possible between the observer and the subjects of the research (Cicourel, 1964; Mehan and Wood, 1975). Alternatively it might arise between researchers and their professional peers and colleagues (McHugh, 1971), as we saw in the cases discussed in Chapter 7 (e.g. Batstone, Boraston and Frenkel, 1977).

However, while the conventionalist or consensus approach to truth recognizes the problems associated with correspondence theory, it does encounter the problem of relativism. As Sayer (1981 p. 6) comments, the 'shattering of innocence' that has arisen through the radical undermining of empiricism by the rejection of the doctrine of the theory-neutrality of observation has often produced a move towards idealism. As such the naïvety of empiricism has given way to possibly more dangerous views in which knowledge is believed not to be subject to any extra-discursive checks. Instead Sayer draws indirectly upon American pragmatism, and more directly upon Marxian traditions, by developing an alternative approach to truth which he terms 'practical adequacy'.

> To be practically adequate knowledge must generate expectations about the world and about the results of our actions that are actually realised .. These expectations in turn are realised because of the nature of the associated material interventions . . . and of their material contents. In other words, although the nature of objects and processes (including human behaviour) does not uniquely determine the content of human knowledge, it does determine their cognitive and practical possibilities for us.
>
> (Sayer, 1984, p. 66)

Here Sayer is in many respects following Kolakowski in differentiating between 'thought objects' and 'real objects'. Kolakowski (1969, p. 75) believes there is an external reality independent of and resistant to human activity; but this is a 'thing in itself' which remains unknowable. Such 'things in themselves' do not have conceptual counterparts; rather, our objects of knowledge – 'things for us' – are constituted by 'active contact with the resistance of nature- . . . [that] . . . creates knowing man and nature as his object at one and the same time'. So as Kolakowski claims, while reality does exist, we can never ultimately know it because of our lack of a theory-neutral observational language; but this is not to say that our engagements with the external world are completely determined by us.

The implications of this issue are further elaborated by Arbid and Hesse (1986). As implied by Kolakowski (1969) they argue that the constraints and tolerance of spatio-temporal reality provide a feedback procedure that enables evaluation of the pragmatic success of our 'cognitive systems' and 'networks of schemata'. This pragmatic criterion prevents 'science' becoming purely an intersubjective representation of, and consensus about, social realities. These schemata allow people to make sense of the world – a world so complex that it is amenable to many interpretations.

For Arbib and Hesse (1986), while such schemata are not individualistic but socially shaped and constructed, they are not socially determined. Rather, since such schemata are guides for action, the pragmatic criterion operates consciously and unconsciously as people adjust and reject schemata when the expectations they support are violated (see also Barnes, 1977). Thus, schemata are ideological, pragmatic and interest-laden in the sense that they are enmeshed with our knowledge of how to interact with the world, and such knowledge of 'how to' is 'intertwined with our knowledge (not necessarily conscious) of our goals and what we wish to achieve through our actions' (Arbib and Hesse, 1986, p. 129).

Law and Lodge (1984, p. 125) attempt to investigate further these social processes through the notion of 'workability', that is, truthfulness in a pragmatic sense. In this they argue that if a theory/network allows people to interact satisfactorily with their environment it is then reinforced, but if, from the stance of theory, their environments become unpredictable and uncontrollable the theory is undermined and is likely to change. Therefore they argue that the workability of a theory is a function of the purposes for which it is used.

The importance of these issues lends force to Morgan's (1983, p. 393) consideration that since the pursuit of knowledge is a particular form of human action that has an essentially social nature, 'it must be understood as being an ethical, moral, ideological and political activity as it is an epistemological one'.

If, therefore, there are any criteria available for evaluating knowledge; they do not relate to some quest for absolute knowledge; rather, they relate to 'the way knowledge serves to guide and shape ourselves as human beings – to the consequences of knowledge, in the sense of what knowledge does to and for humans' (Morgan, 1983, p. 393).

It follows that research embracing practical adequacy maintains the necessity for reflexivity on the part of the researcher. Knowledge, as such, is evaluated in terms of how successfully it may guide action towards the realization of particular objectives which are the expressions of particular interests or needs. This necessarily leads the researcher to reflect upon the partisan nature of his or her research with regard to its human consequences. As Carchedi (1983) argues, this inevitably involves questions such as: for whom and for what does the resultant construction of reality proffer aid? Management researchers should therefore accept their (albeit fallible) role as that of partisan participant in interest-laden dispute and divest themselves of allusions to the role of detached observer (Chubin and Restivo, 1983) occupying a neutral position.

Hence, according to the 'pragmatist' position, the 'truthfulness' of any methodologically corroborated explanation or account would be ultimately available, or testable, only through practice. This makes it incumbent upon the researcher to provide a clear guide to the practical ramifications of the theory and the subsequent practices that would pragmatically test that theory. Therefore as Fay (1975, comments, there would be an

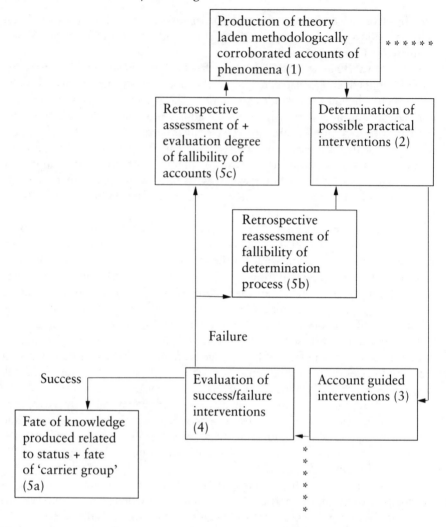

Notes

(i)   The temporal sequence of 1, 2, 3, 4, 5, may in some approaches (eg Action Research or the Clinical Approach) (Schein, 1987) become blurred.

(ii) * * * * * * Intervention of tolerance of reality, ie feedback from external reality.

(iii) For Law and Lodge (1984) the eventual 'fate' of knowledge is mediated by the social status and power of the 'carrier group'.

Figure 9.6   The pragmatist position

explicit recognition that social theory is interconnected with social practice such that what is to count as truth is partially determined by the specific ways in which scientific theory is supposed to relate to practical action . . . Thus the theories of such a science will necessarily be composed of, among other things, an account of how such theories are translatable into action.'

(Fay,1975, pp. 94–95)

The processes by which our methodologically produced and corroborated accounts, or 'cognitive systems', might then be tested by these practical concerns is illustrated below in Figure 9.6.

So, all these considerations regarding the 'truth' imply that research should not stop at the presentation of an account that has been produced and corroborated by the methodologies reviewed and evaluated in this text. Rather, research should proceed at least to identify the practical ramifications of that account and, ideally, should also proceed to test that account through practical interventions into our world so as to get feedback from that external reality.

Suggested further reading

For an extremely useful and easy-to-read introduction to the philosophy of science, we recommend L. Doyal and R. Harris's *Empiricism, Explanation and Rationality*, particularly chapters 1, 2 and 3. Similarly, J. Law and P. Lodge's *Science for Social Scientists* provides an accessible introduction to these issues.

Many of the issues they raise are further elaborated in chapters 1 to 9 of D. C. Phillipps's *Philosophy, Science and Social Inquiry*, which contains an interesting discussion of what he terms 'Hansonism' (i.e. the theory-laden nature of observation).

For those interested in delving further into the implications of pragmatism, both A. Sayer's *Method in Social Science* and J. Margolis's *Pragmatism without foundations* provide comprehensive reviews.

Probably the most incisive considerations of the implications of various philosophical positions for management research, especially that concerned with the study of organizations, are provided by G. Burrell and G. Morgan's *Sociological Paradigms and Organizational Analysis* and G. Morgan's, *Beyond Method*.

Interesting applications of Burrell and Morgan's ideas to managerial issues are to be found in:

1. T. Hopper and A. Powell's 'Making sense of reason into the organisational and social aspects of management accounting: a review of its underlying assumptions';
2. W. F. Chua's 'Theoretical constructions of and by the real' and 'Radical developments in accounting thought';
3. R. A. Hirschheim's 'Information systems epistemology: an historical perspective';
4. D. Gowler and K. Legge's 'Personnel and paradigms: four perspectives on utopia'.

(Full bibliographical details of these works may be found in the References, at the end of this book.)

10
Conclusion: Resolving the Dilemmas in Choosing a Research Strategy

In Chapter 9 we considered some fundamental philosophical issues that are basic to understanding and justifying choices of research strategy. We conclude this book by examining the influence of these philosophical matters on the practical choices of strategy, research design and technical method(s) which need to be made by every researcher. The philosophical, social, political and practical influences on the researcher's conceptualization of the research problem, which we considered in detail in previous chapters, are summarised diagrammatically in Figure 10.1. First, we briefly review the link between philosophical and practical matters, then the nature of the research process in reality, and finally the dilemmas that face the would-be researcher in making choices of strategy, design and method, and pointing to ways through what may seem at first sight to be something of an impasse.

The diversity and complexity of the issues to which we directed attention in Chapter 9 need to be related to the practical problems that arise in management research. In so doing, however, we bear in mind that guides to methodological choices 'if interpreted too literally [they] exert a confining and diversionary hold on imagination as interest in the classification 'map' replaces interest in the 'territory' (Morgan, 1983, p.41). Morgan goes on to say that his purpose in *Beyond Method* is 'to analyse research strategies in a way that moves beyond method so that we can consider the logics of engagement that link researcher and researched . . . rather than on the labels used to denote similarities and differences among them' (ibid).

While we raised this cautionary note about the idealized nature of the rational research model when referring to it in Chapters 1 and 2, we nevertheless felt that at that stage it was necessary to provide some structure for the novice researcher, at least as a rough guide. However, the rational model of the traditional methods textbook, which presents the research process as an idealized, neat series of logically directed steps does not of course provide a description of the way in which research is actually conducted. Rather like the managerial process, which until recently was idealized by textbooks as a logical, orderly one of planning,

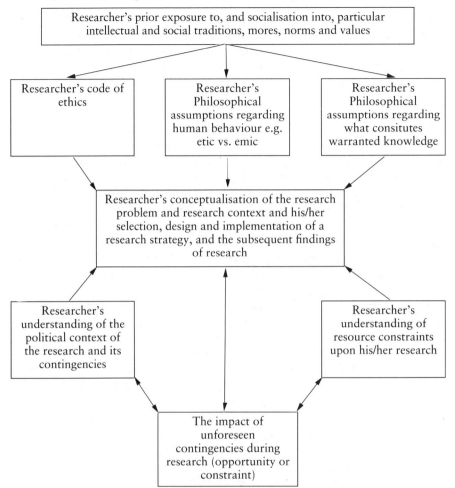

Figure 10.1 The impact upon research of philosophical, social, political and practical dilemmas

controlling and the like (Mintzberg, 1973), there is now widespread recognition of the view that 'idiosyncrasies of person and circumstance are at the heart, not the periphery of the scientific enterprise' (Bell and Newby, 1977, p. 9).

This idiosyncrasy has of course been the justification for the growing number of candid first-person accounts of the research process by experienced researchers (e.g. Hammond, 1964; Morgan, 1983; Bryman, 1988) but even these rarely record the way methodological preferences are determined. It is also difficult to build up a general picture from them as they are often highly anecdotal. In this book, while we have tried to recognize the 'quirkiness and messiness' (Bryman, 1988, p. 1) of the research process that researchers experience, we have also endeavoured to steer a course between descriptions of cases, philosophical underpinning and some generalized practical directions of use to the intending researcher. This short concluding chapter has this last objective particularly in mind.

First, we point up some differences between the rational, reconstructed logic of the textbook account and the actual research process. We then attempt to make some sense of the complexities faced by researchers and indicate some solutions to the evident dilemmas in choice of research strategy by reviewing and further conceptualizing the approaches considered in earlier chapters.

The research process in practice

If the research process is to be improved it is important to be aware of its actual practice rather than some idealized simplification that is often portrayed by books on research methodology. Methodological choices do not seem to be made in the ways frequently suggested in conventional methods textbooks.

In this regard a comment is made by Morgan (1983, p. 11), which occurred to him when working in the field as a young researcher, of the unreality of many texts on methods: he was 'struck by the realisation that the conduct of empirical research was much more problematic than as presented in textbooks and that the results of such research must be much less solid than appeared from a reading of scientific reports'.

Pettigrew (1985a, p. 222) too describes the research process as best 'characterised in the language of muddling through, incrementalism, and political process than as rational, foresightful, goal-directed activity'. Martin (1982) agrees, likening the research process to the 'garbage can' model of organizational choice used by Cohen, March and Olsen (1972) to typify decision-making in organizations. For example, she mentions that in the rational model a passive role is assigned to resources, rather than as a determining factor in the selection of a theoretical problem and choice of method. Similarly, the rational model's implicit advocacy of problems being contingent with methods clearly in many cases does not accord with practice. Methodological considerations frequently determine which theoretical problems are addressed, and indeed which solutions are discovered. Not only this but the choice of method is often fundamentally driven by the cultural upbringing of the researcher (Bygrave, 1989). There is also the view basic to the rational model which suggests that any methodological choice should lead to the same theoretical conclusions. There are of course many well-known examples where this is not so, such as Herzberg, Mausner and Snyderman's (1959) two-factor theory of motivation, which seems to attract empirical support only when tested through Herzberg's own methodology. The same phenomenon also seems true of experiments to test the riskiness of decision-making in groups, mentioned in Chapter 2, where the empirical evidence seems to depend on the design of the instrument used (Brown, 1965).

Kulka (1982), too, examines the actual research process, as opposed to the theoretical rational model, by considering it sequentially, with many amusing anecdotal instances. He suggests, for example, that the choice and formulation of research problems are more frequently related to the availability of funding – rather than resources being a peripheral matter as orthodoxy would have us believe. Examples that confirm this view in the United Kingdom are the current academic research growth industries in small businesses or the technological determinant in organizations, both government inspired. Topic selection is also influenced by ease of access and, bearing in mind Rowan's (1974, pp. 87–8) somewhat cynical view of research by experimental social psychologists, by considerations such as its cost, a handy, readily available data source (e.g. students), and that it is expeditious and 'publishable whether what is produced is worth knowing or not'. Further, it seems to be the case that researchers largely choose the research strategy with which they are most familiar, giving little attention to alternatives. Kulka (1982) instances many cases of nothing less than chaos in the execution of research designs, especially so in data collection. Lest these views should prove too daunting, however, he also quotes Becker.

> As every researcher knows there is more to doing research than is dreamt of in philosophies of science, and texts in methodology offer answers to only a fraction of the problems one encounters. The best laid research plans run up against unforeseen contingencies in the collection and analysis of data; the data one collects may prove to have little to do with the hypothesis one sets out to test; unexpected findings inspire new ideas. No matter how carefully one plans in advance, research is designed in the course of its execution. The finished monograph is the result of hundreds of decisions, large and small, made while the research is under way and our standard texts do not give us procedures and techniques for making those decisions . . . It is possible, after all, to reflect on one's difficulties and inspirations and see how they could be handled more rationally the next time around. In short one can be methodological about matters that earlier had been left to chance and improvization and thus cut down the area of guesswork.
>
> (Becker, 1965, pp. 602–3)

Research choices: resolving the dilemmas

McGrath (1982) aptly uses the term 'dilemmatics' to describe the study of research choices in which it is clear there are no ideal solutions, only a series of compromises. Dilemmas are to be found at all levels of the research process: strategic, design and methodological.

Consider the research strategies in Figure 10.1: they are shown as related to one another in different ways, matrix fashion. The strategies are shown in Figure 10.2 on dimensions derived from the literature: on the vertical axis, prescriptive, obtrusive (Runkel and McGrath, 1972) from the 'outside' (Evered and Lewis, 1981) and deductive at one end and, at the other, descriptive, unobtrusive from the 'inside', and inductive. On the horizontal axis we use the terms 'general' and 'extensive' (Sayer, 1984) at one end, and at the other 'particular' and 'intensive'. We then place our four strategies – experiments, action research and quasi-experiments, survey research, and ethnography outlined in Chapters 4 to 8 – in these four quadrants. It should of course be noted that both action research and surveys fit uncomfortably into their respective quadrants (II and III). Surveys, especially if analytic, have many of the characteristics of experimental research design and accordingly are most appropriately located in quadrant I. Descriptive surveys on the other hand are best located in quadrant III. Action research, with

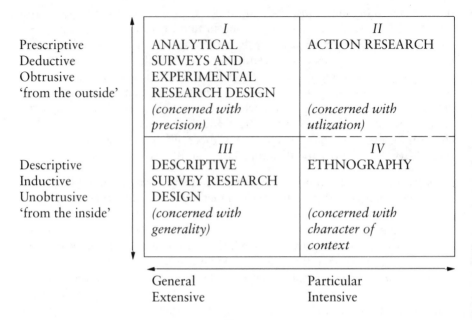

	I	II
Prescriptive Deductive Obtrusive 'from the outside'	ANALYTICAL SURVEYS AND EXPERIMENTAL RESEARCH DESIGN *(concerned with precision)*	ACTION RESEARCH *(concerned with utlization)*
	III	IV
Descriptive Inductive Unobtrusive 'from the inside'	DESCRIPTIVE SURVEY RESEARCH DESIGN *(concerned with generality)*	ETHNOGRAPHY *(concerned with character of context*
	General Extensive	Particular Intensive

Figure 10.2   Choosing research strategies

its prime aim of effecting change, is, as we have seen, regarded by many as most likely to achieve this objective if carried out inductively (Van de Vall, Bolas and Kang, 1976; Argyris, 1980, 1985). Accordingly, although action research is placed in quadrant II it is separated diagrammatically by a broken line to indicate that deductive and inductive methodologies may both be used, sometimes simultaneously.

The nature of the dilemma faced by the researcher is therefore clear, for the experimental researcher is concerned primarily with precision, the survey methodologist with generality, the ethnographer with the character of the particular context and the action researcher with issues of utilization. To focus exclusively on the primary concerns of any of these strategies will necessarily limit the others. As Morgan (1983, p. 378) asks, 'What do we do with the diversity once we have explored and understood it?'

Morgan goes on to define five approaches to the dilemmas, based on work by Churchman (1971) Feyerabend (1975) and Mason and Mitroff (1981). First, any attempt to find some evaluatory test which will determine the merits of a particular strategy will run into the problems of relativism discussed in the previous chapter. Similarly, the search for an integration or synthesis of strategies to find some common ground is apparently not possible given different paradigmatic research assumptions, for by accepting one set of assumptions we may deny others. A third approach is that assumptions and knowledge should be judged by their usefulness. This is the contingent view that there is no optimal way of undertaking research but, rather, that it depends on its practical utility to the interests it serves. The fourth approach – operationalized, for example, by Mason and Mitroff (1981) in an attempt to discuss the assumptions underlying corporate planning – accepts the dilemmas as inevitable and attempts to counterpose the insights from different perspectives to reach a new understanding. This Morgan, (1983) terms the dialectic approach similar to the multi-method research strategy, or, in Brewer and Hunter's (1989) terms, 'style'. In their view this not only enables weaknesses to be cancelled out but rather, and more particularly, allows phenomena to be studied by juxtaposing different paradigms and metaphors (Morgan, 1986). We should

> accept all research strategies as having something to offer but attempt to use their competing insights within the context of a single analysis . . . learning from diversity by using conflict and debate as a means of exploring and expanding our understanding. Synthesis, if it emerges, only occurs at the final stage of analysis in a form of understanding that attempts to recognise and yet go beyond original formulations of the problem and all the conflicts that these generate.
>
> (Morgan, 1983, p. 380)

Finally, there is the approach of Feyerabend, (1975), which adopts a complete relativism in that every research strategy may have something to offer and that anything goes.

We therefore come to the conclusion that all research approaches may have something to offer and that there is no independent form of evaluating different research strategies in any absolute terms. The last three stategies above are all based on the notion that every research strategy has utility but, broadly the consensus seems to be in favour of multi-method strategies, or something close to option four above. By multi-method we imply a strategy that requires not only a convergence of substantive findings derived from a diversity of methods of study but also debate about the contribution of each approach used: debate that is possible only if a detailed methodological justification is available to students of the research.

Justifying the research approach: an example

A good example of an attempt at justification in practice is contained in Mintzberg's (1973) work, which was referred to in Chapter 7 and to which we now turn before finally considering other practical examples of methodological pluralism. Mintzberg (as we have previously noted), having decided that he wished to undertake studies of managers' jobs to reveal how managers in reality behaved, first reviewed previous studies of managerial work and then the research methods employed. He distinguished seven methods: secondary sources; interview and questionnaire; critical incident and sequence of episodes; diary; activity sampling; and unstructured and structured observation (Table 10.1). As we have previously noted, his research strategy would broadly fall into the ethnographic quadrant of Figure 10.2.

Mintzberg reviewed these potential methods, listing their advantages and disadvantages and the ways in which each might be most appropriately used to achieve his research objective of discovering what managers actually do. For example, he rejected secondary sources as not allowing the researcher to be

Table 10.1   Seven methods to study managerial work

Method	Applications	Major advantage(s)	Major disadvantage(s)	Appropriate use
Secondary sources	Neustadt (1960)	Convenient; draws on analyses of others	Data frequently unavailable, inappropriate, or incomplete	To study job of inaccessible manager
Questionnaire and interview	Stogdill, Shartle and Associates (1956)	Convenient	Data of questionable reliability	To study manager's perception of his or her job
Critical incident and sequence of episodes	Flanagan (1954) Marples (1967)	Allows for intense probing	Parts of job not covered by the data	To study certain aspects of job indepth (e.g. decision-making)
Diary	Carlson (1951) Stewart (1965)	Efficient (i.e. large sample possible relative to researcher's time investment)	No help in developing understanding of new dimensions; some problems with interpretation, consistency, and reliability	To study characterisitcs of large sample of differing managerial jobs
Activity sampling	Kelly (1964) Wirdenius (1958)	Efficient; recording by researcher	Little help in developing understanding of new dimensions; non-continuous, hence interpretation difficult	To study observational aspects of different jobs in one location
Unstructured observation	Sayles (1964) Dalton (1959) Hodgson, Levinson and Zaleznik (1965)	Enables researcher to understand new dimensions and to probe	Non-systematic (may lose important data; cannot replicate); inefficient	To study the most complex, least understood aspects of manager's job (content)
Structured observation	Guest (1956) Ponder (1957) Mintzberg (1973) Radomsky (1967)	Enables researcher to understand new dimensions, to probe, to be systematic	Inefficient (consumes much researcher time); difficult to interpret some activities	To study at same time content and characterisitcs of small sample of managers' jobs

Source: Mintzberg, 1973, p. 229 Copyright ©1973 by Henry Mintzberg. Reprinted by permission of Harper & Row, Publishers, Inc.

comprehensive, and further as only very important national figures, in the example quoted US presidents (Neustadt, 1960), would be likely to have generated the depth of data required. While, on the face of it the simplest way to discover what managers do would appear to be to ask them through interviews and questionnaires, these methods were also rejected 'as there is ample evidence from empirical studies cited in Appendix A that managers are poor estimators of their own activities' and there is no evidence that managers can 'translate complex reality into meaningful abstractions' (Mintzberg, 1973, p. 222). Similarly, critical incidents, diary methods and activity sampling were all rejected as some were discontinuous, others gave little help in understanding new dimensions and lacked consistency. Unstructured observation, of the kind to which we referred in Chapter 7 (e.g. Sayles, 1958, 1964; Dalton, 1959), had several advantages to Mintzberg (1973, p. 226) in that it was 'purely inductive . . . nothing need stand between the work . . . [the researcher] . . . observes and the theory he develops save his own ability to interpret.' Further, if items of particular interest arose, or there was a lack of clarity, the researcher was on the spot and could easily discover more. Mintzberg felt, however, that unstructured observation was unsystematic and difficult to replicate; and, further, was perhaps less likely to be comprehensive in that it was open to researcher selectivity. Having then systematically reviewed possible methods Mintzberg turned to what he calls structured observation and, in later reflections on his methods used over a long period and outlined below, 'direct' research (Mintzberg, 1979a). As we have noted earlier, such an approach seemed to offer the advantages of inductive, unstructured observation and systematic recording and reflection, the former preceding the latter.

After several years reflecting on more of his research work using these strategies Mintzberg lists seven basic themes that have characterized his research and act as justification for his approach (Mintzberg, 1979a). After reviewing his research activities, which at the time included one book about organizational structuring (1979b) and another, then in preparation, about 'power in and around organizations' (1980), Mintzberg came to the conclusion that work in the policy area of management has benefited from purely descriptive research. Pure description has, in his view, raised doubts about much that was previously taken for granted – highlighting, for example, that strategy formation is in reality a discontinuous process rather than a formally and rationally planned one as had been previously proclaimed. Second, Mintzberg (1979a, p. 583) believes that the 'field of organization theory has paid dearly for the obsession with rigour in the choice of methodology'. Simpler, more direct methodologies, such as tracing the flow of decisions in an organization, have, he believes, produced more useful results than those which have been significant in only the statistical sense. Small samples, such as the sample of five managers in his research on managerial work (1973), especially in exploratory research should, he feels, be encouraged rather 'than less valid data that were statistically significant' (1979a). Further, his research has been as 'purely inductive' as possible, the first step in induction being what Mintzberg calls 'detective work' (when the researcher looks for order and patterns) and the second the 'creative leap' which entails generalizing beyond one's data. As we have seen this does not of course imply that such research is unsystematic or unfocused, but categories are not abstract and have a close relationship with the organization's actual functioning, often supported with anecdotal evidence. Finally, in his work on organizations, Mintzberg looks for the synthesis of elements into patterns rather than categories coming from 'mechanical data reduction techniques' (Mintzberg, 1979a, p. 588).

This, then, is how one very experienced and influential researcher justifies his methodological approach to investigating the ways in which managers and organizations function. Nevertheless, the pervasive, positivist traditions of our culture die hard, not only in the way students seem obsessed with sample sizes irrespective of research objective and context but also even in their influence on funding bodies. It was, for example, one of the authors' experience to engage in a discussion with a steering group, appointed by a funding body to oversee the research, about the strategy to be pursued at the outset of work to investigate the effects of centrally imposed financial constraints on the management of the public sector of higher education (Gill and Pratt, 1986). The research team favoured in-depth treatment of a limited number of cases in an under-researched and relatively novel area whereas the members of the steering group were concerned about the difficulty of generalizing from the small sample chosen, favouring a survey across all institutions. Generalizability was of course a legitimate worry, but we felt we would be more likely to produce valid findings in a relatively under-researched area if data was taken in depth from a few cases. It was not possible, given the level of resourcing, to pursue an ideal strategy and do both. The alternative – to spread our resources thinly in undertaking a national survey across a very large number of organizations – seemed to us much less desirable, particularly as we believed the data generated would be likely to be trivial and not achieve jointly agreed objectives. It was gratifying that by the end of the project the members of the steering committee had come round to our view.

Multi-methods, linking methods and triangulation

These terms are frequently used interchangeably; some, however, attach special meanings to them. For example, Denzin (1970, p. 297) defines triangulation, a term derived from surveying, as 'the combination of methodologies in the study of the same phenomenon'. Multiple and independent methods, especially if undertaken by different research workers investigating the same problem, should (he argued), if reaching the same conclusions, have greater validity and reliability than a single methodological approach to a problem.

Triangulation is also described as multi-method/multi-trait (Campbell and Fiske, 1959) or convergent validation, and for the most part shares the notion of complementary qualitative and quantitative methodologies rather than competing approaches (Jick, 1979a; Fielding and Fielding, 1986). In Miller and Friesen's (1982) advocacy of longitudinal designs to analyse organizations both qualitative and quantitative methodologies are suggested.

In other treatments triangulation is given a more limited role in, for example, strengthening qualitative research findings by combining participant observation, interviewing and documentary sources (Hammersley and Atkinson, 1983). Many textbook accounts (e.g. H. W. Smith, 1975) advocate multiple methods to address the same problems, on the basis that in this way different methodological strengths and weaknesses will be cancelled out to produce more convincing findings. It should be borne in mind, however, that one of Martin's (1982) myths of the rational research model is that any methodological choice should lead to the same set of theoretical conclusions; and we will consider this matter below. First we provide an example of an attempt to triangulate methodologies.

Jick (1979a) describes his doctoral project (Jick, 1979b) to study the effects of a merger of hospitals on their employees as an example of triangulation. As is usual in merger cases there was high employee anxiety and one of the main purposes of the research was to discover the sources and symptoms of this stress and its impact on the operation of the newly created organization.

On the basis of a review of research methods, especially those designed to collect data on the complex topic of employee stress, Jick decided that there was no ideal, sole method of collecting such data. There were a number of possibilities. He decided he might interview employees; use some indirect form of projective test; ask those interacting with the focal person; systematically observe the person's behaviour; measure physiological symptoms, and so on. Clearly all these strategies had strengths and weaknesses which suggested some form of triangulation, and a design accordingly emerged using a combination of methods. Methods eventually used in practice were surveys distributed to a random sample of the population, followed by semi-structured, probing interviews; interviews were also conducted with supervisors and co-workers to ascertain their observation of particular employees.

In addition, and particularly fruitful, was data based upon unobtrusive measures (Webb *et al.*, 1969) and non-participant observation as well as archival materials. For example, what is described as an 'anxiety thermometer' was developed from an observation by the archivist in one of the organizations that employees frequently used comprehensive newspaper files to compare recent reports of the organization's future with those in the past. Employees were evidently seeking information to relieve their anxieties, and it was hypothesized that the more people visited the archives the higher their level of anxiety. Such data was compared with that derived from other data sources such as interviews and surveys and the hypothesis for the most part confirmed.

Quantitative data sources were used largely to supplement qualitative data but, as Jick observes, 'it is a delicate exercise to decide whether or not results have converged . . . should all components of a multimethod approach be weighted equally? . . . there are no formal tests to discriminate methods to judge their applicability' (Jick, 1979a, p. 607). Nevertheless, in Jick's judgement the various methods taken together produced convergent findings. There were some discrepant findings, but data sources (whether divergent or discrepant) may of course be equally valuable, and discrepant findings are likely to enrich explanations. In this particular case, for example, some employees, known to be highly stressed on the basis of surveys of self-reports, were apparently least likely to visit the archive files. The discrepancy was investigated by conducting further interviews and observations, which helped to reconcile the apparently conflicting data by suggesting that poorly educated employees tended to rely more on oral communications than written documents.

Despite the success of this project, multi-methods are infrequently used in research both in management and business and, for that matter, elsewhere. There are perhaps a number of reasons for this neglect, some practical and some methodological. As we have seen, methodologically triangulation is difficult but practical concerns are probably more crucial. Multi-methods are extremely time consuming and costly and what is more, as Martin (1982) has pointed out, journals tend to have their particular methodological fancies and less preferred methods are accordingly discouraged. For the student setting out to design a project in a limited time the ideal methodological solution of using multi-methods, particularly with methods that are well separated from one another, may be impracticable. However, for students undertaking extended pieces of work such as research degrees, and particularly for those working in research teams, multi-methods may be especially appropriate.

We have tended to use the terms 'triangulation' and 'multi-methods' interchangeably. Brewer and Hunter (1989), however, differentiate triangulation from multi-methods by regarding the former as an aspect of the multi-method approach, to which they give much wider usage and implications. As they suggest, 'theorizing and theory testing, problem formulation and data collection, sampling and generalization, hypothesis testing and causal analysis, social problems and policy analysis, and even the writing and publication of results may benefit from bringing a multimethod perspective to bear on social research' (Brewer and Hunter, 1989, pp. 11–12). We believe this is also true for management research.

Management and research: a conclusion

In Chapter 1 we drew attention to the parallels between the research and managerial processes. We return to this matter in concluding this book, in the belief that management research is useful not only in itself in substantive problem solving but also, through the process of engagement in research, as a means of management development. The process of reflective conversation advocated as a model of research inquiry (Morgan, 1983) is paralleled by Schon's study of five professions, including the managerial (Schon, 1983). Managers cope with uncertainty, complexity, instability and uniqueness and seem to conduct a pattern of reflection in action. As Schon puts it:

> it is clear that managers do sometimes reflect-in-action. Beginning with questions like, What do customers really see in our product? What's really going on underneath the signs of trouble in our organisation? or What can we

learn from our encounters with the competition? managers try to make sense of the unique phenomena before them. They surface and question their intuitive understandings: and in order to test their new interpretations, they undertake on-the-spot experiments. Not infrequently, their experiments yield surprising results that cause them to reformulate their questions. They engage in reflective conversations with their situation.

(Schon, 1983, pp. 264–5)

This behaviour is essentially similar in practice to the position we have suggested for the management researcher. It is our belief that managers, and especially those on part-time programmes such as the MBA, may be readily equipped to act as researchers in their own organizations by building upon what effective managers actually do in practice. If in some way we have facilitated this, particularly by suggesting a broader range of potential research strategies, our work will have been worth while.

Suggested further reading

G. Morgan's *Beyond Method* includes contributions from a large number of authors on a wide range of research strategies. There is a useful introduction and conclusion dealing, among other issues, with the problem of choosing research strategies.

J. E. McGrath, J. Martin, and R. A. Kulka's (1982) *Judgement Calls in Research* contrasts the actual research process with the textbook versions and points up the dilemmas in choosing a research strategy.

On the subject of multi-method strategies the following may be found helpful: N. K. Denzin's *The Research Act: A Theoretical Introduction to Sociological Methods*, N. G. and J. L. Fielding's *Linking Data*, and J. Brewer and A. Hunter's *Multimethod Research: A Synthesis of Styles*. This last we have found especially useful as an advocacy of multi-method approaches to social research applied to all phases of research endeavour. Its only weaknesses, given our objectives, are that it is somewhat theoretical for the naïve management researcher and its examples are derived broadly from the social sciences.

(Full details of these works are given in the References, which follow.)

References

Adler, P. A. and Adler, P. (1987) *Membership Roles in Field Research*, Sage University Paper Series on Qualitative Research Methods, Vol. 6, Sage, Beverly Hills, Calif.

Ahlgren, A. and Walberg, H. J. (1979) Generalised regression analysis, in Bynner and Stribley (1978).

Alderfer, C. (1968) Organisational diagnosis from initial client reactions to a researcher, *Human Relations*, Vol. 27, Fall, pp. 260–5.

Arbib, M. A. and Hesse, M. B. (1986) *The Construction of Reality*, Cambridge University Press.

Argyris, C. (1980) *Inner Contradictions of Rigorous Research*, Academic Press, London.

Argyris, D. (1985) The ethnographic approach to intervention and fundamental change, in Argyris, Putman and Smith (1985).

Argyris, C., Putman, R. and Smith, D. M. (1985) *Action Science*, Jossey Bass, San Francisco.

Armstrong, P. J., Goodman, J. F. B. and Hyman, J. D.(1981) *Ideology and Shop Floor Relations*, Croom Helm, Beckenham.

Asch, S. E. (1951) Effects of group pressure upon the modification and distortion of judgements, in M. Guetzkow (ed.) *Groups, Leadership and Men*, Carnegie Press, Pittsburg, P.A.

Banaka, W. H. (1971) *Training in Depth Interviewing*, Harper & Row, London.

Barnes, B. (1974) *Scientific Knowledge and Sociological Theory*, Routledge, London.

Barnes, B. (1977) *Interests and the Growth of Knowledge*, Routledge, London.

Barnes, J. A. (1979) *Who Should Know What?*, Penguin, Harmondsworth.

Batstone, E., Boraston, I. and Frenkel, S. (1977) *Shop Stewards in Action: The Organisation of Workplace Conflict and Accommodation*, Blackwell, Oxford.

Bechhofer, F. (1974) Current approaches to empirical research: some central ideas, in J. Rex (ed.) *Approaches to Sociology*, Routledge, London.

Bechhofer, F., Elliott, B. and McCrone, D. (1984) Safety in numbers: on the use of multiple interviewers, *Sociology*, Vol. 18. no. 1, pp. 97–100.

Becker, H. S. (1965) Review of P. E. Hammond's *Sociologists at Work*, *American Sociological Review*, Vol. 30, pp. 602–3.

Becker, H. S. (1966) Introduction, in C. R. Shaw, *The Jack Roller: A Delinquent Boy's Own Story*, University of Chicago Press.

Becker, H. S. (1970) *Sociological Work*, Aldine, Chicago.

Bell, C. and Newby, H. (1977) *Doing Sociological Research*, Macmillan, New York.

Bell, J. (1987) *Doing Your Research Project*, Open University Press, Milton Keynes.

Bennett, R. and Gill, J. (1978) The role of research in a regional management centre, *Management Education and Development*, December, pp. 151–61.

Berger, P. L. and Luckmann, T. (1967) *The Social Construction of Reality*, Penguin, Harmondsworth.

Beynon, H. (1973) *Working for Ford*, Penguin, Harmondsworth.

Beynon, H. (1988) Regulating research: politics and decision making in industrial organisations, in Bryman (1988).

Bloor, D. (1976) *Knowledge and Social Imagery*, Routledge, London.

Bloor, M. (1976) Bishop Berkeley and the adenotonsillectomy enigma: an explanation of variation in the social construction of medical disposals, *Sociology*, Vol. 10, pp. 43–61.

Bloor, M. (1978) On the analysis of observational data: a discussion of the worth and uses of inductive techniques and respondent validation, *Sociology*. Vol. 12. pp. 545–2.

Blumer, H. (1954) What is wrong with social theory, *American Sociological Review*, Vol. 19, no. 13, pp. 3–10.

Blumer, H. (1967) *Symbolic Interactionism*. Prentice-Hall, Englewood Cliffs, NJ.

Blumer, H. (1971) Society as symbolic interaction, in A. N. Rose (ed.) *Human Behaviour and Social Processes*, Routledge, London.

Boyd, W. B. and Westfall, R. (1970) Interviewer bias once more revisited, *Journal of Marketing Research*, Vol. 7, pp. 249–53.

Bracht, G. H. and Glass, G. U. (1968) The external validity of experiments, *American Education Research Journal*, no. 5, pp. 537–74

Braithwaite, J. (1985) Corporate crime research: why two interviewers are needed, *Sociology*, Vol. 19, no. 1, pp. 136–8.

Brannen, P. (1987) Working on directors: some methodological issues, in Moyser and Wagstaffe (1987).

Brannen, P., Batstone, D., Fatchett, D. and White, P. (1976) *Worker Directors*, Hutchinson, London.

Braverman, H. (1974) *Labour and Monopoly Capital: The Degradation of Work in the Twentieth Century*, Monthly Review Press, New York.

Brewer, J. and Hunter, A. (1989) *Multimethod Research: A Synthesis of Styles*, Sage Library of Social Research, Vol. 175, Sage, Calif.

Brown, R. (1965) *Social Psychology*, Free Press, Glencoe.

Brunswick, E. C. (1956) *Perception and the Representative Design of Psychological Experiments*, University of California Press, Berkeley.

Bryman, A. (ed.) (1988) *Doing Research in Organisations*, Routledge, London.

Burgess, R. G. (1984) *In the Field: An Introduction to Field Research*, Allen & Unwin, London.

Burgess, R. G. and Bulmer, M. (1981) Research methodology teaching: trends and developments, *Sociology*, Vol. 15, pp. 477–89.

Burrell, G. and Morgan, G. (1979) *Sociological Paradigms and Organisational Analysis*, Heinemann, London.

Bygrave, W. D. (1989) The entrepreneurship paradigm (1): a philosophical look at its research methodologies, *Entrepreneurship: Theory and Practice*, Vol. 14, no. 1. Fall, pp. 7–26.

Bynner, J. and Stribley, K. M. (eds) (1978) *Social Research, Principles and Proceedures*, Longman, London.

Campbell, D. T. (1969) Reforms as experiments, in Bynner and K. M. Stribley (1978).

Campbell, D. T. and Fiske, D. W. (1959) Convergent and discriminant validation by the multitrait – multimethod matrix. *Psychological Bulletin*. Vol. 56., pp. 81–5.

Campbell, D. T. and Ross, H. L. (1968) The Connecticut crackdown on speeding: time series data in quasi-experimental analysis, *Law and Society Review*, Vol. 3, no. 1, pp. 33–53.

Campbell, D. T. and Stanley, J. C. (1963) *Experimental and Quasi-Experimental Designs for Research*, Rand McNally, Chicago.

Campbell, J. P., Daft, R.L. and Hulin, C. L. (1982) *What to Study: Generating and Developing Research Questions*, Sage, London.

Capra, F. (1975) *The Tap of Physics*, Wildwood, London.

Carchedi, G. (1983) Class analysis and social forms, in Morgan (1983).

Carlson, S. (1951) *Executive Behaviour: A Study of the Work Load and Working Methods of Managing Directors*, Strombergs, Stockholm.

Cartwright, D. (1973) Determinants of scientific progress: the case of research on the risky shift, *American Psychologist*, Vol. 28, pp. 222–31.

Checkland, P. (1981) *Systems Thinking, Systems Practice.*, Wiley, Chichester, U.K.

Chua, W. F. (1986a) Theoretical constructions of and by the real, *Accounting, Organisations and Society*, Vol. 11. no. 6, pp. 583–98.

Chua, W. F. (1986b) Radical developments in accounting thought, *The Accounting Review*, Vol. LXI, no. 4, pp. 601–32.

Chubin, D. E. and Restivo, S. (1983) The 'mooting' of social studies: research programmes and science policy in K. D. Knorr-Cetina and M. Mulkay (eds) *Science Observed: Perspectives on the Social Study of Science*, Sage, London.

Churchman, C. W. (1971) *The Design of Inquiring Systems*, Basic Books, New York.

Cicourel, A. (1964) *Method and Measurement in Sociology*, Free Press, Glencoe.

Cohen, D., March, J. G. and Olsen, J. P. (1972) A garbage can model of organisational choice. *Administrative Science Quarterly*, Vol. 17, pp. 1–25.

Cook, T. D. (1983) Quasi-experimentation: its ontology, epistemology and methodology in Morgan (1983).

Cooper, H. M. (1989) *Integrating Research: A Guide for Literature Reviews*, 2nd ed, Applied Social Research Methods Series, Vol. 2, Sage, London.

Covin, J. B. and Slevin, D. P. (1988) The influence of organisation structure on the utility of an entrepreneurial top management style, *Journal of Management Studies*, Vol. 23, no. 3, pp. 217–34.

Cressey, D. (1950) The criminal violation of financial trust, *American Sociological Review*, Vol. 15, pp. 738–43.

Cronbach, L. J. and Meehl, P. E. (1955) Construct validity in psychological tests, in Bynner and K. Stribley (1978).

Cunnison, S. (1966) *Wages and Work Allocation*, Tavistock, London.

Dalton, M. (1959) *Men Who Manage,* Wiley, New York.

Dalton, M. (1964) Preconceptions and methods in *Men who Manage*, in Hammond (1964).

De Bono, F. (1971) *Lateral Thinking for Management*, McGraw-Hill, London.

Denzin, N. K. (1970) *The Research Act; A Theoretical Introduction to Sociological Methods*, Aldine, Chicago.

Denzin, N. K. (1978) *Sociological Methods: A Sourcebook*, McGraw-Hill, New York.

Diesing, P. O. (1972) *Patterns of Discovery in the Social Sciences*, Routledge, London.

Dingwall, R. (1980) Ethics and ethnography. *Sociological Review*, Vol. 28, no. 4. pp. 871–91.

Douglas, J. D. (ed.) (1970) *Understanding Everyday Life*, Routledge, London.

Douglas, J. D. (1976) *Investigative Social Research: Individual and Team Field Research*, Sage, London.

Doyal, L. and Harris, R. (1986) *Empiricism, Explanation and Rationality*, Routledge, London.

Drummond, H. (1989) A note on applying lateral thinking to data collection, *Graduate Management Research*, Summer, pp. 4–6.

Dubs, H. H. (1930) *Rational Induction*, Chicago University Press.

Ehrenberg, A. S. C. (1982) *A Primer in Data Reduction: An Introductory Statistics Textbook*, Wiley, New York.

Eilon, S. (1974) Seven faces of research, *Omega*, Vol. 2, no. 1, pp. 1–9.

Eisenhardt, K. M. (1989) Building theories from case study research, *Academy of Management Review*, Vol. 14, no. 4. pp. 532–50.

Evered, R. and Lewis, M. R. (1981) Alternative perspectives in the organisational sciences: 'inquiry from the inside' and 'inquiry from the outside', *Academy of Management Review*, Vol. 6, no. 3, pp. 385–95.

Fay, B. (1975) *Social Theory and Political Practice*, Allen & Unwin, London.

Fetterman, D.M. (1989) *Ethnography: Step by Step*, Applied Social Research Methods Series, Vol. 17, Sage, Beverly Hills, Calif.

Feyerabend, P. (1975) *Against Method*, New Left Books, London.

Fielding, N. G. (1988) Between micro and macro, in N. G. Fielding (ed.) *Actions and Structure*, Sage, London.

Fielding, N. G. and Fielding, J. L. (1986) *Linking Data*, Sage University Paper Series on Qualitative Research Methods, Vol. 4, Sage, Beverly Hills, Calif.

Flanagan, J. C. (1954) The critical incident technique, *Psychological Bulletin.* Vol. 51, pp. 327–58.

Frame, P. G. (1987) *The management of stringency and the nature of organisational sub-cultures*, unpublished Ph.D. thesis, Sheffield City Polytechnic.

Frey, J. H. (1989) *Survey Research by Telephone*, 2nd ed, Sage, London.

Friedman, M. (1953) *Essays in Positive Economics*, University of Chicago Press.

Gadamer, H. (1975) *Truth and Method*, Sheed and Ward, London.

Galliers, R. D. (1985) In search of a paradigm for information systems research, in Mumford *et al.* (1985).

Garfinkel, H. (1967) *Studies in Ethnomethodology*, Prentice-Hall, Englewood Cliffs, NJ.

Gauld, A. and Shotter, J. (1977) *Human Action and the Psychological Investigation*, Routledge, London.

Geertz, C. (1973) *The Interpretation of Cultures*, Basic Books, New York.

Giddens, A. (1976) *New Rules of Sociological Method*, Hutchinson, London.

Giddens, A. (1978) Positivism and its criticisms, in T. Bottomore and R. Nesbit (eds.) *A History of Sociological Analysis*, Heinemann, London.

Giddens, A. (ed.) (1979) *Positivism and Sociology*, Heinemann Educational, London.

Giddens, A. (1984) *The Construction of Society*, Polity Press, London.

Gill, J. (1985) *Factors Affecting the Survival and Growth of the Smaller Company*, Gower Studies in Small Business, Gower, Aldershot.

Gill, J. (1986) Research as action: an experiment in utilising the social sciences, in Heller (1986).

Gill, J. (1988) Providing effective help to infant business in areas of high unemployment. *International Small Business Journal*, Vol. 7, no. 2, pp. 43–51.

Gill, J. and Pratt, J. (1986) *Responses to Financial Constraint of Institutions of Higher Education in the Public Sector*, Department of Education and Science, London.

Gill, J., Golding D. and Angluin, D. (1989) Management development and doctoral research, *Management Education and Development*, Vol. 20, pt. 1, pp 77–84.

Gladwin, C. H. (1989) *Ethnographic Decision Tree Modelling*, Sage University Paper Series on Qualitative Research Methods, Vol. 19, Sage, Beverly Hills, Calif.

Glaser, B. G. and Strauss, A. L. (1967) *The Discovery of Grounded Theory*, Aldine, Chicago.

Glidewell, J. C. (1959) The entry problem in consultation, *Journal of Social Issues*, Vol. 15, no. 2, pp. 1–59.

Godsland, J. M. and Fielding, N. G. (1985) Children convicted of grave crimes, *Howard Journal of Criminal Justice*, Vol. 24, no. 3, pp. 282–97.

Goffman, E. (1968) *Asylums*, Penguin, Harmondsworth.

Goffman, E. (1969) *The Presentation of Self in Everyday Life*, Penguin, Harmondsworth.

Goffman, E. (1971) *Interaction Ritual*, Allen Lane, Penguin Press, Harmondsworth.

Gold, R. (1958) Roles in sociological field observation, *Social Forces*, Vol. 36, no. 3, pp. 217–23.

Golding, D. (1977) An attempt to gain commitment for organisation development in an engineering company in the north of England, unpublished M.Sc. thesis, Sheffield City Polytechnic.

Golding, D. (1979) Some symbolic manifestations of power in Industrial Organisations, unpublished Ph.D. thesis, Sheffield City Polytechnic.

Golding, D. (1986) On becoming a manager, *Organisation Studies*, Issue 2, Special Issue: Organisation Symbolism, Vol. 7, no. 2, pp. 193–8.

Gorman, R. A. (1977) *The Dual Vision*, Routledge, London.

Gouldner, A. W. (1954a) *Wildcat Strike*, Harper & Row, New York.

Gouldner, A. W. (1954b) *Patterns of Industrial Bureaucracy*, Free Press, Glencoe, N.Y.

Gouldner, A. W. (1962) Anti-minotaur: the myth of a value-free sociology, *Social Problems*, Vol. 9, Winter, pp. 199–213.

Gouldner, A. W. (1970) *The Coming Crisis of Western Sociology*, Heinemann, London.

Gowler, D. and Legge, K. (1986) Personnel and paradigms: four perspectives on utopia, *Industrial Relations Journal*, Vol. 17, pp. 225–35.

Grafton-Small, R. (1985) *Marketing managers: the evocation and structure of socially negotiated meaning*, unpublished Ph.D. thesis, Sheffield City Polytechnic.

Green, P. E. (1978) *Analysing Multivariate Data*, Hinsdale H. Dryden Press,

Gubrium, J. F. and Silverman, D. (eds) (1989) *The Politics of Field Research*, Sage, London.

Guest, R. H. (1955–6) Of time and the foreman, *Personnel*, Vol. 32, pp. 478–86.

Habermas, J. (1974a) *Theory and Practice*, Heinemann, London.

Habermas, J. (1974b) Rationalism divided in two: a reply to Albert, in Giddens (1979).

Hammersley, M. and Atkinson, P. (1983) *Ethnography: Principles in Practice*, Tavistock, London.

Hammond, P. E. (1964) *Sociologists at Work: Essays on the Craft of Social Research*, Basic Books, New York.

Hanson, N. R. (1958) *Patterns of Discovery*, Cambridge University Press.

Harvey-Jones, J. (1989) *Making it Happen: Reflections on Leadership*, Fontana, London.

Heller, F. (ed.) (1986) *The Use and Abuse of Social Science*, Sage, London.

Herbelein, T. H. and Baumgarter, R. (1978) Factors affecting response rates to mailed questionnaires: a quantitative analysis of the published literature. *American Sociological Review*, Vol. 43, no. 4, pp. 447–62.

Hersen, M. and Barlow, D. H. (1976) *Single Case Experimental Designs: Strategies for Studying Behaviour Change*, Pergamon, New York.

Herzberg, F., Mausner, B. and Snyderman, B. (1959) *The Motivation to Work*, Wiley, New York.

Hindess, B. (1977) *Philosophy and Methodology in Social Science*, Harvester, Hassocks.

Hirschheim, R. A. (1985) Information systems epistemology: an historical perspective in E. E. Mumford *et al.* (1985).

Hodgson, R. C. Levinson, D. J. and Zaleznik, A. (1965) *The Executive Role Constellation: An Analysis of Personality and Role Relations in Management*, Harvard Business School, Division of Research, Boston, Mass.

Hooker, C. A. (1973) Empiricism, perception and conceptual change. *Canadian Journal of Philosophy*, Vol. 3, pp. 59–75.

Hopper, T. and Powell, A. (1985) Making sense of reason in the organisational and social aspects of management accounting: a review of its underlying assumptions, *Journal of Management Studies*, Vol. 22, no. 5, pp. 429–65.

House, R. J. (1970) Scientific investigation in management, *Management International Review*, Vol. 4/5, no. 10, pp. 139–50.

Howard, K. and Sharp, J. A. (1983) *The Management of a Student Research Project*, Gower, Aldershot.

Hunt, J. C. (1979) *Psychoanalytic Aspects of Fieldwork*, Sage University Paper Series on Qualitative Research Methods, Vol. 18, Sage, Newbury Park, Calif.

Janis, I. L. (1972) *Victims of Groupthink*, Houghton Mifflin, Boston, Mass.

Jantsch, E. (1967) *Technological Forecasting in Perspective*, OECD, Paris.

Jaques, E. (1951) *The Changing Culture of a Factory*, Tavistock, London.

Jick, T. J. (1979a) Mixing qualitative and quantitative methods: triangulation in action, *Administrative Science Quarterly*, Vol. 24, December, pp. 602–11.

Jick, T. J. (1979b) Process and impacts of merger: individual and organisational perspectives, unpublished Doctoral Dissertation, New York State School of Industrial and Labor Relations, Cornell University.

Johnson, J. M. (1975) *Doing Field Research*, Free Press, Glencoe.

Johnson, P. D. (1989) The impact of the disclosure of accounting information upon aspects of industrial relations, unpublished Ph.D. thesis, Sheffield City Polytechnic.

Junker, B. H. (1960) *Fieldwork*, University of Chicago Press.

Keat, R. and Urry, J. (1975) *Social Theory as Science*, Routledge, London.

Kelly, J. (1964) The study of executive behaviour by activity sampling, *Human Relations*, Vol. 17, pp. 227–87.

Kelman, H. C. (1967) Human use of human subjects: the problem of deception in social psychological experiments, in Bynner and Stribley (1978).

Kidder, L. H. and Judd, C. M. (1986) *Research Methods in Social Relations*, 8th Ed, Holt Rinehart and Winston, London.

Kish, L. (1965) *Survey Sampling*, Wiley, New York.

Kolakowski, L. (1969) Karl Marx and the classical definition of truth, in *Marxism and Beyond*, Pall Mall Press, London.

Kolb, D. A., Rubin, I. M. and McIntyre, J. M. (1979) *Organisational Psychology: An Experiential Approach*, Prentice Hall, London.

Kotter, J. P. (1982) *The General Managers*, Free Press, Collier Macmillan, London.

Krausz, E. and Miller, S. H. (1974) *Social Research Design*, Longman, London.

Kuhn, T. (1970) *The Structure of Scientific Revolutions*, 2nd Ed, University of Chicago Press.

Kulka, R. A. (1982) Idiosyncrasy and circumstance: choices and constraints in the research process, in McGrath, Martin and Kulka (1982).

Laing, R. D. (1967) *The Politics of Experience and the Birds of Paradise*, Penguin, Harmondsworth.

Lane, T and Roberts, K. (1971) *Strike at Pilkingtons*, Fontana, London.

Law, J. and Lodge, P. (1984) *Science for Social Scientists*, Macmillan, London.

Lawler, E. E. and Rhode, J. R. (1976) *Information and Control in Organizations*, Goodyear, London.

Lessnoff, M. (1974) *The Structure of Social Science*, Allen & Unwin, London.

Lewin, K. (1946) Action research and minority problems, *Journal of Social Issues*, Vol. 2, no. 4, pp. 34–46.

Lindesmith, A. R. (1952) Comment on W. S. Robinson's The logic and structure of analytic induction, *American Sociological Review*, Vol. 17, pp. 492–3.

Linstead, S. A. (1984) Ambiguity in the workplace: some aspects of the negotiation and structuration of asymetrical relations, unpublished Ph.D. thesis, Sheffield City Polytechnic.

Lumley, R. (1978) A study of industrial relations on a large construction site, unpublished Ph.D. thesis, Sheffield City Polytechnic.

Lupton, T. (1963) *On the Shop Floor*, Pergamon, Oxford.

Lupton, T. (1971) *Management and the Social Sciences*, Penguin, Harmondsworth.

McAuley, J. M. (1985) Hermeneutics as a practical research methodology in management, *Management Education and Development*, Vol. 16, pt. 3, pp. 292–9.

McCall, G. J. and Simmons, J. L. (1969) *Issues in Participant Observation*, Addison-Wesley, Wokingham.

McCracken, G. (1988) *The Long Interview*, Sage University Paper Series on Qualitative Research Methods, Vol. 13, Sage, Beverly Hills, Calif.

McGrath, J. E. (1982) Dilemmatics: the study of research choices and dilemmas in McGrath, Martin and Kulka (1982).

McGrath, J. E., Martin, J. and Kulka, R. A. (1982) *Judgement Calls in Research*, Sage, London.

McGrath, M. A. (1989) An ethnography of a gift store: trappings, wrappings and rapture- *Journal of Retailing* Vol. 65, no. 4, Winter, pp. 421–9.

McHugh, P. (1971) On the failure of positivism, in Douglas (1971).

Madge, J. H. (1953) *The Tools of Social Science*, Longman, London.

Mant, A. (1977) *The Rise and Fall of the British Manager*, Macmillan, London.

Maranell, G. M. (ed.) (1974) *Scaling: A Sourcebook for Behavioral Scientists*, Aldine, Chicago.

Margolis, J. (1986) *Pragmatism without Foundations*, Blackwell, Oxford.

Marples, D. L. (1967) Studies of managers – a fresh start?, *Journal of Management Studies*, Vol. 4, pp. 282–99.

Martin, J. (1982) A garbage can model of the research process, in McGrath, Martin and Kulka (1982).

Maslow, A. M. (1943) A theory of human motivation, *Psychological Review*, Vol. 50, pp. 370–96.

Mason, R. O. and Mitroff, I. I. (1981) *Challenging Strategic Planning Assumptions*, Wiley, New York.

Mattick, J. P. (1986) *Social Knowledge*, Hutchinson, London.

Mead, G. H. (1934) *Mind, Self and Society*, Chicago University Press.

Mehan, H. and Wood, H. (1975) *The Reality of Ethnomethodology*, Wiley, London.

Miles, M. and Huberman, A. M. (1984) *Qualitative Data Analysis*, Sage, Beverly Hills, Calif.

Milgram, S. (1963) Behavioural Study of Obedience. *Journal of Abnormal Social Psychology*, Vol. 67, pp. 371–8.

Milgram, S. (1974) *Obedience to Authority*. London, Tavistock.

Mill, J. S. (1874) *A System of Logic*, Longman Green, London.

Miller, D. and Friesen, P. H. (1982) The longitudinal analysis of organisations, *Management Science*, Vol. 28, no. 9, pp. 1013–34.

Miller, E. J. (1983) *Work and Creativity*, Occasional Paper no. 6, The Tavistock Institute of Human Relations, London.

Mintzberg, H. (1973) *The Nature of Managerial Work*, Harper & Row, New York.

Mintzberg, H. (1979a) An emerging strategy of 'direct' research, *Administrative Science Quarterly*, Vol. 24, December, pp. 582–9.

Mintzberg, H. (1979b) *The Structuring of Organisations*, Prentice-Hall, Englewood Cliffs, NJ.

Mintzberg, H. (1980) *Power In and Around Organisations*, Prentice-Hall, Englewood Cliffs, NJ.

Mitchell, J. C. (1983) Case and situational analysis, *Sociological Review*, Vol. 31, pp. 187–211.

Mitroff, I. I. (1974) *The Subjective Side of Science*, Elsevier, Amsterdam.

Morgan, D. H. J. (1972) The British Association scandal: the effect of publicity on a sociological investigation, *Sociological Review*, Vol. 20, no. 2, pp. 185–206.

Morgan, G. (ed.) (1983) *Beyond Method*, Sage, London.

Morgan, G (1986) *Images of Organisation*, Sage, London.

Moser, C. A. and Kalton, G. (1971) *Survey Methods and Social Investigation*, Heinemann, London.

Moyser, B. and Wagstaffe, M. (eds) (1987) *Research Methods for Elite Studies*, Allen & Unwin, London.

Mumford, E. E., Hirschheim, R., Fitzgerald, G. and Wood-Harper, A. T. (eds) (1985) *Research Methods in Information Systems*, Elsevier Science Publishers BV, Amsterdam.

Myers, C.S. (1924) *Industrial Psychology in Great Britain*, Cape, London.

Neurath, O. (1959) Sociology and physicalism, in A. J. Ayer (ed.) *Logical Positivism*, Free Press, New York.

Neustadt, R. E. (1960) *Presidential Power: the Politics of Leadership*, Wiley, New York.

Nichols, T. and Armstrong, P. (1976) *Workers Divided*, Fontana, London.

Nie, N. H., Hull, C. H. and others (1975) *Statistical Package for the Social Sciences*, 2nd edn, McGraw-Hill, New York.

Noble, F. (1989) Organisational design and the implementation of office information systems, unpublished Ph.D. proposal, Sheffield City Polytechnic.

Oppenheim, A. N. (1966) *Questionnaire Design and Attitude Measurement*, Heinemann, London.

Parnes, S. J., Noller, R. B. and Bondi, A. M. (1977) *Guide to Creative Action*, Charles Scribner's Sons, New York.

Payne, S. (1951) *The Art of Asking Questions*, Princeton University Press.

Pedler, M., Banfield, P., Boraston, I., Gill, J. and Shipton, J. (1990) *The Community Development Initiative: A Story of the Manor Employment Project in Sheffield*. Avebury, Gower, Aldershot.

Pettigrew, A. M. (1985a) Contextualist research: a natural way to link theory and practice, in E. E. Lawler, A. M. Mohrman, S. A. Mohrman, G. E. Ledford, T. G. Cummings and Associates, *Doing Research that is Useful for Theory and Practice*, Jossey Bass, San Francisco.

Pettigrew, A. M. (1985b) *The Awakening Giant: Continuity and Change in ICI*, Blackwell, Oxford.

Phillipps, D. C. (1987) *Philosophy, Science and Social Inquiry*, Pergamon, Oxford.

Phillipps, E. M. and Pugh, D. S. (1987) *How to Get a PhD*, Open University Press, Milton Keynes.

Ponder, Q. D. (1957) The effective manufacturing foreman, in E. Young (ed.) *Industrial Relations Research Association Proceedings of the Tenth Annual Meeting*, Madison, Wisconsin, pp. 41–54.

Popper, K. R. (1957) *The Poverty of Historicism*, Routledge, London.

Popper, K. R. (1967) *Conjectures and Refutations*, Routledge, London.

Popper, K. R. (1972a) *Objective Knowledge*, Clarendon Press, Oxford.

Popper, K. R. (1972b) *The Logic of Scientific Discovery*, Hutchinson, London.

Pratt, V. (1978) *The Philosophy of the Social Sciences*, Methuen, London.

Pugh, D. S. (ed.) (1971) *Organisation Theory: Selected Readings*, Penguin, Harmondsworth.

Punch, M. (1986) *The Politics and Ethics of Fieldwork*, Sage University Paper Series on Qualitative Research Methods, Vol. 3, Sage, Beverly Hills, Calif.

Quine, W. V. (1960) *World and Object*, Harvard University Press, Cambridge, Mass.

Radomsky, J. (1967) *The problem of choosing a problem*, unpublished M.S. thesis, Sloan School of Management, Cambridge, Mass.

Rapoport, R. N. (1970) Three dilemmas in action research, *Human Relations*, Vol. 23, no. 6, pp. 499–513.

Reed, M. (1985) *Redirections in Organisational Analysis*, Tavistock, London.

Reeves, T. K. and Harper, D. (1981) *Surveys at Work: A Practitioner's Guide*, McGraw-Hill, London.

Revans, R. W. (1971) *Developing Effective Managers*, Longman, London.

Revans, R. W. (1980) *Action Learning: New Techniques for Management*, Blond & Briggs, London.

Rickert, H. (1962) *Science and History: A Critique of Positivist Epistemology*, Van Nosrand, London.

Robinson, W. S. (1951) The logic and structure of analytic induction, *American Sociological Review*, Vol. 16, pp. 812–18.

Roethlisberger, F. J. and Dickson, W. J. (1939) *Management and the Worker*, Harvard University Press, Cambridge, Mass.

Rorty, R. (1979) *Philosophy and the Mirror of Nature*, Princeton University Press.

Rose, M. (1975) *Industrial Behaviour: Theoretical Development since Taylor*, Allen Lane, Harmondsworth.

Rosenberg, M. J. (1968) *The Logic of Survey Analysis*, Basic Books, New York.

Rosenthal, R. (1966) *Experimenter Effects in Behavioural Research*, Appleton Century Crofts, New York.

Rosenthal, R. and Rosnow, R. L. (1975) *Primer Methods for the Behavioural Sciences*, Wiley, London.

Rowan, J. (1974) Research as intervention in N. Armistead (ed.) *Reconstructing Social Psychology*, Penguin, Harmondsworth.

Roy, D. (1960) 'Banana time' – job satisfaction and informal interactions, *Human Organisation*, Vol. 18, no. 2, pp. 156–68.

Rummel, R. W. and Ballaine, W. C. (1963) *Research Methodology in Business*, Harper & Row, New York.

Runkel, P. J. and McGrath, J. E. (1972) *Research on Human Behavior: A Systematic Guide to Method*, Holt Rinehart & Winston, New York.

Ryan, A. (1970) *The Philosophy of the Social Sciences*, Macmillan, London.

Sanday, P. R. (1979) The ethnographic paradigm(s), *Administrative Science Quarterly*, Vol. 24, December, pp. 527–38.
Sayer, A. (1981) Abstraction: a realist interpretation, *Radical Philosophy*, Vol. 28, pp. 6–15.
Sayer, A. (1984) *Method in Social Science*, Hutchinson, London.
Sayles, L. (1958) *The Behavior of Industrial Work Groups*, Wiley, New York.
Sayles, L. (1964) *Managerial Behaviour: Administration in Complex Organisations*, McGraw-Hill, New York.
Schein, E. H. (1970) *Organisational Psychology*, 2nd edn, Prentice-Hall, Englewood Cliffs, NJ.
Schein, E. H. (1987) *The Clinical Perspective in Fieldwork*, Sage University Paper Series on Qualitative Research Methods, Vol. 5, Sage, Beverly Hills, Calif.
Schon, D. A. (1983) *The Reflective Practitioner: How Professionals Think in Action*, Temple Smith, London.
Schutz, A. (1964a) The problem of social reality, in Schutz (1967).
Schutz, A. (1964b) *Collected Papers Volume II*, Martinus Nijhoff, The Hague.
Schutz, A. (1966) *Collected Papers Volume III*, Martinus Nijhoff, The Hague.
Schutz, A. (1967) *Collected Papers Volume I*, 2nd edn, Martinus Nijhoff, The Hague.
Schutz, A. (1970) Reflections on the problem of relevance, in M. Zander (ed.) *The Way of Phenomenology*, Pegasus, New York.
Scott, C. (1961) Research on mail surveys, *Journal of the Royal Statistical Society*, Vol. xxiv, no. 124, pp. 143–205.
Shotter, J. (1975) *Images of Man in Psychological Research*, Methuen, London.
Simons, R. (1987) Accounting control systems and business strategy: an empirical analysis, *Accounting, Organisations and Society*, Vol. 12, no. 4, pp. 357–74.
Smart, B. (1975) *Marxism and Phenomenology*, Routledge, London.
Smircich, L. (1983) Studying organisations as cultures, in Morgan (1983).
Smith, G. M. (1975) Business and management studies: a guide to the information network, *Journal of Management Studies*, May, pp. 194–209.
Smith, H. W. (1975) *Strategies of Social Research: The Methodological Imagination*, Prentice-Hall International, London.
Smith, H. W. (1978) in H. McShane and Smith, H. W., *No Mean Fighter*, Pluto Press, London.
Sofer, C. (1961) *The Organisation from Within*, Tavistock, London.
Spencer, A. C. (1980) Some issues arising from the role relationships of the non-executive director, unpublished Ph.D. thesis, Sheffield City Polytechnic.
Spencer, A. C. (1983) *On the Edge of the Organisation*, Wiley, Chichester.
Spinelli, E. (1989) *The Interpreted World*, Sage, London.
Stewart, R. (1965) The use of diaries to study managers' jobs, *Journal of Management Studies*, Vol. 2, pp. 228–35.
Stewart, R. (1967) *Managers and their Jobs*, Macmillan, London.
Stewart, R. (1982) *Choices for Management*, McGraw-Hill, London.
Stogdill, R. M. Shartle, C. L. and Associates (1956) *Patterns of Administrative Performance*, Research Monograph No. 81, Ohio State University, Bureau of Business Research, Columbus, Ohio.
Summers, G. F. (1970) *Attitude Measurement*, Rand McNally, Chicago.
Susman, G. I. (1983) Action research: a socio-technical systems perspective, in Morgan (1983).
Susman, G. I. and Evered, R. D. (1978) An assessment of the scientific merits of action research, *Administrative Science Quarterly*, Vol. 23, pp. 582–602.
Tiles, M. (1987) A science of Mars or of Venus?, *Philosophy*, Vol. 62, no. 241, pp. 293–306.
Tinker, T. and Lowe, T. (1982) The management science of the management sciences, *Human Relations*, Vol. 35, no. 4, pp. 331–47.

Trist, E. L., Higgin, G. W., Murray, H. and Pollock, A. B. (1963) *Organisational Choice: Capabilities of Groups at the Coalface under Changing Conditions. The Loss, Rediscovery and Transformation of a Work Tradition*, Tavistock, London.

Trow, M. (1957) A comment on participant observation and interviewing: a comparison. *Human Organisation*, Vol. 16, no. 3, pp. 33–5.

Turner, B. A. (1971) *Exploring the Industrial Sub-Culture*, Macmillan, London.

Turner, B. A. (1988) Connoisseurship in the study of organisational cultures, in Bryman (1988).

Unwin, N. (1986) Beyond truth, *Mind*, Vol. XV, pp. 300–17.

Van de Vall, M., Bolas, C. and Kang, T. S. (1976) Applied social research in industrial organisations. An evaluation of functions, theory and methods, *Journal of Applied Behavioural Science*, Vol. 12, no. 2, pp. 158–77.

Vitalari, N. P. (1985) The need for longitudinal designs in the study of computing environments, in Mumford *et al.* (1985).

Walker, C. R. and Guest, R. H. (1957) *Man on the Assembly Line*, Yale University Press, New Haven.

Wallace, W. (1971) *The Logic of Science in Sociology*, Aldine, Chicago.

Warmington, A. (1980) Action research: Its methods and implications, *Journal of Applied Systems Analysis*, Vol. 7, pp. 23–39.

Watson, T. J. (1977) *The Personnel Managers: A Study in the Sociology of Work and Employment*, Routledge, London.

Wax, R. H. (1971) *Doing Fieldwork*, University of Chicago Press.

Webb, E. J., Campbell, D. T., Schwartz, R. D. and Sechrest, L. (1969) *Unobtrusive Measures*, Rand McNally, Chicago.

Webb, S. and Webb, B. (1975) *Methods of Social Research*, Cambridge University Press. First published 1932.

Westwood, S. (1985) *All Day Every Day*, Pluto Press, London.

Whitley, R. (1984a) The fragmented state of management studies: reasons and consequences, *Journal of Management Studies*, Vol. 21, no. 3, pp. 331–48.

Whitley, R. (1984b) The scientific status of management research as a practically oriented social science, *Journal of Management Studies*, Vol. 21, no. 4, pp. 369–90.

Whyte, W. F. (1948) *Human Relations in the Restaurant Industry*, McGraw-Hill, New York.

Whyte, W. F. (1984) *Learning from the Field*, Sage, London.

Wilson, A. T. M. (1961) The manager and his world, *Industrial Management Review*, Vol. 3, no. 1, pp. 1–26.

Winkler, J. T. (1987) The fly on the wall of the inner sanctum: observing company directors at work, in Moyser and Wagstaffe (1987).

Wirdenius, H. (1958) *Supervisors at Work*, The Swedish Council for Personnel Administration, Stockholm.

Wiseman, J. P. (1978) The research web, in Bynner and Stribley (1978).

Wright, M. (1986) The make–buy decision and managing markets: the case of management buy-outs, *Journal of Management Studies*, Vol. 25, no. 4, pp. 443–64.

Yeomans, K. A. (1973) *Applied Statistics: Statistics for the Social Scientist: 2*, Penguin, Harmondsworth.

Yin, R. K. (1981) The case study crisis: some answers, *Administrative Science Quarterly*, Vol. 26, pp. 58–65.

Yin, R. K. (1984) *Case Study Research: Design and Methods*, Applied Social Research Series, Vol. 5, Sage, Beverly Hills, Calif.

Young, K., Fogarty, M. P. and McRae S. (1987) *The Management of Doctoral Studies in the Social Sciences*, Occasional Paper no. 36, Policy Studies Institute, London.

Zelditch, M. (1962) Some methodological problems of field studies, *American Journal of Sociology*, Vol. 67, pp. 556–76.

Znaniecki, 6F. (1934) *The Method of Sociology*, Farrar and Rinehart, New York.

Glossary of Terms

Action learning A form of management development which, in essence, involves 'learning to learn-by-doing with and from others who are also learning-to-learn by doing' (Revans, 1980, p. 288). The process is inductive rather than deductive as managers are asked to solve actual organizational problems. It crucially depends upon the 'set' or group as a vehicle for learning by its members with a 'set adviser' to facilitate progress. Its variants in situations throughout the world are described by Revans (1980).

Analysis The processes by which a phenomenon (e.g. a managerial problem) is conceptualized so that it is separated into its component parts and the interrelationships between those parts, and their contribution to the whole, elucidated.

Analytic induction A research methodology concerned with the inductive development and testing of theory.

A posteriori Outcome of, and dependent on, experience or observation.

A priori Prior to, and independent of, experience or observation.

Cognition The act or process of knowing.

Concepts Abstractions which allow us to order our impressions of the world by enabling us to identify similarities and differences in phenomena and thereby classify them.

Consensus theory of truth The notion that the veracity of an account or theory is determinable only through agreement between the resarcher and his or her professional peers, or between the researcher and the subjects of his or her research.

Control group A group of subjects in an experiment who do not experience the action of the independent variable or experimental treatment.

Conventionalism Another term to describe the consensus theory of truth.

Correspondence theory of truth A notion that the truthfulness of an account or a theory is determinable by direct comparison with the facts of an external and accessible reality. If they fail to correspond the theory or account must be rejected.

Deduction The deduction of particular instances from general inferences. It entails the development of a conceptual and theoretical structure which is then tested by observation.

Dependent variable The phenomenon whose variation the researcher is trying to explain or understand.

Emic A form of explanation of a situation or events that relies upon elucidation of actors' internal logics or subjectivity.

Empiricism The idea that valid knowledge is directly derived from sense-data and experience.

Epistemology The branch of philosophy concerned with the study of the criteria by which we determine what does and does not constitute warranted or valid knowledge.

Etic A form of analysis which relies upon explanations that impose an external logic or frame of reference upon subjects so as to explain their behaviour.

Experimental group A group of subjects in an experiment who experience the action of the independent variable or experimental treatment.

Extraneous variable A phenomenon whose variation might cause some variation in the dependent variable and thus provide rival explanations of any observed variability in the dependent variable to that suggested by the independent variable.

Grounded theory The outcome of inductive research, that is, theory created or discovered through the observation of particular cases.

Hermeneutic circle The notion that no observation or description is free from the observer's interpretation based upon his or her presuppositions and projection of his or her values, theories, etc., on to phenomena.

Hermeneutics A discipline concerned with the interpretation of literary texts and/or meaningful human behaviour.

Hypothesis A tentative proposal that explains and predicts the variation in a particular phenomenon.

Ideographic An approach to social science that emphasizes that explanation of human behaviour is possible only through gaining access to actors' subjectivity or culture.

Independent variable A phenomenon whose variation notionally explains or causes changes in the dependent variable.

Indexicality The problem that people vary their behaviour according to their interpretation of the situation in which they find themselves.

Induction
General inferences induced from particular instances, or the development of theory from the observation of empirical reality.

Methodology The study of the methods or procedures used in a discipline so as to gain warranted knowledge.

Multi-method research May often be used synonymously with triangulation, as multiple measurement is perhaps the multi-method strategy's most familiar application. However, with Brewer and Hunter (1989) we use the term 'multi-method research' more widely, to include its application to all phases of the management research process.

Multivariate analysis A generic term for the use of various statistical procedures to indicate the amount of variance in the dependent variable which can be attributed to the action of each independent and extraneous variable.

Naturalism This term can have two opposing meanings:
1. That the methodologies of the natural and physical sciences (e.g. physics) provide a blueprint that should be followed by the social sciences.
2. The necessity to investigate human action in its natural or everyday setting and that the researcher must avoid disturbing that setting.

Nominalism The notion that what people take to be an external objective reality has no real existence independent of subjects' cognitive efforts.

Nomothetic Approaches to social science that seek to construct a deductively tested set of general theories that explain and predict human behaviour.

Ontology The study of the essence of phenomena and the nature of their existence.

Operationalization   The creation of rules which indicate when an instance of a concept has empirically occurred.

Paradigm   Usually taken to mean a way of looking at some phenomenon. A perspective from which distinctive conceptualizations and explanations of phenomena are proposed.

Phenomenology   A study of how things appear to people – how people experience the world.

Positivism   An approach that emphasizes the use of the methods presumed to be used in the natural sciences in the social sciences.

Practical adequacy   Criterion that determines the truthfulness of knowledge through consideration of the extent to which such knowledge generates explanations regarding the results of human action that are actually realized. In other words, the extent to which knowledge is practically useful.

Random sample   A sample in which all members of the specific populations from which the sample is drawn have an equal chance of selection.

Realism   May be divided into 'metaphysical realism' and 'epistemological realism'. The former considers that reality exists independently of the cognitive structures of observers, while the latter considers that reality is cognitively accessible to observers. Much of realism entails both views, although some realists would claim that, while reality does exist independently of our efforts to understand it, it is not cognitively accessible.

Reflexivity   The monitoring by an ethnographer of his or her impact upon the social situation under investigation.

Relativism   The notion that how things appear to people, and individuals' judgement about truth, are relative to their particular paradigm or frame of reference.

Reliability   A criterion that refers to the consistency of the results obtained in research.

Theory   A formulation regarding the cause and effect relationships between two or more variables, which may or may not have been tested.

Theory-dependent   This term refers to the way in which human practical activities entail acting upon the imperatives deriving from theoretical conjectures about, and explanations of, phenomena.

Theory-laden   This term refers to the way in which the prior values, knowledge and theories of an observer influence what he or she sees during observation.

Theory-neutral observation language   The idea that it is possible to test precisely a theory through observation of empirical reality which is readily open to neutral inspection by the observer.

Triangulation
1. The use of different research methods in the same study to collect data so as to check the validity of any findings.
2. The collection of different data upon the same phenomena, sometimes using different researchers so as to validate any findings.
3. Collecting data upon the same phenomenon at different times and places within the same study.

Validity   There are three types of validity:
1. Internal validity is the extent to which the conclusions regarding cause and effect are warranted.
2. Population validity is the extent to which conclusions might be generalized to other people.
3. Ecological validity is the extent to which conclusions might be generalized to social contexts other than those in which data has been collected.

Verstehen   A term used to explain the actions of subjects by understanding the subjective dimensions of their behaviour.

Index